FREE eGUIDE!

Enter this code at primagames.com/code to unlock your FREE eGuide:

VK6F-HJPS-ZBK3-GJD

CHECK OUT OUR eGUIDE STORE AT PRIMAGAMES.COM

All your strategy saved in your own personal digital library!

Mobile Friendly:
Access your eGuide on any web-enabled device.

Searchable:
Quickly find the strategies you need.

$9.99 Value:
Strategy where, when, and how you want it.

BECOME A FAN OF PRIMA GAMES!

Subscribe to our Twitch channel twitch.tv/primagames and join our weekly stream every Tuesday from 1-4pm EST!

*Tune in to **PRIMA 365** on our YouTube channel youtube.com/primagamesvideo for a new video each day!*

Aberdeenshire

3234042

MOBILE GAMING: GO PLAY!

TABLE OF CONTENTS

ANGRY BIRDS 2

Developer	Rovio Entertainment
Publisher	Rovio Entertainment
Year Released	2015
Platforms	iOS, Android
Type	Puzzle
ESRB Rating	E
Cost	Free to download

$ IN-GAME PURCHASES
In-game currency

Game Overview

Angry Birds 2 is the direct sequel to one of the first mega-hits of mobile gaming. There are a few updates in the sequel, but the gameplay remains firing a bird from a slingshot at crass pigs.

What You Need to Know

The pigs are back and need to be run out of town. At your disposal are a slingshot, a number of birds, and a handful of magic spells. With the exception of the **Tower of Fortune**—which is a simple guessing game—the challenges that were added are essentially the same as playing through levels, except you're going head-to-head against other players.

Flinging Birds and Taking Names

In the main adventure, you advance along a path as you complete each level. Challenges generally take place in one level. Before you begin a level, you can add one copy of each spell available to you. Levels typically have more than one set of pigs to clear out, which is indicated by the circles at the top of the screen.

Your arsenal for taking out these pigs is a combination of **birds** and **spells**, which appear as **cards** on the bottom left of the screen. If you want to switch out your current bird or spell, tap one of the other two visible cards. Face-down cards in the deck can't be selected.

Destruct-O-Bar

One of the new features is the **Destruct-O-Bar**, which appears in the upper right corner. Scoring points gradually fills the bar. When the bar is completely full, you're rewarded a **bonus card** to your deck. The card will be a bird or spell that isn't already in the deck. A second way to earn a bonus card is to knock out a **golden pig head**. Taking out a golden pig head instantly fills the Destruct-O-Bar. If you're close to filling the bar, do not aim at golden pig heads! Save those for nearly empty bars or for when you're down to your last card and there are multiple pigs left to get.

Active Environment

The environment has also gotten into the act in *Angry Birds 2*. **Red flowers** swallow, then expectorate, anything that gets too close, regardless of the object's size. **Fans** and **steam vents** blow debris and alter the trajectories of your birds and debris. **Slime flows** catch loose objects in their current and deposit them in a new area. When the **fire ring** appears, the first bird through it ignites, then explodes upon impact. It's possible to use all of these changes to your advantage with a little practice.

Those Tricky Pigs

Another big change is the pigs. A number of the green nuisances have picked up weapons, arming themselves with items ranging from blasters to wands. These pigs fire at your birds as they approach (or rocket at them in the case of the pig with a jetpack) and either knock down your birds, turn them into random objects, or just steal their momentum so you can't use the bird's special ability.

The biggest change to pigs is the addition of **boss pigs**. Boss pigs are huge and don't take much damage from bird strikes, even direct hits. When you face one of the boss pigs, your goal is usually to clear a path and roll the big pig off the screen.

In-App Purchases

The primary in-app purchases are rose-colored gems, which are spent to continue playing levels and challenges when your attempts come up short. Offers to buy other in-game currency, such as black pearls, pop up from time to time. There's no real need to buy anything. Everything can be earned from playing the game or waiting for your lives to regenerate.

TIPS

Increasing Your Score

Scoring points is what earns bonus cards and wins most challenges. You score points by taking out pigs and destroying their structures with the fewest birds possible.

There are three additional ways to boost your score. First, collect **feathers** and rank up your birds. Second, collect **hats**, or buy them with black pearls. Birds wearing hats enjoy a score multiplier. Finally, collecting complete sets of hats unlocks **slingshots with score multipliers**. The more sets of hats you collect, the greater the multiplier for your slingshot. Spells rank up based on the levels of your birds and slingshot.

The Flock

Red

The bird you have from the start comes with a **shout** ability. The shout is effective against tall buildings, especially when it's aimed at the middle or top of them. The energy of the shout passes through barriers, so it can take out pigs despite not breaking down the structures sheltering them.

The Blues

The Blues' ability remains **splitting into three birds** after leaving the slingshot as a single bird. They excel at destroying blue objects (glass/ice). They're also a good choice to get past armed pigs, provided they are split before getting into that pig's range.

Chuck

The triangular Chuck's ability is a **burst of speed**, He excels at destroying wooden structures. He's also your best bet when you need to hit a pig that's far away from the slingshot. Once his ability kicks in, he zips in a straight line until he crashes into an object or flies out of view.

Matilda

Matilda is a double threat to pigs. When you tap the screen, she drops an **explosive egg** with so much force that she is propelled upward with incredible momentum. The egg isn't as powerful as Bomb, but it still packs a punch. To maximize her destructive potential, aim Matilda so she falls between two structures. As she passes over the first structure, release her egg to destroy its base. Her upward momentum should send her crashing into the second structure. She's also great at taking out pigs behind tough structures. Aim her over the pig (it doesn't matter how high!) and drop her egg when she's directly overhead.

Silver

Silver is the newcomer to the flock. She has a **loop** ability that may require some practice before you can use it effectively. She zips forward before curling upward into her loop. She's fantastic for taking out targets that are guarded by terrain. Where other birds can only fly past the target or crash into the terrain, her loop allows her to flip around and score hits.

Bomb

The aptly named Bomb **explodes** with great force. Tapping the screen detonates him instantly, or he blows up shortly after his first contact with a pig or object. The energy of the explosion travels in all directions with equal force and is capable of destroying thick stone pieces. Aim him at the base of a tower to bring it down in one shot.

Terence

There's not much subtlety with this monster. Terence's only ability is his **immense size**, which makes him almost unstoppable after he gets going. Terence is more than capable of trashing entire levels on his own. Only a considerable build-up of stones will stop him. Aim Terence at distant structures so that his path takes him through closer ones.

Spells

There's no need to aim spells. Just pull back the slingshot and fire. The spells take care of the rest.

Golden Ducks

Golden ducks that resemble a bath toy fall from the sky and blanket everything below. They don't have any real ability other than weight. They'll crush pigs and topple buildings if enough of them settle on a roof.

Blizzard

Frost coats everything in the area, making the material incredibly brittle. Some structures might collapse under their own weight, but most won't. Follow up Blizzard with the Blues for maximum destruction.

Hot Chili

Golden Ducks and Blizzard can be used anytime, but Hot Chili is really only good for taking out the pigs in one location, unless there are explosive crates nearby. Hot Chili targets one pig, which ignites and explodes. It doesn't matter how well protected the pig is because this spell ignores structures.

Pig Inflater

A ray gun zaps multiple pigs in the level and causes them to expand to comical proportions. The expanded pigs usually crush or topple structures if they're on top of them. However, pigs closer to the ground or on sturdy platforms may survive the growth.

Mighty Eagle

There's not much to say about this spell. It's a free pass to clearing an area. If you use it, you advance.

ASPHALT XTREME

Developer	Gameloft
Publisher	Gameloft
Year Released	2016
Platforms	Android, iOS, Windows
Type	Off-road rally racing
Suggested Age	10+
Cost	Free to download

IN-GAME PURCHASES

Stack of Credits, Stack of Tokens, Suitcase of Tokens, Pile of Tokens, Pile of Credits, Trunk of Credits, Trunk of Tokens, Suitcase of Credits, Booster Pack IV, Trunk of Credits, Starter Offer

Game Overview

Asphalt Xtreme is the first off-road racing game in Gameloft's series of Asphalt racing games (*Asphalt Urban GT 1* and *2*, *Asphalt 3-9*, *Asphalt 3D*, *Airborne*, *Overdrive*, *Nitro*, and *Street Storm*).

Asphalt Xtreme features 35 licensed cars, with new cars continuing to be added. Sorted into five performance classes (D, C, B, A, S), there are seven categories of vehicles: **buggy, SUV, pickup, rally car, monster truck, truck,** and **muscle car.** Each vehicle type has its own strengths and weaknesses, keeping the game interesting, competitive, and well balanced.

There are five race types in single and multiplayer modes: **Classic, Versus, Infected, Elimination,** and **Knockdown.** The eight locations each have up to four unique tracks. You can race in Mongolia, Thailand, Egypt, Norway, Detroit (U.S.A.), France, Coachella Valley (U.S.A.), and Asia.

The gameplay in a nutshell is to come in first while completing course objectives. Winning is made easier when you destroy objects and drift in the turns. These two actions fill your turbo meter faster, and the more turbo you can use the quicker you can get ahead of the pack and maintain the lead.

What You Need to Know

There's a lot going on under the hood of *Asphalt Xtreme*. Here's what you need to know to rule the road…

Credits and Tokens

Credits are earned by completing races and objectives within races. **Credits** are used to purchase upgrades, while **tokens** are used to speed up oil changes and upgrade times (you can also choose to watch video advertisements to do the same and save your tokens). Tokens are also used to purchase **special event fuses, event tickets,** and **pro boxes**.

Stars

Stars are earned by winning races in Career mode. You can win up to three stars on each course in Career mode by completing the race and its other two specific objectives. You need to earn 40 stars to unlock multiplayer mode.

Blueprints

Blueprints are acquired from boxes. You can build new vehicles with nothing more than a few required blueprints.

Boxes

Boxes contain tech cards and blueprints. There are five kinds of boxes: 1-card-box, iron, bronze, silver, and gold. All the boxes can contain any card, but only certain boxes have a higher chance of dropping a certain type of card. There are also special occasion boxes: daily boxes, a 4-hour-box, an expert kit box, a specialist box, and a champions box. Boxes are opened as soon as they are obtained. Boxes are free or earned by winning races in Career mode.

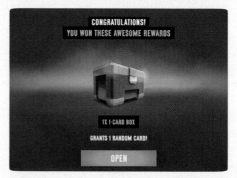

Cards

There are three types of cards: **elite, material,** and **part and tech cards.** You need these to upgrade vehicles. The only way to access upgrades 5-10 is to use an elite card, but these are only obtainable if all other specs are at level 4 or 9 correspondingly.

Oil

All vehicles have an **oil indicator** with 20 segments. You must maintain your oil to keep racing and stay competitive. The oil meter is live, so if you let it go below 6 segments and you start a race, you'll see your performance suffer during the race as it dips lower. Your vehicle is unusable when an oil change is needed. It costs credits and time to get an oil change. You can either watch an advertisement or pay tokens to erase the time penalty. The higher the vehicle class, the more time it takes for an oil change. Switch vehicles if you don't want to wait, or pay to clear the oil change time.

Nitro

Nitro is king in this game. Everything you do during a race revolves around clean driving and the strategic use of **nitro**. If you're colliding with vehicles, picking up nitro power-ups, drifting around corners, performing tricks off ramps, or destroying objects, then you're filling up your **nitro meter.**

Every vehicle has three nitro meter segments (unless you have the **extra tank** booster). Each nitro hit takes one segment per press of the nitro button.

Performing stunts, hitting obstacles, drifting, and destroying opponent vehicles fills the white fill bar below the nitro meter. A full white fill bar grants you one segment of nitro. A good trick to learn early is to drift often and perform stunts and destroy vehicles while in a nitro boost to continually fill up nitro while using it. When the continuous nitro chain is executed nothing can stop you.

Long Nitro

Long nitro is triggered at a key moment after draining a nitro segment. It's a nitro blast that drains the entire nitro gauge instead of one section and lasts three times longer than a single blast. Press the nitro button as soon as a drained nitro segment reaches the low (red) 10 percent mark. This means that the nitro bar needs your visual attention more so than in previous versions of *Asphalt* games. You need to take your eye off the race, because you can't rely on feel, as each vehicle type has its own nitro consumption rate (but for the most part, each vehicle category has the same nitro duration). So, get familiar with the audio cue so you know the exact moment to press nitro again without taking your eye off the course.

Boosters

Before each race you are given the opportunity to purchase boosters to help you get the upper hand in the race. You pay with hard-earned tokens or blueprints. Or sometimes if you're lucky, they're free. Keep your eyes open for those free ones.

◆ Boosted Wheels: These make you immune to hindering terrain. The effect lasts for 15 minutes.

◆ Nitro Recharger: Shortens the duration for the nitro refill bar to refill, giving you a nitro segment more quickly. This lasts for 10 minutes.

◆ Extra Tank: Lasts for two hours and costs 25 tokens or 18,500 credits but only gives you a 30 percent capacity boost to your nitro bar.

◆ Overclock: Acts like a tuning kit by enhancing every performance statistic by a small amount. It lasts for 15 minutes after activation.

◆ Double Credits: This booster lasts for four hours and costs 50 tokens or 37,000 credits. It gives you double the credit rewards won after each race.

Race Modes

Classic

You versus seven other racers. The first to cross the finish line wins. You win three stars for coming in first, two for second, and one for third. You can also win two additional stars for completing the two special objectives (besides coming in first, which is always the first objective).

Versus

This is a one-on-one race exactly like a Classic race except that you face off against just one racer using a different car. Monster trucks and pickup trucks act as head-on traffic and must be avoided or you risk wrecking your vehicle. You win three stars for first place and one for second place.

Infected

Nitro power-ups make you infected, as does bumping into other vehicles that are infected. Being infected turns you green and gives you unlimited nitro boost (which is activated automatically). Picking up nitro bottles increases bonus infected time. The virus wears off when the infection timer runs out. Wrecking kills the virus immediately.

To gain the most infection time possible, be in last place on purpose, and as soon as the warm-up expires, run into and infect everyone ahead of you. Touch them or wreck the healthy racers while infected to spread the virus, which adds 10 seconds to your infection. If you wreck an infected racer you only gain 5 seconds.

To have a 45-second timer at the start, be in last place while touching the 7th-place racer, then wreck them as soon as you become infected.

Elimination

A certain amount of time is given to the eight racers (190-225 seconds). There's a 15-second warm-up time, while the elimination period usually lasts 15-30 seconds. The timer turns red if you are in last place. The key is to be in first when the timer runs out. You get three stars for first but get two stars if you are eliminated and in second place or one star for third. A couple of bonus stars are available, and one is usually for a perfect run.

Knockdown

You face seven other racers, and the goal is to knock down (wreck) more target vehicles than the competitors. The targets are other cars that travel along the course, which are randomly spawned. The challenge ends when the maximum number of knockdowns is reached or when the timer runs out, in which case the player with the most knockdowns wins.

If you are tied when the timer runs out, then you enter Sudden Death mode and 30 seconds is added to the clock. The first one to do a knockdown wins. If no one gets a knockdown in that time, then whoever was ahead of the other in the course wins.

Getting more knockdowns than any other racer earns you three stars. There's no second or third place prize, but accomplishing bonus objectives can earn you additional stars.

Destroy Everything

Destroying objects earns you a quicker nitro recharge. Using nitro wins races. You can destroy most anything that is not terrain. So run through boxes, barrels, obstructions, and fences as well as other vehicles. When you wreck them, it's called a knockdown, and this also fills your nitro refill meter.

Bonus Objectives

You can get up to five stars per race in Career mode: three for coming in first and two more for completing a couple of more track-specific objectives. Sometimes you may need to go back to the race with a different vehicle to accomplish these objectives. Make sure to get all the stars possible from each track to earn the coveted card box and the materials needed to upgrade cars.

Upgrades

Materials and parts are needed to upgrade vehicles. Vehicles need to be upgraded to stay competitive. Make sure to secure all the bonus stars possible from Career courses. This is the quickest way to materials.

Drift-Nitro Chains

Perform a **drift** by tapping the brakes in a fast, sharp turn. Doing so awards you with a quickly filled nitro refill bar, which leads to faster nitro refills. To chain nitro hits together, execute a nitro hit when the meter is full (three bars) and then press it again when the bar turns red to achieve **long nitro**. Drift in the turns while in nitro speed to refill the meter as it's draining. And then continue to the next nitro hit when the meter is full again. Repeat as many times as you can.

Multiplayer Races

You can also earn card boxes from playing live players in multiplayer mode. For every three races you win you earn a card box. This is unlocked after earning 40 stars. Multiplayer can take a toll on your vehicle. Be prepared for oil changes like you would in Career mode.

Best in Acceleration

Buggies are the quickest off the starting line. They are the lightest vehicles, which makes them great for stunts but very vulnerable to knockdowns by heavier vehicles. The strategy for speed is to use a buggy and use its speed to stay away from heavier vehicles looking to wreck you. The Ariel Nomad is one of the best buggies.

Best in Destruction

Monster trucks and **pickups** make up for slower speeds by being able to effortlessly knock down other vehicles and fences. Look for the special shortcuts closed off by heavy gates that only trucks can plow through. These shortcuts will make up for the truck's slower speed. The more you destroy the more nitro you can earn to keep up with and pass the other racers. The Ford 3-Window Coupe is one of the best well-rounded trucks.

Best in Nitro

Rally cars, such as the Volkswagen Beetle GRC, are tops in nitro refill speed and drifting. However, consider the Unimog U 4023. It may seem slow, but when you chain together the nitro hits you can add a consistent 27 mph boost to the truck, which makes it very competitive.

Best in Stunts

Buggies not only are fast but are also the best choice for performing stunts.

Again, the Ariel Nomad is the top choice for pulling off stunts and stringing together drift and nitro combos.

Best in Speed

Muscle cars are the top choice for speed. You can't go wrong with the Chevrolet Camaro SS, Subaru WRX STI GRC, or the Dodge Challenger SRT8. A good **rally car** can keep up, though, since they handle better and have better nitro performance. **Muscle cars** burn through nitro faster than any other vehicle.

Best All-Around

To get the best all-around vehicle type, you should try using an SUV like the Range Rover Evoque. They are durable, have good speed and handling, and are big enough to destroy smaller vehicles when in a nitro boost. Nitro boosts last the longest when using an SUV. Just don't expect much from them in the stunt category.

Freebies

To get ahead quickly, be sure to get in the game every day so you can take advantage of the **daily login rewards, free boxes,** and **free tokens.** You can also go to Token Packs and watch a video for free tokens beyond the daily five videos to watch.

AVP: EVOLUTION

Developer	Angry Mob Games
Publisher	Fox Digital Entertainment, Inc.
Year Released	2013
Platforms	Android, iOS
Type	Third-person action
Suggested Age	17+
Cost	$2.99

 IN-GAME PURCHASES
Xeno points, honor points, Predalien and Battle Generator Bundle

Game Overview

On a distant planet, the blood feud between predator clans continues to rage. In a final attempt to eradicate the Jungle Hunter clan, the **super predators** secure the capabilities of an unlikely and unwilling species, the **aliens**. Play as both alien and predator, the deadliest creatures in the universe.

What You Need to Know

Gameplay

As an alien, you are tasked with fighting **colonial marines** as well as destroying the super predators to free your species from slavery. As a Jungle Hunter predator, you must eliminate the **alien queen** to prevent the super predators from annihilating your clan.

The game features finishing moves and character upgrades via ability enhancements and armor and weapon unlockables. The 19 campaign missions and 12 side missions can be played in either Normal or Hard mode.

Controls

A joystick appears on-screen when you touch your thumb on the left side of the screen. Use this to control character movement. For more precise control, aim the camera by sliding your right thumb on the right side of the screen. Together you can manage a good amount of control over your character. The on-screen **A** and **B** buttons control **attack** and **block**, respectively. The following actions are available using the on-screen controls:

- ◆ Movement
- ◆ Attack/fatalities
- ◆ Switching weapons
- ◆ Sense (xenomorph)
- ◆ Facehugger call (xenomorph)
- ◆ Plasma energy (predator)
- ◆ Cloak (predator)
- ◆ Alien vision (predator)
- ◆ Thermal vision (predator)

Predator Moves

The predator has three view types. These are accessed by tapping on the T at the top right corner. Thermal vision, for example, allows you to see trip mines. The predator can switch weapons by pressing the weapon toggle icon in the top right corner and then selecting one of the weapon icons to the left and bottom of the weapon toggle.

Xenomorph Moves

The **xenomorph** can **wall-climb** in areas with a yellow glow. Approach the glow at the wall and press forward and the block button to get onto the wall. It can also climb through vents to find better vantage points and access to new areas otherwise unreachable. Pressing the **facehugger icon** releases one or two facehuggers into the room to attack your enemies.

Typical Predator Weapon Combos

A = right slash

A + A = right + left slash

A + A + A = right + left + right slash

A + A + A + A = dash slash

A + B = power kick

A + A + B = scissor split

Hold A = impale slash

A + A + A + hold A = upward slash

Typical Xenomorph Claw Combos

A = right slash

A + A = right + left slash

A + A + A = right + left + right slash

A + A + A = overhead slash

A + A + A + hold A = uppercut

A + B = spin slash

A + A + B = ground slam

Hold A = heavy right slash

Purchases

There are several places where AVP allows you to part with your hard-earned cash. From the Level Select menu you can access the Predator Bundle or the store.

Predalien & Battle Generator Bundle

Accessed from the Level Select menu, this bundle costs $1.99 and allows you to create customized levels for the alien-predator hybrid, the predalien. With the battle generator you can choose your terrain and the enemies you'll go up against.

Store

The store is also accessed from the Level Select menu or from the Pause menu during gameplay. Here you use your xeno and honor points to purchase body parts, weapons, and armor if you have reached the level required to access them—and if you have the available points. If you don't have the points, you can buy them. Press the Buy button or the Get Points button at the top of the item categories to access the store, where you can purchase bundles of points.

XENO POINTS	HONOR POINTS	COST	BONUS
700,000	700,000	$49.99	75%
200,000	200,000	$19.99	25%
90,000	90,000	$9.99	10%
40,000	40,000	$4.99	—

Execution Opportunity

Repeatedly and rapidly press the attack button and combo sequences to carve away an enemy's health until a **skull icon** appears above the opponent's head and another appears below your attack controls. This means you can execute a fatality. Press the corresponding skull on the bottom right corner of the screen.

This is typically a three-swipe combo that starts with two specific swipe direction arrows and ends with a choice of three directional arrows. When more than one command appears on the screen at once, just choose which direction you want to swipe—it does not change execution type. This ends with an execution animation and refills a portion of your health meter.

Full Health Bar

Keep the health bar full by performing as many executions as possible for either predator or xenomorph.

Harvest Execution

You'll lose the power to use the facehugger ability for a short amount of time after you've performed the xenomorph's Harvest Execution.

Dash

You can cover more ground by performing a dash move. Simply tilt the virtual control stick in the desired direction and then press B. This is also a good way to evade ranged weapons.

Blocking

Many enemies have shields or other methods of blocking that prevent any of your attacks from doing damage. To counter this, don't forget to block yourself, which you can do by pressing B while standing still. Wait for an opening (just after the opponent attacks) to come out of the block and counterattack.

Upgrading

Both the alien and predator earn xeno and honor points independently of each other. You won't get far without upgrading your characters. Use these points in the store to upgrade your character's offensive and defensive skills with new weapons, body parts, and armor.

Stealth

Unlike the xenomorph, the predator doesn't have stealth skills in the beginning of the game, so don't attempt to sneak up on enemies.

Buckets of Xenomorph and Honor Points

To get crazy amounts of xenomorph and honor points, play either **Temple Wars** (mission 9) for xenos or the predator mission 8, **Temple Descent**, which pits you against waves of humans. Playing either of these side missions earns you the most points, especially if you play them for over 20 minutes. After 30 minutes, you'll rack up 300,000 or more points, which will buy you anything you want without having to pay cash at the store.

Shielded Androids

To kill shield-armored androids, use the A + A + B combo two or three times. Their shields drop off shortly after. If you're a xeno, use Acid Pool next, followed with a dash attack. If predator, use Smart Disc and Net Guns.

Kill the Queen

As predator, shoot the queen with the Berserker Plasma Cannon or Smart Disc while keeping your distance. This wears her health down and keeps you healthy by not engaging in close combat. When she charges, dash and hide behind columns. When she falls, dash to her and strike her to finish her off.

Finding Items

Predators look for hidden **skulls** and xenomorphs look for hidden **eggs**. If you've lost track of what hidden items you're missing, simply click on the locked bonus missions; they indicate which hidden items (by level) you still need to find to unlock them.

To help you find the items more easily, equip the full Chopper armor set (gun, mask, armor) for predator and the Berserker armor for xenomorph.

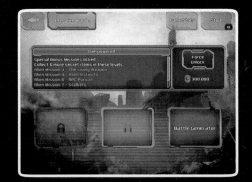

13

BADLAND

Developer	Frogmind Games
Publisher	Frogmind Games
Year Released	2013
Platforms	iOS, Android
Type	Puzzle
ESRB Rating	E
Cost	Free to download

$ IN-GAME PURCHASES
Full version ($3.99)

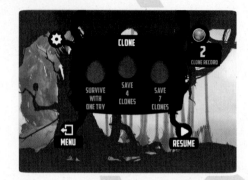

Game Overview

Don't let the simple controls of Badland fool you. This is a deceptively tricky side-scrolling puzzle game set in a dim and unforgiving world. You primarily play as Clony, a rotund bat-like creature that emerges from a garbage chute as the game begins.

What You Need to Know

The free-to-download version of *Badland* allows you to play a significant portion of the game before you commit to a full purchase. The gameplay doesn't change with the full version—you simply get more of it.

The game is set up for you to tackle incrementally more difficult challenges in each level. Your tries aren't limited, and there are checkpoints along the way that cut down the need to repeat puzzles you already passed.

Flap to the Finish

One command controls Clony and other characters: **Tap** or **hold** your finger on the screen and they flap their wings. Each flap propels them upward and forward.

Your initial goal on every level is to reach the end. The game offers three **missions** per level. Completing missions and saving clones unlocks **achievements**.

The Environment

The easy control scheme is there to balance out the difficult navigation necessary to reach the end of every level. Despite the vivid backdrop of the game, your path is entirely in shadow. There are few visual cues to indicate how solid, how movable, or how deadly the objects lining your path are.

Spinning blades may slice up Clony or flick him in a different direction. Thin pieces of environment may yield when pressure is applied, or they may require lifting from below. Long stretches of thick pipes will have one section that gives way when enough weight lands on it. All you have to guide you through each level is experience earned through trial and error and the certainty that there's at least one way to get past every puzzle.

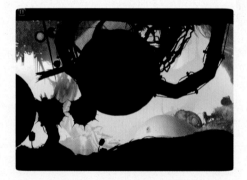

Clones

Clones are part power-up and part bonus life, and they come in two varieties: single (spawns one clone) and super (spawns 10 clones). When your character approaches one, a copy of the character pops up and reacts to your command exactly like the original. Clones often appear in groups, so you may be in control of five or six or 10 copies of your character simultaneously. The number of clones is a good indication of the difficulty of the path ahead.

Any copy of your character that reaches the end counts as clearing the level, whether it's a clone or what you started with. Saving clones serves mission requirements on some levels, and saving an increasing number of clones is required to unlock additional levels.

Power-ups

Small shapes with glowing bits are almost always power-ups. You don't always need to reach a power-up, because they will come to you. Power-ups are drawn to your character and clones, and will even track them through walls. The effect of any power-up absorbed by a clone is spread to every copy on the screen.

There are five pairs of power-ups in addition to the clone and super clone. There are two power-ups each for **roll** (clockwise or counterclockwise motion), **size** (increase or decrease size), **speed** (faster or slower clones), and **time** (speed up or slow down the passage of time). The **cling** power-up allows clones to stick safely to surfaces briefly (even spinning fans), while the **bounce** power-up provides a rebound effect when a clone comes into contact with anything.

Multiplayer

There are two flavors of multiplayer: coop and versus. The gameplay is the same as the single-player game, which includes sharing the same screen. Each player selects a color and starting character, and is then assigned an area of the screen to control their character.

In **coop**, everyone works together to reach the end of a level. Characters lost during the level will respawn when another player activates a clone power-up.

Versus mode is a survival race that uses distinct levels. You win by either reaching the end first or being the last clone standing. Power-ups are absorbed by the first character that reaches it, and the effects are not shared.

In-App Purchases

The full version of Badland, which includes additional levels and the level editor in addition to blocking advertisements, is available for $3.99 as an in-app purchase.

Clear Vision

Keep your finger to a spot on the screen that doesn't block your view. Remember that touching the screen only initiates wing flaps. Your character doesn't fly to where you touch the screen.

Patience and Persistence

You won't complete every mission on your first run through any level, so use early attempts to study the puzzles you must pass to reach the end. Once you are familiar with the layout of the level, go back with the goal of completing missions or saving as many clones as you can.

Clones Are Interchangeable

Until you're familiar with navigating the levels and are trying to complete missions or climb leaderboards, treat clones as cannon fodder. Don't worry about keeping track of the original character in the midst of clones. For all intents and purposes, every copy on the screen is your character. The environment treats them the same, and power-ups react to them the same way.

Tight Formation

When you're working on increasing the number of clones that reach the end of a level, keep them bunched up as much as you can. If your lead clone moves too far ahead, land for a moment and let the rest catch up. If your flock is strung out, use the terrain to collect everyone before continuing.

Split Path Problems

Hit a fork in the road and can't continue despite trying both paths? Are there two power-ups in close proximity, but neither helps you get past the next puzzle? You need clones! More specifically, you need to split up the clones between the two paths or to reach the different power-ups. Keeping two groups that aren't together moving in unison is one of the trickiest skills to master in *Badland*.

Power-Ups as Clue or Ruse

In many cases, available power-ups are the key to getting through sections of a level, such as when a size-decreasing power-up precedes a narrow opening. Just don't assume that every power-up you see is necessary, because that would be straightforward, and *Badland* isn't known for being straightforward. During your initial playthrough of a level, ignore power-ups (except for clones, which are always good for you) unless they're obviously necessary to continue.

Versus Victories

The key to winning versus multiplayer matches is to get ahead of the pack. Staying in the lead puts you first in line for power-ups and makes it much less likely to be caught up in a bottleneck near a hazard.

BATTLE OF POLYTOPIA

Developer	Midjiwan AB
Publisher	Midjiwan AB
Year Released	2016
Platforms	Android, iOS
Type	4X/Turn-based strategy
Suggested Age	12+
Cost	Free to download

IN-GAME PURCHASES
Additional tribes, multiplayer

Game Overview

The Battle of Polytopia is a 4X game that places you in command of a small city, garrisoned by a single unit. Under your guidance, the tribe **eXplores** the world, **eXpands** its territory and knowledge, and builds its military to **eXploit** unaffiliated villages and **eXterminate** its rivals.

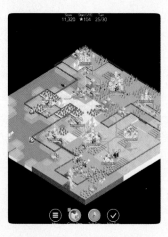

TRIBE	FREE / BUY	STARTING ADVANTAGE
Xin-Xi	Free	Climbing tech
Imperius	Free	Organization tech
Bardur	Free	Hunting tech
Oumaji	Free	Riding tech
Kickoo	Buy	Fishing tech
Hoodrick	Buy	Archery tech
Luxidoor	Buy	Level 3 city + city wall
Vengir	Buy	Smithery tech
Zebasi	Buy	Farming tech
Ai-Mo	Buy	Meditation tech
Quetzali	Buy	Shields tech
Aquarion	Buy	Modified technology tree, unique water units

Each turn begins with harvesting the resource (stars), which you may expend in different ways. **Stars** are used to harvest natural resources, construct buildings and improvements, muster military units, and research technology. Since your stars are limited, you must balance how they are spent in order to maximize their benefit to your tribe.

What You Need to Know

There are two game modes for single player. In **Perfection,** the tribe with the highest score after 30 turns wins. To achieve victory in **Domination,** you must be the last tribe standing, but there is no turn limit. The multiplayer versions of these games are **Glory** and **Might.** Glory is similar to Perfection, but you aim for a point total with no turn limit. In Might, you win by capturing all the capital cities of your rivals.

Conquer the World

Each game takes place on a map with randomly generated terrain that is tailored to the tribe in a given area of the map. Each playable tribe has a starting advantage (see table) and distinct looks for their units. There are four tribes available immediately—**Xin-Xi, Imperius, Bardur,** and **Oumaji**—but the rest must be purchased. As an incentive, purchasing a tribe also unlocks multiplayer.

Cities

There are two ways to add cities to your empire. The most common way is to send out your military units to find villages, which become level 1 cities after conversion. The other way is to invade another tribe's city and convert it. More cities, and larger cities, mean more star production per turn and greater potential production of the units necessary to explore and conquer.

There are two ways to grow individual cities: harvesting natural resources and constructing buildings and improvements. There's no downside to growing a city larger, other than expending stars that could be used elsewhere.

Harvest Natural Resources

Natural resources don't grow over time, which means you should harvest them as early as possible. All you need to do is learn the requisite technology and have enough stars available to complete the work. The majority of resources increase the nearest city's population when they're harvested. A few, notably **whales**, turn into stars.

Construct Buildings

Buildings require more planning because each square can hold only one building, meaning you're limited by the borders of each city. **Farms, mines, ports, lumber huts,** and **temples** add population. **Sawmills, windmills,** and **forges** also add to your population, but they can't be built until after one of the previous buildings has been constructed. **Customs houses** increase star production for every port adjacent to one.

Monuments

Monuments are special buildings that serve as rewards for completing special tasks. Monuments add three to the population of the nearest city and points to your score. They require an open space for building but don't eat into your reserve of stars.

Connected Capital

Roads and **ports** also boost the populations of your capital and each city connected to it. All you need is an unbroken path (roads and white-colored shipping lanes in the water) to make the connection. Roads can be built on improved squares without impacting the buildings on them. Shipping lanes pop up between two friendly ports with a shared coastline. For inland cities, connect your city to its port with a road.

Units

Units perform two functions: They explore the world and project force. Since there are no peace treaties in *Battle of Polytopia*, you're essentially at war with every other tribe on the map at all times.

Send out units to explore the world, convert villages, and engage with enemy units. Keep some units in your home territory. Without protection, your cities will fall into the hands of your enemies.

Villages and Ruins

In addition to the villages that turn into cities, there are ruins that yield bonuses that you don't want to leave for your opponents.

The possible rewards from ruins are a giant, an undiscovered technology, a population boost of three to your capital, an explorer, a battleship, or 10 stars.

Each city can produce one unit per turn, and each city can support only as many units as it has population notches. Black dots inside notches indicate the number of units currently supported by each city.

Naval Units

Ground units that move onto ports become **boats.** At the cost of stars, boats can be upgraded to **ships,** and ships can be upgraded to **battleships.** Any upgrades are lost when a unit returns to land. If a previously upgraded unit returns to port, it starts over as a boat.

Attack, defense, and movement for naval units are based on the type of naval unit (boat, ship, battleship), but the unit's health carries over. For example, a giant at sea, whether as a boat, ship, or battleship, has the same health as the giant on land.

Unit Skills

The skills for a unit appear on the **Build** window (when you muster one in a city). For naval units, they appear on the **Upgrade** window.

SKILL	DESCRIPTION
Carry	Unit can travel on coastal water squares. After Navigation has been researched, unit can travel on all water squares.
Convert	Unit converts opponent into a friendly unit.
Dash	Unit may attack after moving.
Escape	Unit may move after attacking, even if it moved prior to attack.
Heal	Unit restores health to friendly units in adjacent squares.
Persist	Unit may attack again provided its previous attack killed an opponent.
Scout	Unit has wider field of view.
Swim	Unit moves freely between land and water (Aquarion-only ability)

Tech Tree

Tap the flask at the bottom of the screen to bring up the Tech Tree. The circles represent all the technologies in the game, which are organized into three tiers. Tier 1 technologies are closest to the center. Individual tier 2 technologies become available after certain tier 1 technologies are purchased. Tier 3 technologies are unlocked with tier 2 technology purchases.

Tier 1 technologies have an initial research value of five stars. Tier 2 ones cost six, and tier 3 techs cost seven. However, each city added to your empire increases those costs by one, two, or three depending on the tier. A tier 3 technology, **Philosophy,** decreases the cost of research.

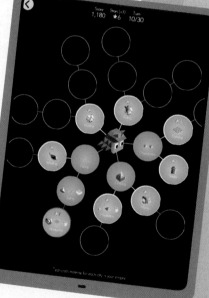

In-App Purchases

To play as a tribe beyond the original four, you must purchase them. Six human tribes (Kickoo, Hoodrick, Vengir, Zebasi, Ai-Mo, and Quetzali) are $0.99 each. The Aquarion and Luxidoor are more: $1.99 and $2.99, respectively. To unlock multiplayer, you must purchase at least one tribe. Purchasing tribes also expands the number of tribes you can play against in Perfection and Domination games.

TIPS

Explore Aggressively

Villages are the best way to boost your stars per turn and unit construction capabilities. In addition, it's much better to meet opposing tribes closer to their cities than to your cities. Meeting a new tribe often results in a reward of technology or stars.

There are no bad results from exploring **ruins,** so get to them before any opponents do. If you reveal a village and a ruin on the same turn, always go to the ruin first. The potential rewards are too great to put off.

Giant Reinforcement

Monuments and giants make a great back-up plan for defending vulnerable large (level 5+) cities. Since you can place a monument at any point before the game ends to get the points from it, hold them in reserve. Grow the city's population just shy of what it needs to reach the next level. If that city is invaded, place a monument in its border and select super unit. The giant that spawns will kick out the invader. You must do this before the invader has a chance to convert!

Swarms of Ships

Because every ship uses a ranged attack, you can turn even basic warriors into a devastating flotilla. Move units through your docks and into the water, then use them to support any remaining land units. Soften up enemy units from the water and finish them off with your units still on dry land.

Specialize Tech

Pick one end path for tech choices and stick to it. If you jump around trying to get everything, your army of *almost* swordsmen, catapults, and battleships will be overwhelmed by actual swordsmen, catapults, or battleships. You can always fill in your Tech Tree after your enemies are ground to dust.

Temple Scores Improve over Time

There are four types of temple buildings: temples (unlocked with Free Spirit), forest temples (cheaper to build, unlocked with Spiritualism), mountain temples (unlocked with Meditation), and water temples (unlocked with Aquatism).

Temples are fantastic investments in games where points matter, provided you build them early enough. Temples upgrade every three turns after being built, which increases their value to your score. Temples start out at 100 points and max out at 400 points 12 turns later.

City Upgrade Options

Each time your city levels up, you are given a choice of rewards. The first choice is +1 star production or an explorer. Go with production unless you really need to see what's nearby in a hurry; for example, if it's late in the game and you need to explore a few bits of the map to finish the Explorer task.

At level 3, you can either add a wall around the city or get a one-time bonus of five stars. City walls are a considerable boost to units behind them. Go with the wall unless you're confident the city will never come under attack.

At level 4, you choose between a population increase of three for the city or border growth. Border growth is generally the better option since you can improve the newly claimed squares to increase the city's population. If the squares outside the city are already claimed by other cities, then choose the instant population boost.

At level 5 and beyond, your options are a park or a super unit (giant). The park is worth 250 points, which helps in Perfection and Glory mode but is worthless in Domination. Giants tend to trample most other units in fights, especially when you create a battleship with the health of a giant.

Bonus Tapping

Tap on a square inside your home territory until a bunny appears. This unit is not under your control, so be careful. It has the Crush skill, which allows it to destroy improvements as well as units. The bunny is disabled in multiplayer.

Tap and hold a square anywhere in the sky to get the Sunbringer achievement. The list of achievements appears as an option in the Throne Room.

BEHOLDER

Developer	Warm Lamp Games
Publisher	Alawar Entertainment
Year Released	2016
Platforms	Windows, Mac, Linux, Android, iOS
Type	Adventure, strategy
Suggested Age	12+
Cost	$2.99 on mobile; $9.99 on PC; $14.99 on consoles

$ IN-GAME PURCHASES
Yes

Game Overview

You are Carl, a government-installed landlord of a multistory apartment building in a dark, dystopian world, in a totalitarian State that controls every aspect of its citizens' lives. The State employs you to spy on your tenants. This entails breaking into apartments when tenants are out; installing spy cameras; and stealing their personal items and selling them—or, if the items are prohibited, using them for evidence to get them arrested.

The State demands that you report anyone violating their laws or plotting dissident activities against the State to the authorities. However, you have a choice. You can either become a puppet of the State or side with those tenants who suffer from the same oppressive laws as you.

Every decision you make affects the way the story develops. This means there are multiple outcomes at the end of the game, which are a sum of the decisions you've made.

What You Need to Know

Characters

Beholder is all about its characters: talking to them, getting to know them, spying on them, and turning on them or helping them out (your choice). Talk to characters with exclamation marks above their heads to accept quests. Sometimes these only appear if you express interest in their lives (deeply conversing with them). Other tasks are given over the phone, but we'll cover that next.

Following is a list of all the characters in the game (in alphabetical order by first name), along with all the vital information you need to progress.

IMAGE	NAME	MOVE-IN TIME	INTERESTS	PERSONAL ITEMS	SPECIAL ITEMS	TASKS	INVOLVED IN THESE TASKS	NOTES
	Anna Stein	Carl's wife. Moves in with him.	—	—	• Veil • Golden brooch	• Martha Is Sick • Martha's Doctor • Life-Threatening Condition • Seasonal Fruit • Weather at Home • The Last Jerk • Chocolate Candy • Broken TV • Bedtime Stories • Bills, Bills, and More Bills • Grocery Money • Weird Note	• Trust and Care • Wedding Preparations	This is Carl's (your) wife. She's 40 years old, a housewife, and can be found in the basement (your apartment).
	Airel Johnson	Ten hours after the propaganda truck parks outside.	• Smokes a pipe. • Was in the Battle of Aglow. Find medal in his apartment. • Find dumbbells in his apartment. • Likes to travel. Find world map in his apartment. • Find stamp album in his apartment. • Takes photos. Find camera in his apartment. • Plays chess. Find chess in his apartment.	• Dumbbells • World map • Stamp album • Camera • Chess • Passport • Sweater • Pistol • Blue shirt • Tiger balm • 3 books • Film • Green tie • Blue tie • Spyglass • Hard hat	• Medal	—	• Glory to the War Hero • The Butcher from Agloe	A famous and respected war hero. He's 40 years old and is a propagandist who lives alone. If you report him, you're fined $100 for "Code 732: High-ranking military officers are beyond your scope of responsibility." Drinks and caviar cost you $1500. If warned about the assassination attempt, you can eliminate the revolutionary at the corner of the apartment building.
	Albert Meineke	After Danton's call regarding Antoine, or 10 hours after Antoine leaves.	• Find fake passport in his apartment. • See him smoking, or find tobacco in his apartment. • See him cooking. • Find chess in his apartment. • Find fishing rod in his apartment. • Find foreign letter in his apartment. • Find wine in his apartment. • Foreign spy: talk to Albert.	• Fake passport • Tobacco • Foreign letter • Fishing rod • Chess • Wine • Passport • Blue shirt • Robe • Pocket watch • Foreign money • 3 records • Soda • Salt • Cook book	• Fake passports • Liebespirit	• Document Theft • The Hunt for an Engineer • Homeland Will Never Forgive	• The Last Jerk • Saving a Life	A spy from the enemy country, Albert is a 35-year-old male who is unemployed and lives alone. He can help you and your family escape by paying $10,000 in "Homeland Will Never Forgive," and an additional $10,000 if the fake passports are stolen from his apartment.
	Alloisius Shpak	After "Crime and Punishment" is completed.	• Find stamp album in his apartment. • Find wine in his apartment. • Find dumbbells in his apartment. • Find tennis kit in his apartment. • Find ship model in his apartment. • Find spyglass in his apartment.	• Stamp album • Wine • Dumbbells • Tennis kit • Ship model • Spyglass • Passport • Whiskey • Parts • Chocolate candy	• Whiskey • Liebespirit • Cruise tickets	• Lonely Alloisius • Love on the Phone • Gathering Data • Wedding Preparations	• Difficult Conversation • Martha's Doctor • Life-Threatening Condition	Alloisius claims to be a famous cardio surgeon. He's a 47-year-old well-known doctor who lives alone. He's gullible and lonely, but this can be turned around if you complete "Lonely Alloisius." He stops talking to you if it's said that Sarah is an impostor (if she's chosen in the mission "Lonely Alloisius."
	Anjei Rothaar	Moves in during "Creator's Life," when asking Antoine Grubic to move in.	• Dangerous tendencies. Find broken bottle in his apartment. • Find violin in his apartment. • Find Molotov cocktail in his apartment. • Find soccer ball in his apartment. • Find dumbbells in his apartment. • Find bow and arrows in his apartment. • Talk to him to learn he wants to go to war to kill people.	• Violin • Passport • Blue shirt • Pocket watch • Soccer ball • Broken bottle • Knife • Molotov cocktail • Dumbbells • Bow and arrows		—	—	A 21-year-old male who is unemployed and lives alone. He's constantly ready to attack. If he's accused of the propaganda truck's explosion, he will kill Carl (you).
	Antoine Grubic	Shows up 24 hours after the box is handed to Fulfledle Brukich, or after solving problems with the box (if stolen from Fulfledle), or 10 hours after refusing the box.	• Smokes a pipe. See him smoking in his apartment. • Government Worker. Find note in his apartment, or call Ministry after spotting him doing something illegal. • Find tennis kit in his apartment. • Likes art. Find reproductions in his apartment. • Find ship model in his apartment. • See him drinking.	• Tobacco • Tennis kit • Reproductions • Ship model • Passport • Sweater • Boots • Blue shirt • Robe • Vine • Leaflet • Blueprints • Fish • Screwdriver • Pistol • Blue dress • World map • 6 books • Sock • Newspaper	• Note	• Creator's Life	• Under Suspicion • Weird Note	A 45-year-old male press-room master who lives alone. His awkward gaze and darting eyes belie his confidence in his own invincibility. Code 3087. This subject is under State protection.

Characters (continued)

IMAGE	NAME	MOVE-IN TIME	INTERESTS	PERSONAL ITEMS	SPECIAL ITEMS	TASKS	INVOLVED IN THESE TASKS	NOTES
	Bastian Walner	After receiving the mission "The Hunt for an Engineer."	• Find chess in his apartment. • Find Turkish coffee pot in his apartment. • Find spyglass in his apartment. • Find manuscript in his apartment. • Find ship model in his apartment.	• Chess • Spyglass • Turkish coffee pot • Ship model • Manuscript • Passport • Eyeglasses • Hard hat • Book • Insulating tape • Fish • Wine • Parts • Factory access card • First aid	• Top secret blueprints	• But What If She…	• The Hunt for an Engineer • Homeland Will Never Forgive	A 45-year-old chief engineer, Bastian lives with Clara Walner and loves to draw and create blueprints. He doesn't feel worthy of Clara, his wife. He believes suicide is the right thing for him after her affair.
	Bruno Hempf	Does not move in.	—	—	—	• Accession	—	Bruno is your boss from the Ministry. This is who you report the tenants to. Visits twice in the game, once to be introduced and later to help you get a better grade on your test.
	Bruno Noel	Five hours after giving the pistol to Dora.	—	• Rum • Newspaper • Blue tie • Green tie • Sock • Blue sock • Red sock • Boots • Sweater • Trousers	—	—	—	This aggressive unemployed male is 40 years old and is unemployed and lives with Dora Noel.
	Carl Stein	This is you. Moves in Day 1.	—	—	—	—	• He's involved in all the tasks	You're a male landlord who lives in the basement of the apartment building. You're married to Anna and have two children: Patrick and Martha. It's your job to spy on your tenants.
	Clara Jacque	After "Love on the Phone" is completed.	• Dreamy nature. Find five books in her apartment. • Drinks coffee and alcohol. See her drinking and find Turkish coffee pot in her apartment. • Smokes a pipe. See her smoking. • Likes fine arts. Find reproductions in her apartment.	• Turkish coffee pot • Reproductions • 5 books • Purple blouse • Passport • Cardigan • Blue blouse • Handbag • Slouch hat • Blue dress • Red dress	• Cruise tickets	• Drunk and Happy	• Complaints About Clara • Love on the Phone	Clara is a 30-year-old female who lives with Alloisius Shpak and isn't a good choice for any man. Judging by the news, Clara is an adventurer. One should expect anything from her.
	Clara Jacque-Walner	When Bastian Walner moves in.	• Dreamy nature. Find five books in her apartment. • Drinks coffee and alcohol. See her drinking and find turkish coffee pot in her apartment. • Smokes a pipe. See her smoking. • Likes fine arts. Find reproductions in her apartment. • Cheats on her husband. Talk to Feodosius Ruan or see her cheating in her apartment.	• Turkish coffee pot • Reproductions • 5 books • Purple blouse • Passport • Cardigan • Blue blouse • Handbag • Slouch hat	• Strawberry soap		But What If She…	Clara is a 30-year-old female who lives with her husband, Bastian Walner. She's unemployed and a newlywed. They seem an odd match, but it works.
	Dora Noel	After posting propaganda posters around the apartment block.	• Drinks. See her drinking. • Find ice skates in her apartment. • Seamstress. Find a purple dress in her apartment. • Dreamy nature. Find five books in her apartment. • Sleeps poorly. Observe her sleeping. • Victim of domestic violence. Talk to Dora.	• Ice skates • 5 books • Purple blouse • Passport • Cardigan • Blue blouse • Knife • Records (1–3) • Rat poison • Thimble and needle	—	• Insomnia • Fear and Hate	—	A young 29-year-old music teacher who lives alone, Dora has been abused by her husband, with little care for her family. She'll kill him if he shows up to the apartment block. She's the only tenant who can move someone into their apartment without Carl (you) knowing.
	Fulfledle Brukich	After explosions and panic in the streets of Krushvice, 6.	• Works out. Find dumbbells in his apartment. • Dangerous tendencies. Find broken bottle in his apartment. • Find Tobacco in apartment or see him smoking. • Find soccer ball in his apartment. • Find bow and arrows in his apartment. • See him drinking. • Find a fishing rod in his apartment.	• Bow and arrows • Broken bottle • Dumbbells • Turkish Coffee pot • Empty bottles • Tobacco • Soccer ball • Passport • Blue shirt • Robe • Pocket watch • Rum • Bag of candy • Fishing rod	—	—	• Mystery Box	This university student is 20 years old, lives alone, and is a revolutionary for the New Tomorrow Movement. If you use Rep Points, he tells you a story about the origin of his name. You'll be killed by him if you don't give him the box and peacefully agree with him. After you give him Danton's package, he leaves the apartments within a few days.
	Feodosius Ruan	Does not move in.	—	—	—	—	—	This is Bastian Walner's boss. He's having an affair with his wife, Clara Walner.

IMAGE	NAME	MOVE-IN TIME	INTERESTS	PERSONAL ITEMS	SPECIAL ITEMS	TASKS	INVOLVED IN THESE TASKS	NOTES
	Gerda Birkenfeld	Moves in with her mother.	• Find tennis kit in her apartment. • Find ice skates in her apartment. • Smokes a pipe. See her smoking. • Dangerous Tendencies. Find broken bottle in her apartment.	• Tennis kit • Ice skates • Broken bottle • Purple blouse • Passport • Blue blouse • 3 books • Empty bottles • Chocolate bar • Wine • 2 records	—	—	• Patriotic Production	Gerda is a 20-year-old female who lives with her mother. She's unemployed, has a patriotic nature, and is always whispering something about our Dear Leader.
	George Danton	Does not move in.	—	—	•Box •Leibespirit	•Mystery Box •Danton's Request •Under Suspicion •No More Propaganda •The Butcher from Agloe	•The Last Jerk •Weird Note	George is a revolutionary for the New Tomorrow movement. He helps you escape in "To Go Or Not To Go?" by reducing the price. You will be killed if you report the planned murder on Airel Johnson.
	Georg Dreiman	After situation with Airel Johnson has been solved. If she was killed, then after the call from Danton. If Airel was left alive, then after the newspaper release.	• See him smoking or find tobacco in his apartment. • Find dumbbells in his apartment. • Find fishing rod in his apartment. • Find world map in his apartment.	• Tobacco • Dumbbells • World map • Fishing rod • Passport • Sweater • Blue shirt • Robe	—	• To Go or Not to Go?	—	Georg is a 45-year-old CAT employee who lives with Krista-Maria Dreiman. He can help you and your family escape the country if you get to know Georg and his circumstances at the border.
	Inga Birkenfeld	During the time the propaganda truck is parked outside. If Danton is not helped, then after it explodes. If helped, then after the call from Danton or Ministry.	• Likes fine arts. Find reproductions in her apartment. • Keen on astronomy. Find spyglass in her apartment. • Performs amateur theater. Find theatre mask in her apartment. • Writing a novel. Find manuscript in her apartment. • Find Coin collecting album in her apartment.	• Reproductions • Spyglass • Chess • Theatre mask • Manuscript • Coin collecting album • Thimble and needle • Passport • Cardigan • Blue blouse • Foreign money • Handbag • Shoes • Brooch • Still • Star atlas	—	• Saving a Life	• Pick Up the Phone • Patriotic Production	Ingra is a 48-year-old chemist who lives with her daughter, Gerda Birkenfeld. She suffers from bronchitis and is a fanatical patriot.
	Irving Munch	After talking to Georg about leaving the country.	• Find chess in his apartment. • Smokes a pipe. See him smoking or find tobacco in his apartment. • Find stamp album in his apartment. • Find fishing rod in his apartment. • Find world map in his apartment. • Drinks. See him drinking. • Likes to draw. Find paints in his apartment. • Disgusted by propaganda posters. Talk to him.	• Chess • Tobacco • Stamp collection • Fishing rod • World map • Paints • Passport • Old sweater • Old shoes • Blue shirt • Pocket watch	—	—	• Ministry Order	This 70-year-old caretaker lives alone, is honest, and loves art. Suspiciously similar to Mark Ranek. Keeps items and sells them when they become illegal.
	Jacob Manishek	Is moved in Apartment 2 in beginning of the game.	• Likes to gamble. Find deck of cards and dice in his apartment. • Dangerous tendencies. Find broken bottle in his apartment. • Smokes a pipe. See Jacob smoking. • Doesn't make trouble. Find empty bottles in his apartment. • See him drink alcohol.	• Deck of cards and dice • Broken bottle • Empty bottles • Record • Old sweater • Mittens • Old shoes • Newspaper • 3 books	—	—	• Crime and Punishment	This 45-year-old man lives alone in Apartment 2 and is a slippery snake of a guy. He's rude to you and threatens your family when you exit conversations with him. Talking to your family gives you the option to talk seriously with Jacob. He produces drugs in his apartment. In the mission "Crime and Punishment," you can blackmail him for an extra $2000.
	Jeanne Oehrn	Does not move in.	—	—	—	—	—	Jeanne is a strong woman campaigning for women's rights. If you donate to her cause, Wise Leader wins the cockfight.
	Jones Popanedo	After "Crime and Punishment" is completed.	• Likes to gamble. Find deck of cards and dice in his apartment. • See him smoking or find tobacco in his apartment. • Find coin collection in his apartment. • See him drinking. • Dangerous tendencies. Find broken bottle in his apartment.	• Passport • Sweater • Boots • Blue shirt • Rove tobacco • Wine • Whiskey • Rum • Salt • Jeans • 3 records • 2 sodas • Coin collecting album • Empty bottles • Broken bottle • Deck of cards and dice	• Canned fish	• Great Offer • Making Up	• Farewell, Motherland!	Jones is a 40-year-old coal barge bosun who lives alone. He's impatient and moves away if you don't pay attention to his quests. He kills you if you don't agree with him during conversations.

Characters (continued)

IMAGE	NAME	MOVE-IN TIME	INTERESTS	PERSONAL ITEMS	SPECIAL ITEMS	TASKS	INVOLVED IN THESE TASKS	NOTES
	Justas Markovich	Does not move in.	—	—	—	—	• No More Propaganda	This technician has a weakness for alcohol and money.
	Klaus Schimmer	Is in apartment in the beginning of the game.	• Smokes a pipe. See him smoking, or find tobacco in his apartment. • Takes photos. Talk to Maria Schimmer during "That Which is Hidden Will Be Revealed," or find film in his apartment. • Wine steward. Talk to Rosa Ranek, or find wine in his apartment. • Find chess in his apartment. • Enjoys modeling. Talk with Mark Ranek or find ship model in his apartment. • Plays piano. See him playing or find sheet music in his apartment. • Likes to draw. Find paints in his apartment. • See him drinking.	• Paints • Ship model • Chess • Film • 7 books • Book • Boots • Blue shirt • Robe • Tobacco • Blue tie	• 2 books • 2 books • Teddy bear	• Papers Please! • Farewell, Motherland!	• Trust and Care • That Which Is Hidden Will Be Revealed • Ministry Order • Making Up	Klaus is a 40-year-old tobacco salesman who lives with Maria Schimmer in Apartment 1. He and his wife used to own the apartment building, but the State seized it. He fought the action, causing the authorities to hold a grudge. He can help reduce the cost of escaping the country by $10,000 if you give him cruise tickets in "Farewell, Motherland!" He kills you if you're rude to him. If you choose to report him during "Ministry Order," he's beaten and arrested. If he's ransomed to Jones during "Making Up," he attempts to escape the country on the barge, but it crashes and sinks, killing him. If you give him cruise tickets, he and Maria escape the country. If a report is written on Maria and she's arrested, Klaus commits suicide.
	Krista-Maria Dreiman	Moves in with husband Georg Dreiman when his requirements are completed.	• Seamstress. Find purple blouse in her apartment. • Likes to travel. Find world map in her apartment.	• Purple blouse • World map • Shoes • Green jacket • Blue blouse • Straw hat • Chocolate candy • Chocolate bar • Red dress • Thread	—	—	—	Krista is a 46-year-old jeweler who lives with her husband, Georg Dreiman. She's a sweet lady with a charming smile.
	Leo Gvizdek	Ten hours after Fulfledle moves in.	• Smokes a pipe. See him smoking or find tobacco in his apartment • Find dumbbells in his apartment. • Find fishing rod in his apartment. • Find soccer ball in his apartment. • Find Turkish coffee pot in his apartment. • Drinks. See him drinking.	• Tobacco • Fishing rod • Dumbbells • Soccer ball • Turkish coffee pot • Passport • Sweater • Blue shirt • Robe • Factory access card • Mittens • Wrench • Hard hat • Engine oil • Record	—	• Spick and Span! • All-In	• Horns & Hoofs	Leo is a 45-year-old turner who lives alone. He won the labor lottery and is in town for a celebration of his winnings.
	Maria Schimmer	Moved in when you did.	• Corresponds with foreigners. Find foreign letter in her apartment. • Find Turkish coffee pot in her apartment. • Performs in an amateur theater. Find theatre mask in her apartment. • Dreamy Nature. Find five books in her apartment. • Drinks. See her drinking. • Plays violin. See her playing.	• Turkish coffee pot • Theatre mask • Foreign letter • Passport • Blue skirt • Handbag • Slouch hat • Red dress • 5 books	• Pot • 2 books	—	• Ministry Order • Trust and Care • That Which Is Hidden Will Be Revealed • Gathering Data	Maria is a 35-year-old literature teacher who lives with her husband, Klaus, in Apartment 1. She commits suicide if you hint to Klaus being shot after his arrest. She kills you if you're rude after Klaus's arrest.
	Margaret Zauer	After "Creator's Life," when asking Antoine Grubic to move into the apartments.	• Find cook book in her apartment. • Find chess in her apartment. • Enjoys gardening. Find gardening magazine in her apartment. • Find Turkish coffee pot in her apartment. • Plays violin. Find violin concerto in her apartment. • Find tobacco in her apartment.	• Cook book • Chess • Gardening magazine • Turkish coffee pot • Violin concerto • Tobacco • Passport • Rum • 3 books • Whiskey • Wine • Empty bottles	—	—	—	Margaret is a 60-year-old librarian who lives alone. She's a typical old lady who will kill you if you confess to her what you did to books. She can be accused of the truck's explosion.
	Mark Ranek	Moved in at beginning of game.	• Find chess in his apartment. • Drinks. See him drinking. • Collects stamps. Find stamp album in his apartment. • Likes to fish. Talk to Rosa Ranek or find fishing rod in his apartment. • Smokes. See him smoking, or find tobacco in his apartment.	• Stamp album • Tobacco • Fishing rod • Chess • Passport • Old sweater • Old shoes • Blue shirt • Robe • Pocket watch • Green tie • Sweater • Tiger balm • Pistol	• Absentee certificate	• Missing Glasses	• That Which Is Hidden Will Be Revealed • Papers, Please! • Missing Glasses	Mark is a 65-year-old archive employee in Apartment 3, living with his wife, Rosa Ranek. Code 4087. This subject is under State protection.

IMAGE	NAME	MOVE-IN TIME	INTERESTS	PERSONAL ITEMS	SPECIAL ITEMS	TASKS	INVOLVED IN THESE TASKS	NOTES
	Martha Stein	This is your daughter. She lives with you.	—	• Ball • 4 books • Colored pencils • Wooden block • Duck • Stacking toy	—	• Ambulance	• Trust and Care • Missing Glasses	Martha is your daughter, a six-year-old girl who stays home with her mother. Code 1689, children under the age of 14 are under their parents' patronage. If a report is written on Martha, you will be arrested instead. Martha enjoys chocolates, sweets, cartoons, and games. She has a weak immunity, and she will eat any apples left in the basement.
	Nathan Kehler	Does not move in.	—	—	• Liebespirit • Money	—	• Great Offer • The Last Jerk	Nathan is a trader. He's normally found outside of Krushvice, 6 and sells a wide variety of items. After items are sold, it costs triple the sale price to buy them back. He buys anything.
	Patrick Stein	This is your son. He lives with you.	—	—	• Glasses	• Date Night • Faraway Lands • On the Brink of Expulsion	• Trust and Care • Local Opposition • Missing Glasses	Patrick is your son. He's 17 and a university student. He lives with you in the basement. He can be expelled if his tuition isn't paid. He can help the family escape in "To Go or Not to Go?" You need to give him the cruise tickets from the mission "Faraway Lands." He'll kill you if you report his mother to the State. Patrick is ambitious and commits rash acts.
	Public servant	Does not move in.	—	—	—	—	—	This is a policeman. He always works with a partner and never talks to you. Public servants always check reports and keep an eye on theft, whether it's you or a tenant. Removes dead bodies from the apartments.
	Rosa Ranek	Lives in apartments in beginning of game.	• Likes to cook. Talk to Mark Ranek, or find cook book in her apartment. • Knits. Find ball of yarn in her apartment. • Writing novel. Find manuscript in her apartment. • Enjoys gardening. Find gardening magazine in her apartment.	• Cook Book • Ball of yarn • Manuscript • Gardening magazine • Passport • Chocolate bar • First aid • Slouch hat	• Veil • Aspirin	—	• That Which Is Hidden Will Be Revealed • Making Up • Lonely Alloisius • Gathering Data • Wedding Preparations • Great Offer • Martha Is Sick	This 71-year-old cafeteria cook lives in apartment 3 with husband Mark Ranek. She's a sweet old lady who's calm and talkative. She hasn't seen her son in years.
	Rowena Petracke	Moves in during the mission asking for Antoine Grubic's move.	• See Rowena smoking. • Makes weird mechanisms at home. Find unfinished device in her apartment. • Suffers from migraines. Talk to her to discover this. • Performs in an amateur theater. Find theatre mask in her apartment. • Enjoys Modeling. Find ship model in her apartment. • Takes photos. Find film in her apartment.	• Unfinished device • Theatre mask • Ship model • Film • Thimble and needle • Purple blouse • Passport • Cardigan • Blue blouse • Comb • Camera	—	—	—	Rowena is a 43-year-old pipeline operator who lives alone. She's a modern woman and a feminist. She can be accused of the truck's explosion.
	Sarah Wattermach	After talking to Rosa in "Lonely Alloisius," she visits the apartment block.	• Not who she claims to be. Talk to Rosa Ranek. • Loves flowers. Talk to Maria Schimmer. • Doesn't make trouble. Find empty bottles in her apartment. • Likes to cook. Find cook book in her apartment.	• Empty bottles • Cook book • Passport • Meat pie • Purple blouse • Knife • Shoes • Straw hat • 6 books • Empty bottles • Light bulb • Narcotic • Lab coat	• Arsenic	• Difficult Conversation	• Gathering Data • Wedding Preparations	Sarah is a 42-year-old kindergarten teacher who lives with Alloisius Shpak. She's Rosa Ranek's niece. She's a strong and stately woman. Her real name is Vera Rentsi. She's wanted for poisoning, polygamy, theft, and fraud. She can kill you with a poisoned mug of coffee if you speak to her about her real name and force her out of the apartments.
	Sonora Voiko	Only if you advise Leo Gvizdek to share his winnings with your family in "All-In."	• Seamstress. Find purple blouse in her apartment. • Likes to cook. See her cooking. • Find theatre mask in her apartment. • Find Turkish coffee pot in her apartment. • Find five books in her apartment.	• 5 books • Purple blouse • Turkish coffee pot • Theatre mask • Blue blouse • Shoes • Straw hat • Red dress • Eyeglasses • Slouch hat • Handbag • Wine • Light bulb • 2 sodas • Blue skirt • Chocolate candy • Chocolate bar • Thread • Black tea	—	—	—	Sonora is a 46-year-old merchant, an extravagant and fussy woman.

Tasks & Quests

Pick up missions in *Beholder* by talking to anyone with an exclamation point above their head. Other missions only appear if you take special interest in tenants' lives, which means digging deep into conversation threads with them. Other missions are given over the phone, from your boss. The missions are displayed on the left side of the screen in the form of a column of icons, with the character's face associated with that task. Beware that some tasks have time limits; to get the reward from that mission, you must complete it in the time given.

You earn reputation points, money, and sometimes items by completing missions. You spend reputation points by persuading other characters or purchasing surveillance cameras from the State Store. If your reputation dips into negative numbers, you'll be arrested.

Following are details on all the tasks in the game, in alphabetical order.

MISSION	DESCRIPTION	UNLOCKING	TIPS	REWARD	NOTES
Accession	Bruno Hempf issues this early task.	—	• Search your office desk for two cameras. • Talk with your boss on the phone. • Set up two cameras for surveillance in the dining hall, then call the Ministry.	$300 100 RP Unlocks "Crime and Punishment"	—
Affordable Apartment	This task is automatically given. There's no penalty for not completing it.	—	• Complete the repairs and lease any apartment.	Unlocks "Mystery Box."	
All-In	Leo Gvizdek asks for your advice on what to do with his lottery winnings.	Twelve hours after you finish "Spick and Span!"	• Persuading him to invest in fruit and berry development yields $10,000. • Persuading him to help his family results in his sister moving in. • Persuading him to invest in the savings bank results him dying on the way. • Persuading him to invest in cattle development results in him losing all his money and being fired. Costs you 500 RP and earns you $5000.	$0 to $10,000	—
Ambulance	Martha Stein wants you to find the medicine chest for her games.	—	• Purchase the first aid kit for $200.	50 RP	—
Bedtime Stories	Anna Stein asks you to buy a radio for your daughter.	—	• Buy a radio from Nathan Kehler for $2250.	100 RP	—
Bills, Bills, and More Bills	Anna Stein issues this mission. You have 24 hours to complete. Anna (wife) needs money to pay for municipal services.	—	• Give her $700.	50 RP	24 hours to complete. Failure costs 50 RP, and also $1500 for the bill.
Broken TV	Anna Stein asks you to repair your TV.	Given early in the game. Speak to Anna. You can agree or choose not to. Agreeing is better.	• Purchase repair tools for $50. • Go to the TV in the basement and select the option to repair it.	50 RP	—
But What If She…	Bastian Walner suspects his wife of cheating on him and asks you to follow her.	Complete "The Hunt for an Engineer."	• Find solid evidence of Clara having an affair. • Talk to him or Clara. • Accept Clara's bribe and talk to Bastian.	Top secret blueprints	
Change Is Coming	The Ministry wants you prepared for the inspection.	Complete "Completion Report."	• Be prepared for the inspection.	Game finale	—
Chaos and Anarchy	Ministry needs you to remove the anti-government poster from the front of the building immediately.	—	• Get the tools needed from your desk in your office. • Go to the top floor. • Click on the banners to cut them down.	Unlocks "Local Opposition."	—
Citizen Registration	Ministry needs you to write reports on the tenants.	Complete "Patriotic Production."	• Write five characteristics on tenants.	—	—
Chocolate Candy	Anna Stein issues this quest. You should buy candy for your wife.	—	• Buy a chocolate candy from Nathan Kehler. • Give the chocolate to Anna.	50 RP	—
Complaints About Clara	Ministry orders you to take care of the noisy tenant.	—	• Find Clara as a girlfriend instead of Sarah. To do this, browse through the mailbox and mail when you get the quest concerning the doctor's loneliness.	$5000 Cruise tickets (talk to Clara)	12 hours to complete.
Completion Report	This mission appears automatically. You must call the Ministry.	Complete "Ministry Order."	• Call the boss from the office phone.	500 RP Unlocks "Propaganda."	—
Creator's Life	Antoine Grubic issues this mission. You need to move Antoine Grubic into the apartments.	—	• Antoine asks you to get him some supplies. • Find the paints in the basement on the table. • Find a pair of scissors in the basement. • Give supplies to Antoine.	—	36 hours to complete.

MISSION	DESCRIPTION	UNLOCKING	TIPS	REWARD	NOTES
Crime and Punishment	Ministry mission. Watch Jacob Manishek. Use cameras bought from the store.	Complete "Accession."	• Search Apartment 2 and install camera(s). • Get data on Jacob Manishek. • Call Ministry to get reward. • Wait for Jacob to make drugs in apartment to gather evidence. • Write a report on Jacob to get another reward. • Repair Apartment 2 to prepare for new tenant. • Find a tenant—either Alloisius Shpak or Jones Popanedo. • Call Ministry after tenant moves in to collect reward.	$500, 50 RP $1000, 250 RP $1000, 50 RP $1000, 250 RP	48 hours to complete. If you fail, you're arrested.
Date Night	Patrick Stein wants money so he can take a girl on a date.	—	• Give Patrick $550 for the tickets. • You can also spend another $20 for flowers.	50 RP	12 hours to complete. Failure costs 50 RP.
Danton's Request	George Danton gives you this mission on the phone. Move Antoine Grubic into the apartments.	—	• Make repairs on apartment. • Move Antoine Grubic in.	$3000	—
Difficult Conversation	Sarah Wattermach issues this mission. Tell the doctor about the Raneks' niece.	—	• Talk to Alloisius Shpak about the woman on the porch.	—	—
Document Theft	Albert Meineke asks you to obtain three passports.	—	• Get three passports by stealing from tenants or from belongings previous tenants have left behind. • Give the passports to Albert. • Agree to help with the blueprints.	$2000 Unlocks "The Hunt for an Engineer."	—
Drunk and Happy	Clara Jacque asks for booze.	Complete "Love on the Phone."	• Give Clara any kind of booze. She comments on the quality of the booze you give her. You can give her whiskey or wine.	$500	—
Farewell, Motherland!	Klaus Schimmer wants your help escaping.	Complete "Papers, Please!"	Option 1: The Coal Barge If Jones Popanedo is a tenant, he provides the task "Great Offer," where you sell canned fish for at least $3000. Accept to get canned fish, and give it to Nathan Kehler. He returns with $1500 from canned goods. Take this to Jones and offer to earn money. Carl offers up the Schimmers to work for Jones on the coal barge. Talk to Klaus. Jones, Klaus, and Maria all move out and escape on the barge. Option 2: The Holiday Cruise Obtain the cruise tickets from Alloisius Shpak at the end of "Lonely Alloisius" and "Love on the Phone." Or from Alloisius or Clara Jacque at the end of "Lonely Alloisius" and "Complaints About Clara." Hand the tickets to Klaus. Klaus and Maria move out and escape on the cruise.	$3000	If you choose "The Holiday Cruise" route, Klaus and Maria help you escape the country at the end of the game by lowering the price of escape by $10,000.
Empty House	This mission is automatically given. Move in new tenants immediately.	—	• Lease any apartment.	—	8 hours to complete. If you fail, you're arrested.
Fear and Hate	Dora Noel issues this mission. She wants you to find a gun for her.	Complete "Insomnia."	• Dora wants protection from her husband. Find a gun for Dora. • Mark Ranek, Airel Johnson, and Antoine Grubic all have pistols in their apartments, or you can buy one for $6000. • Give Dora the gun.	$1000 700 RP	48 hours to complete. No penalties for not completing in time.
Faraway Lands	Patrick Stein wants money to travel abroad.	Complete "On the Brink of Expulsion."	Give Patrick (your son) $20,000, or give him the cruise tickets.	—	48 hours to complete. If you fail, you're penalized $5000 and 250 RP.
Gathering Data	Alloisius Shpak wants you to gather data on Sarah.	Complete "Difficult Conversation."	• Talk to Maria Schimmer, or see Sarah cooking. • Talk to Rosa Ranek about Sarah to find out she's not who she says she is. • Call Ministry to report Sarah, or talk to Sarah and accept her bribe. • Tell Alloisius what you found out about her liking flowers. He won't speak to you anymore.	Unlocks "Wedding Preparations."	48 hours to complete. No penalty if you fail.

Tasks & Quests (continued)

MISSION	DESCRIPTION	UNLOCKING	TIPS	REWARD	NOTES
Great Offer	Jones Popanedo offers to pay you to sell his canned goods.	—	• Give the canned goods to Rosa Ranek (this results in food poisoning at the cafeteria, and Rosa refuses to pay for the canned goods). • Talk to Jones Popanedo. He becomes angry and demands $3000. • Pay Jones, or use RP to diffuse the dispute, or send the Schimmers on a barge as payment. • An alternative is to sell the canned goods to the merchant with the top hat. He pays $1500. This is the same result as if you give Rosa the canned goods.	Unlocks "Making Up."	—
Glory to the War Hero	This is a Ministry mission. You need to rent the apartment to General Airel Johnson.	—	• Rent an apartment to the general. • You'll be fined $500 and $1000 for having him in your building. • One day later you receive "The Butcher from Agloe" mission.	Unlocks "The Butcher from Agloe."	24 hours to complete. If you fail, you're arrested.
Grocery Money	Anna Stein needs grocery money.	—	• Give your wife $500.	50 RP	—
Horns & Hoofs	You receive an anonymous phone call about moving Leo Gvizdek in.	—	• Move Leo Gvizdek into an apartment. • Purchase a green tie ($195), or steal one. • When Leo asks for advice, persuade him to invest in Horns & Hoofs.	$5500 Leo moves out.	During "All In," you can convince Leo to invest his winnings in cattle development at a cost of 500 RP.
Homeland Will Never Forgive	Albert Meineke wants you to acquire the blueprints from Bastian Walner.	Complete "The Hunt for an Engineer."	• Talk to Bastian and complete "But What If She…" • Give the blueprints to Albert after Bastian gives them to you.	—	—
Insomnia	Dora Noel wants you to find her a sleeping bag.	Watch Dora's sleep pattern.	• Talk to Dora after seeing her struggling with sleep. • Buy sleeping aid from the merchant. • Give the pills to Dora.	250 RP Unlocks "Fear and Hate."	—
Life-Threatening Condition	Anna Stein wants you to find the money to treat Martha.	—	• Find money by stealing or gathering things to sell. • Gather illegal items from the merchant and blackmail tenants, profile them, or report them.	1000 RP Unlocks "Seasonal Fruit."	80 hours to complete. Fail, and Martha dies.
Local Opposition	This is automatically unlocked. You need to tell Patrick to stop hanging the anti-government posters.	Complete "Chaos and Anarchy."	• Talk to Patrick about the posters. • Answer the call from Ministry. • Agree to turn your son in, and he will be taken to corrections. • Refuse to turn your son in, and "Chaos and Anarchy" continues.	Unlocks "Pick Up the Phone."	—
Lonely Alloisius	Alloisius Shpak asks you to find him a girlfriend.	—	Option 1 Dial the number you get in the mail. You're asked to wait for a callback. They accept the offer and arrive. Tell Alloisius about the girl. Buy a chocolate bar from Nathan Kehler, or steal one. Give it to Alloisius, and he goes on the date. When he returns, ask him what happened. He asks if his girlfriend can stay with him. Agree and get $500, but deny and get $1000. Clara Jacques arrives and moves in with Alloisius. After some game hours, he asks you to get rid of Clara. If you refuse, this mission ends with no reward, Alloisius leaves permanently, you get a call from Ministry, and "Complaints About Clara" unlocks. Then you can evict Clara in one of these ways: • Talk to Clara and demand she leaves, -1000 RP. • Talk to Clara and bribe her for -$5000. • Talk to Clara and ask her. This unlocks "Love on the Phone" and ends this mission. Purchase an illegal item from Nathan Kehler, or steal one, then plant evidence in Clara's apartment and write a report. Option 2 Comfort Rosa Ranek concerning lonely Alloisius, then tell Alloisius about his new girlfriend. Sarah Wattermach arrives. Greet her and tell Alloisius about her. She moves in with him and eventually he wants info: "Gathering Data" unlocks.	Option 1 unlocks "Drunk and Happy," "Missing Glasses," and "Complaints About Clara." Option 2 unlocks "Gathering Data." "Wedding Preparations," "Difficult Conversation" and "Love on the Phone" are unlocked either way.	36 hours to complete.
Love on the Phone	Alloisius Shpak's girlfriend is bugging him. He wants you to evict her.	Complete "Drunk and Happy."	• Clara asks you to find Alloisius' cache. If you do this, she leaves. • Talk to Alloisius about family jewels. If asked about the perfect place to hide something, he reveals a location. Tell Clara the location. She steals the item and leaves. • Talk to Alloisius. He gives you the cruise tickets and leaves the apartments.	Cruise tickets	—
Making Up	Jones Popanedo needs money before he leaves.	Complete "Great Offer."	• Give Jones the money he needs by pulling it out of your saved money, or steal and sell items.	—	70 hours to complete. No penalties if you don't complete in time.
Martha's Doctor	Anna Stein says the pills didn't work for Martha. She wants you to find a doctor.	Complete "Martha Is Sick."	• Talk to Alloisius, and he examines Martha. He tells you he needs $20,000 to save her life.	150 RP	36 hours to complete. Failure costs 150 RP.
Martha Is Sick	Anna Stein asks you to find aspirin for Martha.	—	• Steal aspirin from the Schimmers in Apartment 1. • Or buy it from Nathan Kehler. • Or trade Rosa Ranek a cardigan for it. The cardigan can be stolen from apartments or purchased from Nathan Kehler.	50 RP	30 hours to complete. Failure costs 50 RP.
Ministry Inquiry	Ministry wants you to help Ingra Birkenfeld settle in.	Complete "Pick Up the Phone."	• Help Ingra Birkenfeld settle in the house.	Unlocks "No More Jokes."	48 hours to complete. Failure costs $15,000.

MISSION	DESCRIPTION	UNLOCKING	TIPS	REWARD	NOTES
Ministry Order	Ministry wants you to find a way to evict Klaus Schimmer from Apartment 1.	Complete "That Which Is Hidden Will Be Revealed."	Option 1: Report Klaus • If no book is in Apartment 1, buy illegal item from Kehler, or steal one from tenant. • Place item in furniture in Apartment 1, clicking on red text to add it as evidence. Use this to report Klaus. Option 2: Help Klaus Escape • Talk to Klaus. Truthfully tell him about your task. Offer to help him. Then insist on it. This unlocks "Papers, Please!" • Complete "Papers, Please!" and "Farewell, Motherland" to complete this mission.	$3000 500 RP Unlocks "Completion Report."	240 hours to complete. If you fail, you're arrested. If you help Klaus escape, then you are fined when Mark Ranek moves out.
Missing Glasses	Mark Ranek asks you to help him find his glasses.	—	• Talk to Martha (your wife). • Give Martha Chocolate, stolen or purchased. • Confront Patrick Stein to get the missing glasses. • Return to Mark. If you tell the truth about Patrick using the glasses for school, you earn $500.	$500	—
Mystery Box	George Danton asks you to give a box to Fulfledle Brukich.	—	• Talk to Fulfledle Brukich. • Give the box to Fulfledle Brukich.	$3000	—
No More Jokes	Ministry wants you to find the bomb in the apartment building.	Complete "Ministry Inquiry."	• Locate the bomb in the washroom. • Take the device. • Call Ministry.	Unlocks "Tick Tock BOOM!"	24 hours to complete. Fail, and the building explodes.
No More Propaganda	George Danton calls and asks you to reprogram the propagation machine to send out messages encouraging revolution.	—	Option 1 • Tempt Justas Markovich with a bottle of rum. • Use a screwdriver to open the panel. • Enter the code 21/12/1864 (Great Leader's B-day). • Set the frequency to 101.9. Option 2 • Follow Option 1 up to frequency entry. • Set the frequency to 81.6 .	—	48 hours to complete. Asking Justas to leave ahead of schedule fails the mission. When talking about the car, you either use 500 RP or $5000 to change the settings. The screwdriver is either in your apartment or purchased. Option 2 leads to a $3000 reward, but Ministry fines you that much. Option 1 earns you the "Bad Time Stories" Achievement.
On the Brink of Expulsion	Patrick Stein needs more money to pay for school.	—	• Give Patrick $15,000, or refuse and be fined the same amount. Let him work in the mines, and you end up sending him abroad. He becomes lost and ends up in the wrong country.	750 RP	48 hours to complete.
Papers, Please!	Klaus Schimmer asks you to get his absentee certificate from the city archive, giving him a way to escape the country.	Complete "That Which Is Hidden Will Be Revealed."	• Talk to Mark Ranek and ask to help Klaus. Be honest about your intentions during the conversation. • Mark wants whiskey as a bribe. Buy from Kehler or get it from Alloisius (which he gives you if you tell him you've heard of him when you first talk to him). • Or bribe Mark with $500 and compliments, or $1000 with no compliments. • Mark leaves the building. Talk to him when he returns to get absentee certificate.	Unlocks "Farewell, Motherland!"	If you choose to bribe Ranek with either whiskey or money, you're fined $3000 later when the Raneks move out.
Patriotic Production	An unidentified terrorist calls and orders you to kill Ingra Birkenfeld.	—	Option 1 • Talk to Ingra about her cough. • Buy a bottle of poison or rat poison. • Give Ingra one of the poisons as a cough remedy. Option 2 • Find foreign coins in Ingra's apartment. • Tell Gerda about her mother disobeying the law.	$5000 Unlocks "Citizen Registration."	—
Pick Up the Phone	This mission is given automatically. Pick up the phone.	Complete "Local Opposition."	• Take the roll of fabric (from the mission "Local Opposition") to blame someone, and make a report for the Ministry of the person you blamed.	Unlocks "Repairs."	6 hours to complete. If you don't pass, you're arrested and the game is over. There are eight total "Pick Up the Phone" missions.
Propaganda	Ministry wants you to hang three banners in the hallways.	Complete "Completion Report."	• Hang the three banners in the hallways on different floors of the building.	$1000	24 hours to complete. You're penalized $1000 if you fail.
Repairs	Ministry wants you to repair everything that's broken in the building.	Complete "Pick Up the Phone."	• Purchase electrician's kits and cabinetmaker's kits for $50 each. • Repair everything that's broken in the building.	—	48 hours to complete. Failure costs $2000.
Saving a Life	Ingra Birkenfeld asks you to help her leave the country.	Complete "Homeland Will Never Forgive."	• Give her your clean passports, and she leaves immediately. • Evict her for 1000 RP.	—	—
Seasonal Fruit	Anna Stein asks you to bring her an apple.	Complete "Life-Threatening Condition."	• Steal or buy a red or green apple from Kehler. • Give the apple to Anna.	350 RP	24 hours to complete. Failure costs 50 RP.
Spick and Span!	Leo Gvizdek needs a tie.	Complete "Life-Threatening Condition."	• Buy a green or blue tie from Kehler, or steal one from an apartment. • Give Leo the tie.	$300 Unlocks "All-In."	—
That Which Is Hidden Will Be Revealed	Ministry wants you to talk to the tenants about Klaus Schimmer.	Complete "Crime and Punishment."	Part 1 • Talk with Schimmer's wife. • Talk to Mark Ranek. • Talk to Rosa Ranek. Part 2 • Profile Klaus. Part 3 • Call Ministry and report that the task is completed.	$500 15 RP	48 hours to complete. Costs $1000 if not completed in time. When you talk to Mark, be honest to get three pieces of evidence for Klaus (150 RP). You can ask Alloisius about Klaus during Part 1 for smokes info. There are seven more parts to this mission. The final unlocks "Between Life and Death."

MISSION	DESCRIPTION	UNLOCKING	TIPS	REWARD	NOTES
The Butcher from Agloe	George Danton wants you to get evidence that the general is the butcher of Agloe.	Complete "Glory to the War Hero."	Option 1 • Find a medal in Airel Johnson's apartment, confirming George's theory. • Call George Danton to refuse to kill the general. • Alert Airel Johnson about the assassination attempt. • Respond to the Ministry's call. Option 2 • Do Option 1, but agree to kill the general. • Take a bomb from the revolutionists at left street corner and give it to Airel (repercussions will be had). • Or convince Airel to drink rat poison (only available if it's in your inventory—Dora Noel has it in her apartment). • Or lure Airel to street corner to collect champagne—revolutionists will shoot him. • Answer the Ministry's call.	—	—
The Hunt for an Engineer	Albert Meineke wants you to move Bastian Walner into the building. He's an engineer.	Complete "Document Theft."	• Move Bastian and his wife into the building.	Unlocks "Homeland Will Never Forgive."	—
Tick Tock Boom!	Ministry needs you to deactivate the bomb.	Complete "No More Jokes."	• Get the leaflet from the mailbox. It explains how to disarm the bomb. • Interact with the bomb on the washroom floor to figure out which of three bomb types it is. • Take the clippers from your desk. • Return to the bomb and disarm it by clipping wires according to the bomb type seen in the leaflet.	Unlocks "Completion Report."	1 minute to complete. If you fail, the building explodes.
To Go or Not to Go?	Georg Dreiman needs money so he can help you leave the country.	—	• The front cost of emigration is $145,000, but you can lessen the amount by having tickets and friends aboard. For every person you help leave the country, the price is reduced. Help five and no tickets, and the price is $35,000. Help four and no tickets, and the price goes up to $45,000. • Pay Dreiman the amount needed to leave the country.	Game finale	—
Trust and Care	You haven't been paying attention to your family lately. Talk with them.	Complete "Crime and Punishment."	• Talk with Anna. She wants to borrow a pot from the neighbors. • Talk with Maria Schimmer to get the pot for Anna for free. • Talk with Martha; she lost her doll. • You can find the doll in the basement cupboard next to one of the beds. • Talk with Patrick; find books on economics for him. • Buy the book from Nathan Kehler for $2250, or from Klaus Schimmer for free.	—	48 hours to complete.
Under Suspicion	George Danton wants you to follow Antoine Grubic.	Complete "Danton's Request."	• Spy on Grubic and discover him making propaganda posters and reading. • Write a report on these illegal activities. • Answer the Ministry call. • Tell Danton about Grubic, or keep quiet and protect Grubic.	Report on Grubic and get fined $100, but receive $2000 for vigilance.	—
Unexpected Turn	Ministry wants you to find out who blew up the mobile propaganda unit.	Complete "No More Propaganda."	• Search the vehicle outside. • Plant the bomb parts on Margaret Zauer. • Write a report.	—	36 hours to complete. You're arrested if you fail to complete within the time limit.
Weather at Home	Anna Stein asks you to bring a heater home.	Complete "Seasonal Fruit."	• Buy a heater from the merchant for $2250.	450 RP	24 hours to complete. Failure costs you 50 RP.
Weird Note	Anna Stein found a note saying you need to call 89-35-76.	—	• This is part of Danton and Antoine Grubic's storyline. It's a number to call Antoine. He requests to stay with you for a few days. You can choose to agree or refuse to help. If you let him stay, George Danton asks if you've seen him. Give him up or keep him hidden. Keep him hidden, and the Ministry calls you with a reward.	$3000 Ministry reward	—
Wedding Preparations	Alloisius Shpak asks you to find a veil for Sarah.	—	• Talk to Rosa Ranek about the veil, and exchange it for tea. • Talk to Anna about making a veil for Sarah. • Give one of the veils to Alloisius.	250 RP	24 hours to complete.
The Last Jerk	Anna Stein wants you to get medicine for Martha, who's sick again.	Complete "Life-Threatening Condition."	• Purchase Liebespirit for $15,000, or acquire it.	1000 RP	120 hours to complete. Failure costs you 500 RP.

Blissful Sleep

Blissful Sleep is the DLC for Beholder. It's an adventure where you play as Hector Medina, the former building manager, making this a prequel to Beholder that gives you a look at the lives of the tenants before Carl Stein and his family move in. Where Beholder is about totalitarian government, Blissful Sleep focuses on the opening of a euthanasia center. Citizens are directed there when they turn 85. Hector, who is nowhere near that age, has had his birth date recorded incorrectly. Like Carl, Hector is a spy for the State and uses his skills in attempt to get out of this sticky situation. This download costs $1.99.

THE BINDING OF ISAAC: REBIRTH

Developer	Nicalis, Inc.
Publisher	Nicalis, Inc.
Year Released	2014
Platforms	Microsoft Windows, OS X, Linux, PS4, PS Vita, Wii U, New Nintendo 3DS, Xbox One, iOS, Nintendo Switch
Type	Roguelike
Suggested Age	17+
Cost	$14.99

$ IN-GAME PURCHASES
None

Game Overview

The Binding of Isaac: Rebirth is a roguelike action game that features procedurally generated dungeon crawls with hundreds of enemies and bosses, and a gigantic selection of collectibles and items that can change your game. Your goal is to fight your way to the bottom of the basement-dungeons and defeat Isaac's mother so that you can escape with your life.

What You Need to Know

The HUD

The Binding of Isaac: Rebirth has a standard mobile HUD that features the amount of gold, keys, and bombs being carried; your current number of hearts, and the map. The map moves and expands as you enter new rooms. The standard controls for mobile are two circular movement pads in the corners of the screen. However, if you have another type of controller connected to your device, you may change your controller type in the Options section of the Pause menu.

Map

As you progress through the dungeon in *The Binding of Isaac*, your map changes to show helpful information such as the current room you're in, item and pickup icons, and icons for the special rooms in the game. These rooms include boss rooms, treasure rooms, shops, arcades, devil/angel rooms, as well as various locked or hidden rooms.

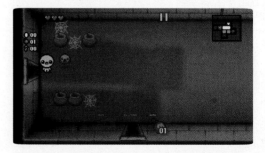

Rocks

Oftentimes rocks are just in your way and act as obstacles, but after you clear a room, take your time and inspect the rocks. A rock featuring a small X indicates treasure inside—blow it up.

Finding a Secret Room

There are two secret rooms in each level of the game, and they always have at least one shopkeeper. Secret rooms are identifiable by a crack in the wall that can be blown up, but not every crack is an entrance to a secret room.

Walking Away

After clearing a room, make a practice of inspecting items and blowing up rocks and other items. Note that sometimes, though, blowing up rocks reveals more enemies. It's not a good idea to engage enemies when you're low on health. If you discover an enemy in a room you've already cleared, consider simply walking out of the room and back in. This clears the new enemy that spawned as a result of your searching.

Don't Waste Your Bombs

If there's something in a room you want to blow up but you're low on bombs, consider a couple of alternatives. Check whether there are any enemies present that drop bombs, and lead them to the thing you want to explode. Another option is to push TNT barrels toward your target and use the tears to blow up the barrels.

Spikes

If there's an item trapped behind a wall of spikes, don't hurt yourself getting it. Place a bomb where its explosion pushes the item away from the spikes.

Making an Escape

Entering a new room, you never know what to expect. As soon as you step inside, the doors lock behind you. If you see an enemy you don't think you can beat yet, keep in mind that the doors should unlock after you've been in a room for 90 seconds, allowing you to escape. Alternatively, you can blow up the doors to open them. However, note that some rooms are immune to both methods.

Making a Bridge

Sometimes you find a room with a chest in the center, but you can't reach the chest because of a large ravine in the floor. Look around— you should find some rocks on your side of the ravine. Place a bomb on the side of a rock facing away from the ravine to blow the rock into the ravine. This creates a bridge for you to safely cross. Go grab the treasure!

BLOONS TD 5

Developer	Kaiparasoft
Publisher	Ninja Kiwi
Year Released	2011
Platforms	PC/Mac, iOS, Android, Xbox One, PS4, Steam
Type	Tower defense
ESRB	E
Cost	$2.99 on mobile; $9.99 on PC; $14.99 on consoles

 IN-GAME PURCHASES

Yes

Game Overview

Bloon TD 5 is the fourth game in the *Bloons Tower Defense* series. This is a tower defense game. The towers are various types of monkeys, gadgets, and traps, each with a unique set of special skills. These skills are used to take out balloons (or Bloons, as they're called in the game) that travel onto the screen through an entry point, follow a path, and then try to exit the screen through an exit point. Your job is to prevent the Bloons from exiting. Each Bloon you burst earns you Monkey Cash and XP, and you continue to upgrade and purchase more towers with those points. Bloons get increasingly difficult to destroy as more and higher-level Bloons (more layers) enter the board at a higher frequency rate. However, there's a particular tower type or trap that exploits each of the Bloons' weakness. And that's *Bloons TD 5* in a nutshell.

What You Need to Know

The quickest way to get up to speed and start beating levels is to understand the Bloon hierarchy and what tower you need to destroy each Bloon type. So first we'll jump into the Bloon tables, and once those Bloons' weaknesses are revealed, we'll discuss the tower types and their strengths. Finally, we'll discuss strategy, and how to easily control the chaos and start winning games and earning metals.

Bloon Types

This table lists all the Bloon types and their characteristics in ascending order, from the most basic to the most advanced. To understand "child of" and "parent to," keep in mind that Bloons encapsulate other Bloons. Since the Red Bloon is at the core of all Bloons, the Red Bloon is a child of (spawned from) a Blue Bloon and is the parent of (spawns) nothing.

IMAGE	BLOON NAME	CHILD OF (SPAWNS FROM)	PARENT TO (SPAWNS)	HITS TO DESTROY	SPEED (1 TO 11)	IMMUNE TO	ROUND APPEARANCE
	Red	Blue	—	1	3	—	1
	Blue	Green	Red	2	4	—	3
	Green	Yellow	Blue	3	5	—	6
	Yellow	Pink	Green	4	10	—	11
	Pink	Black and White	Yellow	5	11	—	15
	Camo	DDT (Bloons Monkey City, Ceramic with Regrowth)	Depends on original Bloon color	11	Depends on original Bloon color	Cannot be detected by most towers (without special upgrades). Dartling Gun, Ninja Monkey, and Spike Factory can detect Camo without upgrades.	24
	Black	Zebra and Lead Bloons	(x2) Pink	11	5	Explosions	20
	White	Zebra and Lead Bloons	(x2) Pink	11	6	Freezing	22
	Lead	—	(x2) Black	23	3	Sharp Projectiles and Lasers	28
	Zebra	Rainbow (spawns 2 Zebras)	(1) Black, (1) White	23	5	Bombs and ice	26
	Rainbow	Ceramic	(x2) Zebra	47	7	Its children are immune to bombs and Ice	35
	Ceramic	MOAB, DDT (spawns 6 Camo Regen Ceramics)	(x2) Rainbow	104	8	Glue (takes one hit to break immunity to Glue)	40
	Massive Ornery Air Blimp (MOAB)	BFB	(x4) Ceramic	616	3	—	46
	Brutal Floating Behemoth (BFB)	ZOMG	(x4) MOABs	3164	1	—	60
	Zeppelin Of Mighty Gargantuaness (ZOMG)	Nothing	(x4) BFBs	16,656	4/5	—	85

Camo Bloons

One of the biggest, earliest obstacles is the Camo Bloon. A single one comes out early to warn you of what's ahead. At Level 33, a group comes out alone, so if you don't have a Ninja Monkey and a Spike Factory, you could be in trouble. There's also a group that comes out last on Level 37. When you start combining them with Ceramic, things get ugly.

Camo Bloons can only be seen by Dartling Guns and Spike Factories. All other towers require upgrades or nearby towers that give them the ability to see Camo. If a tower can't see them, the Camo Bloon passes through undetected and unharmed, even if explosions are occurring all around them. If they have Regrowth, they become extremely dangerous. This table shows how to combat Camo Bloons.

Regrowth Bloon

The heart-shaped Bloon is a Regrowth Bloon. These grow a new layer every second that passes, but they don't surpass their original form (what color they started as). When they have Camo attributes, they become problematic. Monkey Apprentice with the Monkey Sense upgrade and an Engineer with Cleansing Foam are easy ways to counter this.

TOWER	UPGRADE	NOTES
Dart Monkey	Enhanced Eyesight 1st path, 2nd upgrade	Gives better range. With the Triple Darts upgrade, it can destroy three layers of the Camo Bloon. The Juggernaut (1st path, 4th upgrade) pops Camo Leads.
Monkey Sub	Submerge and Support 1st path, 3rd upgrade	It can pop Camos if using Advanced Intel (1st path, 1st upgrade), but only if there's another tower that can see Camo. With Submerge and Support, Camos lose their status when they pass through the green target that appears when submerged.
Monkey Engineer	Cleansing Foam 1st path, 3rd upgrade	Sprays foam that removes Camo and Regen, and pops Leads but cannot detect Camo unless its Camo is first removed with the foam.
Sniper Monkey	Night Vision Goggles 2nd path, 2nd upgrade	Allows detection and shooting of Camo Bloons. Also pops Camo Leads with the Full Metal Jacket upgrade (1st path, 1st upgrade).
Boomerang Thrower	Glaive Lord 1st path, 4th upgrade	Two permanent Glaives orbit the tower and pop an infinite amount of Bloons as long as the Glaives make contact. This also pops Lead Bloons.

TOWER	UPGRADE	NOTES
Ninja Monkey	—	The Ninja Monkey sees Camo with no upgrades. With Double Shot (1/3) or Bloonjitsu (1/4), can pop two to five layers of Camo Bloons. Destroys Camo Leads with a Flash Bomb upgrade (2/3).
Bomb Tower	MOAB Assassin 2nd path, 4th upgrade	This only works if the Camo Bloon is the strongest Bloon on the board, and only pops one layer. This is one of the weakest Camo-popping options.
Ice Tower	Viral Frost 1st path, 4th upgrade Absolute Zero 2nd path, 4th upgrade	Viral Frost causes Frozen Bloons to freeze others that come in contact, Camo Bloons included. Absolute Zero (ability) freezes Camo Bloons, and the Tier 4 Ice Fortress can take away the Camo status.
Glue Gunner	Glue Striker 2nd path, 4th upgrade	Glue Striker (ability) glues everything on-screen, Camos included, no matter if there's Camo-detection support.
Monkey Buccaneer	Crows Nest 2nd path, 2nd upgrade	Allows Buccaneer to hit Camo Bloons.
Monkey Ace	Spy Plane 2nd path, 2nd upgrade	Spy Plane allows Camo Bloon hits. Neva-Miss Targeting (1/3) and Spectre (1/4) need Spy Plane upgrade to pop Camo Bloons.
Super Monkey	Temple of the Monkey God 1st path, 4th upgrade	With a Tier 3 Super Monkey Lair, allows Camo detection—even if another tower with Camo detection is sacrificed.
Monkey Apprentice	Monkey Sense 2nd path, 2nd upgrade	Allows the Monkey Apprentice to hit Camo Bloons.
Monkey Village	Radar Scanner 2nd path, 2nd upgrade	Allows towers within its radius to hit Camo Bloons. The Energy Beacon (1st path, 4th upgrade) can't pop Camo Bloons without this upgrade.
Mortar Tower	Signal Flare 2nd path, 3rd upgrade	Camo Bloons popped by Flares permanently lose their Camo, and the tower cannot detect Camos without this upgrade.
Dartling Gun	No upgrade required	Pops Camo Bloons without upgrades, but needs Depleted Bloontonium (2/2) or Ray of Doom (1/4) to pop Camo Leads.
Spike Factory	No upgrade required	Non-upgraded Spikes pop Camo Bloons, but need White Hot Spikes upgrade (1/2) to destroy Camo Leads.
Heli Pilot	Enhanced IFR Instruments 2nd path, 2nd upgrade	Detects and shoots Camo Bloons, but needs upgrades—Razor Rotors (1/3) or Apache Dartship (1/4)—to pop Camo Leads.
Road Spikes	—	Costs $30 per use. Pops 10 Bloons, including Camo, but doesn't destroy Leads.
Pineapple	—	Costs $25 per use. Has to be timed right, as they explode three seconds after being placed.
Bloonsday Device	(Special Agent)	Gives you temporary control of the orbital strike satellite, whose beam destroys all Bloons on-screen, including Camo Bloons.
Meerkat Spy	(Special Agent)	No attack, but uses his super-keen senses to spot Camo Bloons, granting Camo Detection for all towers within his radius.
Bloonberry Bush	(Special Agent)	Plant this right on the track. Loses a thorn for each Bloon popped, but grows 10 thorns between each round (up to 200). Does not pop Lead.
Angry Squirrel	(Special Agent)	Armed with sharp acorns, it goes berserk and can spot Camo and pop Lead.
Super Monkey Storm	(Special Agent)	Destroys every single Bloon (including Camo) on-screen with a squadron of flying super-powered Laser-beamin' monkeys.

Tower Types

Now that we've covered all the targets, let's talk about the towers. Each tower (mostly made up of monkeys) has two paths of upgrades, and these upgrades are unlocked by reaching a higher rank, which is accomplished by earning XP (popping Bloons). Rank 45 is the point where every tower's fourth tier of upgrades is unlocked. Once tiers are unlocked, you need only have the money to purchase the upgrade in each game. Be aware that the cost of upgrades per game is dependent on the difficulty you select: Easy is the least expensive; Hard is the most expensive.

Keep in mind that once you reach the third-tier upgrades, you must choose either the Path 1 or 2 Tier 4 upgrade, as you cannot have two Tier 4 upgrades on one tower. The following table lists all the towers and their upgrade details and paths.

IMAGE	NAME	RANK UNLOCKED	UPGRADES					NOTES
	Dart Monkey	1		Tier 1	Tier 2	Tier 3	Tier 4	Cheapest tower. If used first, upgrade to Triple Darts, and it could hold its own up to Level 13–15, depending on placement. Path 1 focuses on popping power, and Path 2 increases darts per shot. Since upgrade 1/2 reveals Camo, you don't need a Ninja as soon.
			Path 1	Long-Range Darts	Enhanced Eyesight	Spike-O-Pult	Juggernaut	
				Makes it shoot farther than normal.	Shoots even farther and can detect Camo.	Catapult fires spiked balls that can pop 18 Bloons.	Hurls a giant spiked ball that excels at crushing Ceramics. Unlocks at Rank 21.	
			Path 2	Sharp Shots	Razor-Sharp Shots	Triple Darts	Super Monkey Fan Club	
				Can pop one extra Bloon per shot.	Can pop two extra Bloons per shot.	Throws three darts at a time instead of one.	Ability: Up to 10 nearby Dart Monkeys go Super for 10 seconds. Unlocks at Rank 21.	
	Monkey Sub	20		Tier 1	Tier 2	Tier 3	Tier 4	This is a cheap tower that you can only place in water. Multiple 2/3 upgraded subs can withstand the Ceramic rush. Using Advanced Intel makes it useful for taking out Camos when other towers that can see Camos are in play.
			Path 1	Barbed Darts	Advanced Intel	Submerge and Support	Bloontonium Reactor	
				Makes the Submarine's Darts pop up to three Bloons each.	Allows long-range targeting of Bloons that are in the radius of your other towers.	Activates Submerge, using target option to permanently reveal Camo Bloons in its radius.	Activates Submerge, using target option to detect Camo, pop Bloons, and reduce Water Tower cooldowns 15% (doesn't attack).	
			Path 2	Twin Guns	Airburst Darts	Ballistic Missile	First-Strike Capability	
				Added twin gun doubles attack speed.	Airburst Darts split into three on impact for massively increased popping power.	Ballistic missile seeks its target over any distance and does extra damage to Ceramic and MOAB Bloons.	Ability: A devastating missile strike on the largest Bloon on-screen. Destroys up to a ZOMG Bloon in one go, or many lesser Bloons.	
	Bloonchipper	21		Tier 1	Tier 2	Tier 3	Tier 4	This is one of the most powerful towers in the game. Use this early on to shred everything. The more you upgrade, the more it tears through all layers of any Bloon quickly. You really only need one unless you want to use another further down the line to get Bloons that get past your initial offense. Since some power has been taken from it in updates, consider using a Bomb Tower or the Monkey Ace in its place.
			Path 1	Suckier	Heavy-Duty Suction	Dual-Layer Blades	Super-Wide Funnel	
				Increased suction sucks Bloons in faster.	Higher-wattage motor allows for sucking in heavier Bloons such as Lead Bloons.	Dual-layer Blade array doubly shreds Bloons, taking off two layers instead of one.	Wide funnel can suck in MOAB-class Bloons, which will be shredded for up to three seconds before being ejected.	
			Path 2	Long-Range Suck	Faster Shred	Triple Barrel	Supa-Vac	
				Increases suction range.	More efficient internal componentry decreases the time Bloons take to be shredded.	Triple barrels provide the most efficient Bloon-shredding possible.	Huge burst of suction power brings all nearby non-MOAB Bloons toward it and holds them there until they've been sucked into the tower. Lasts eight seconds.	
	Monkey Engineer	21		Tier 1	Tier 2	Tier 3	Tier 4	This is a good tower to use early on as a solo tower, as with upgrades it can spawn sentries to assist with popping Bloons. Great to use against Camo with the Cleansing Foam upgrade.
			Path 1	Sentry Gun	Fast Engineering	Cleansing Foam	Bloon Trap	
				Creates temporary sentry guns and deploys them nearby.	Increased build speed produces sentry guns more often.	Sprays foam that removes Camo and Regen, and pops Leads.	Trap captures Bloons until full. Can be emptied for cash.	
			Path 2	9-Inch Nails	Larger Service Area	Sprockets	Overclock	
				Massive Nail pops eight Bloons at once, including Frozen Bloons.	Shoot farther, and deploy sentries in a larger area.	Increases sentry fire rate appreciably.	Ability: Target tower becomes super-powered for 60 seconds.	

Tower Types (continued)

IMAGE	NAME	RANK UNLOCKED	UPGRADES					NOTES
				Tier 1	Tier 2	Tier 3	Tier 4	The Tack Shooter is great for putting behind a Bloonchipper to pick up everything it misses. The Ring of Fire is a must. It has no Camo detection on its own. Artic Wind (Ice Tower upgrade), and use with Ring of Fire to destroy Ceramics and Leads. Monkey Beacon does not increase the range of the Tack Shooter.
	Tack Shooter	2	Path 1	Fast Shooting	Even Faster Shooting	Track Sprayer	Ring of Fire	
				Shoots Tacks faster.	Shoots Tacks even faster!	Sprays out 16 Tacks per volley instead of the usual 8.	Shoots a deadly ring of flames instead of Tacks.	
			Path 2	Extra-Range Tacks	Super-Range Tacks	Blade Shooter	Blade Maelstrom	
				Tacks fly out farther than normal.	Tacks go much farther than normal.	Shoots out big razor-sharp Blades.	Ability: Covers the area in a storm of Blades.	
				Tier 1	Tier 2	Tier 3	Tier 4	Infinite range and Camo detection at upgrade 2/2. Set stance to Strong or Last to take advantage of their high damage. Path 1 upgrades are great for Camo, Lead, and Frozen Bloons. With their unlimited range, you can place them anywhere on the map. If you use more than one, make sure their target priorities are different so they don't all go for the same target and miss.
	Sniper Monkey	3	Path 1	Full Metal Jacket	Point Five Oh	Deadly Precision	Cripple MOAB	
				Shots can pop through four layers of Bloons. Can pop Lead and Frozen.	Shots can pop through seven layers of Bloon!	Erases 18 layers of Bloons per shot—enough to destroy a Ceramic.	Immobilizes MOAB-class Bloons for a short time.	
			Path 2	Faster Firing	Night Vision Goggles	Semi-Automatic Rifle	Supply Drop	
				Allows Sniper to shoot faster.	Allows Sniper to detect and shoot Camo Bloons.	Allows Sniper to take multiple shots and attack 3x as fast.	Ability: Drops a crate full of cash.	
				Tier 1	Tier 2	Tier 3	Tier 4	This is a good tower for early-to-mid-game challenges. Turbo Charge can be used for Camo Lead rushes.
	Boomerang Thrower	4	Path 1	Multi-Target	Glaive Thrower	Glaive Ricochet	Glaive Lord	
				Boomerangs can now pop seven Bloons each.	Throws sharper, faster, bigger Glaives instead of Boomerangs.	Glaives now automatically bounce from Bloon to Bloon.	Two permanent Glaives orbit the tower.	
			Path 2	Sonic Boom	Red-Hot 'Rangs	Bionic Boomer	Turbo Charge	
				Sonic Boomerangs can smash through Frozen Bloons.	Red-hot Boomerangs can melt through Lead Bloons.	Throws Boomerangs twice as fast.	Ability: Attacks incredibly fast for 10 seconds.	
				Tier 1	Tier 2	Tier 3	Tier 4	This is a great tower to use first, as its speed can be ramped up quickly and cheaply. Plus, it can take out Camo Bloons. Sabotage Supply Lines is a great ability to have in later levels.
	Ninja Monkey	6	Path 1	Ninja Discipline	Sharp Shurikens	Double Shot	Bloonjitsu	
				Increases attack range and attack speed.	Shurikens can pop four Bloons each.	Throws two Shurikens at once.	Throws five Shurikens at once!	
			Path 2	Seeking Shuriken	Distraction	Flash Bomb	Sabotage Supply Lines	
				Shuriken seeks out and pops Bloons automatically.	Some Bloons become distracted and move the wrong way.	Sometimes throws a flash bomb that stuns multiple Bloons.	Ability: Lasts for 15 seconds. During the sabotage, all new Bloons are crippled to half-speed.	
				Tier 1	Tier 2	Tier 3	Tier 4	Cannot detect Camo alone. If you upgrade beyond Path 1, Tier 2 (Frag Bombs), you'll be locked out of Path 2 upgrades. The same goes for Path 2: if you upgrade past Path 2, Tier 2 (Missile Launcher), you'll be locked out of further Tier 1 upgrades. This is an important tower to have to go up against MOAB-class Bloons. It's a flexible tower.
	Bomb Tower	7	Path 1	Extra Range	Frag Bombs	Cluster Bombs	Bloom Impact	
				Gives tower long attack range.	Each explosion throws out eight sharp fragments for more popping.	Throws out secondary bombs instead of frags.	Bloons become stunned for a short time when they're hit.	
			Path 2	Bigger Bombs	Missile Launcher	MOAB Mauler	MOAB Assassin	
				Larger blast area and more popping power.	More velocity and range, more damage, and faster firing.	Inflicts 10x damage on MOAB-class Bloons.	Ability: Deadly missile seeks the nearest MOAB and destroys it.	

Tower Types (continued)

IMAGE	NAME	RANK UNLOCKED	UPGRADES					NOTES
				Tier 1	Tier 2	Tier 3	Tier 4	This tower is good for slowing down Bloons, allowing your other towers to do their jobs more efficiently. Without upgrades, it's useless against White, Zebra, and MOAB-class Bloons. Suggest keeping it away from your front line, as it can hinder some towers from breaking Frozen Bloons. Absolute Zero is a useful ability at high levels, as it slows down MOABs.
	Ice Tower	8	Path 1	Enhance Freeze	Snap Freeze	Arctic Wind	Viral Frost	
				Larger freeze area that freezes Bloons for longer.	Pop a layer off of each Bloon frozen.	Super-cold aura slows all Bloons in its larger radius.	Frozen Bloons freeze other Bloons that come in contact.	
			Path 2	Permafrost	Deep Freeze	Ice Shards	Absolute Zero	
				Larger blast area and more popping power.	Freezes two layers, extending the slow duration.	Razor-sharp shards fly out when Frozen Bloons pop.	Ability: Freezes all Bloons on-screen temporarily.	
				Tier 1	Tier 2	Tier 3	Tier 4	No Camo detection until you upgrade it with Glue Striker, which takes awhile and is expensive. This is one of the least-used towers, even though it can eat through layers of Bloons. Money spent on other towers is usually better for strategy.
	Glue Gunner	9	Path 1	Glue Soak	Corrosive Glue	Bloon Dissolver	Bloon Liquefier	
				Glue soaks through all layers of Bloons.	Glued Bloons pop one layer every few seconds.	Extreme solvents melt two layers every second.	Pops once instantly and liquefies Bloons ten times every second!	
			Path 2	Stickier Glue	Glue Splatter	Glue Hose	Glue Striker	
				Makes Glue effect last much longer.	Splatters Glue across eight Bloons at a time.	Shoots Glue more than 3x as fast!	Ability: Glues everything on-screen temporarily.	
				Tier 1	Tier 2	Tier 3	Tier 4	This tower must be set in water or in a Portable Lake (Special Agent). After you purchase the third upgrade in a path, you can only purchase the first two upgrades in the other path. It's nice to pair this up with a farm and an Apprentice.
	Monkey Buccaneer	11	Path 1	Faster Shooting	Longer Cannons	Destroyer	Aircraft Carrier	
				Shoots its big Darts faster.	Much longer range.	Attacks super duper fast!	Launches fast strafing Monkey Ace pilots.	
			Path 2	Grape Shot	Crow's Nest	Cannon Ship	Monkey Pirates	
				Adds a spray of four sharp grapes.	Allows the Buccaneer to hit Camo Bloons.	Adds a powerful, independently firing cannon to the Buccaneer.	Ability: Grapples the nearest MOAB and brings it down.	
				Tier 1	Tier 2	Tier 3	Tier 4	Make sure to choose your flight path to work best with your map. It can fly a circle, or two differently oriented figure-eights. Circle usually does best, as figure-eights could send it off-screen. This is one of the weakest towers but is good as a support tower to help keep Bloon count down.
	Monkey Ace	12	Path 1	Rapid Fire	Sharper Darts	Neva-Miss Targeting	Spectre	
				Shoots Darts more often.	Monkey Ace Darts can pop eight Bloons each!	Darts seek out and pop Bloons intelligently.	Missiles pierce through anything and pop two layers.	
			Path 2	Pineapple Present	Spy Plane	Operation: Dart Storm	Ground Zero	
				Drops an exploding pineapple every three seconds.	Allows Monkey Ace to hit Camo Bloons.	More Darts = win.	Ability: Drops a devastating bomb that destroys all Bloons and damages MOAB class.	
				Tier 1	Tier 2	Tier 3	Tier 4	This is a tower best used toward the end of a game because of the expense involved. You must upgrade to make it as effective as you would expect. A few Sun Gods can hold off swarms of MOABs. This tower is extremely fast.
	Super Monkey	13	Path 1	Laser Blasts	Plasma Blasts	Sun God	Temple of the Monkey God	
				Fast-firing twin Laser beams pop twice as much as before. Each Laser pops two Bloons instead of one.	Plasma vaporizes everything it touches. Shoots twice as fast as individual Laser blast, each popping four Bloons, and is able to pop Lead.	It is said that Bloons should never touch the sun. This is an unstoppable power and an upgrade to strive for.	Tower sacrifices enhance and modify Temple's awesome arsenal. It demands a sacrifice! Use at your own risk.	
			Path 2	Super Range	Epic Range	Robo Monkey	Technological Terror	
				Increases attack range.	Why settle for super when you can have epic? This gives Super Monkey ultimate attack range.	Half Super Monkey, half killer robot of death (not quite as coveted as Sun God). Can pop Frozen and Lead even if Path 1 isn't upgraded.	Ability: Destroys all Bloons within short radius of tower, completely. Does 1000 damage to MAOB-class Bloons and can hit Camo.	

Tower Types (continued)

IMAGE	NAME	RANK UNLOCKED	UPGRADES						NOTES
	Monkey Apprentice	14			Tier 1	Tier 2	Tier 3	Tier 4	This is a popular tower because of its affordability, to help pop Camo Lead. Since the Apprentice pushes balloons, it's a good idea to put it near the end of the path. They can pop Lead without upgrades, so you could use this instead of a Bomb Tower early on.
				Path 1	Intense Magic	Lightning Bolt	Summon Whirlwind	Tempest Tornado	
					Shoots larger and more powerful magic bolts.	Unleash the power of lightning to zap many Bloons at once.	Whirlwind blows Bloons off the path, away from the exit, but also removes Ice and Glue.	Pops Bloons and blows them faster, farther, and more often.	
				Path 2	Fireball	Monkey Sense	Dragon's Breath	Summon Phoenix	
					The Apprentice adds a powerful fireball attack to its arsenal.	Allows the Monkey Apprentice to hit Camo Bloons, but doesn't help other towers detect them.	Spews endless flames at nearby Bloons.	Ability: Super-powerful phoenix wreaks Bloon havoc for 20 seconds.	
	Monkey Village	15			Tier 1	Tier 2	Tier 3	Tier 4	This is a support tower and is recommended for use on your front line as early as you can afford to take advantage of Radar Scanner and Monkey Intelligence Bureau upgrades. Try putting a few Super Monkeys within its range toward the end of the game. You can't stack the powers of multiple Monkey Villages placed within range of each other.
				Path 1	Monkey Beacon	Jungle Drums	Monkey Town	Energy Beacon	
					Increases attack range by 15% of all towers in its radius.	Jungle drums inspire nearby towers to attack 15% faster.	Bloons popped near the Monkey Town get 50% more cash per pop.	Nearby ability cooldowns reduced by 20%.	
				Path 2	Monkey Fort	Radar Scanner	Monkey Intelligence Bureau	MIB Call to Arms	
					Increases the popping power of all nearby towers by 1.	Allows all towers within its radius to hit Camo Bloons.	Allows all nearby towers to pop all Bloon types, and increases its range.	Ability: Increases attack speed, pierce, and range for towers in radius for 10 seconds.	
	Banana Farm	16			Tier 1	Tier 2	Tier 3	Tier 4	Use this to create a money farm. Place three or four next to each other. Use the Banana Farmer (Special Agent) to collect the Bananas automatically (when placed nearby). Money Bank negates the use of the Banana Farmer. Having a money farm is pivotal to your survival in later levels. The increased money flow allows you to purchase much-needed towers sooner. Upgrade them with Path 1, Tier 1 as soon as you buy one. Consider selling some farms to upgrade one or two to Tier 4.
				Path 1	More Bananas	Banana Plantation	Banana Republic	Banana Research Facility	
					Grows three big bunches of Bananas.	Generates seven big bunches each round.	Generates 13 big bunches of Bananas every round. $520 per round without Valuable Bananas. This prevents you from Path 2, Tier 3-4 upgrades.	Produces five boxes of Bananas every round. Each box is worth $200. Unlocked at Rank 36.	
				Path 2	Long-Life Bananas	Valuable Bananas	Monkey Bank	Banana Investments Advisory	
					Bananas last 25 seconds longer on-screen before disappearing.	Increases the value of each Banana or box of Bananas by 50%. Purchase this if you only want to pursue full Path 2 upgrades, or if you've maxed out Path 1.	No longer drops Bananas but deposits them directly into your account. Creates $450 per round, plus 10% interest. Holds up to $5000. Locks Path 1, Tier 3-4.	Increases money generated to $1000 per round, increases interest to 20%, and max held at a time to $20,000 per round. Unlocked at Rank 36.	
	Mortar Tower	17			Tier 1	Tier 2	Tier 3	Tier 4	This is a popular tower. It's effective at bombarding the front line and other areas where Bloons are bottlenecked. Burny Stuff is its first upgrade that allows you to damage Black and Zebra. The Tier 4 upgrades are both useful in the final levels.
				Path 1	Increased Accuracy	Bigger Blasts	Bloon Buster	The Big One	
					Makes your Mortar shots more accurate. The targeting reticle becomes 60% smaller.	Heavy ordinance delivers a bigger explosion radius. Explosions are bigger.	Smash through two layers of Bloons at once! Doesn't damage Black or Zebra.	Devastating explosions each pop three layers of Bloons. Pops Black and Zebra.	
				Path 2	Rapid Reload	Burny Stuff	Signal Flare	Artillery Battery	
					Increases the attack speed of the Mortar. Also reloads faster.	Pops additional Bloons two seconds after impact. Burns Black and Zebra Bloons.	Camo Bloons popped by Flares permanently lose their Camo. This allows towers without Camo detection to attack Camo. Removes Camo status.	Ability: Immobilizes and bombards the entire screen for five seconds. Doesn't fully affect MOAB but stuns them.	

Tower Types (continued)

IMAGE	NAME	RANK UNLOCKED	UPGRADES				NOTES
			Tier 1	Tier 2	Tier 3	Tier 4	
	Dartling Gun	18	**Path 1** Focused Firing — Greatly reduces the spread of the gun.	Faster Barrel Spin — Makes gunfire much faster.	Laser Cannon — Rapid-fire plasma can pop 13 Bloons each and also pops Frozen Bloons.	Ray of Doom — The Ray of Doom is a persistent solid beam of Bloon destruction.	This tower aims its gun wherever your mouse or finger is placed on the screen. A 4/2 upgraded Dartling Gun outmatches a 4/2 Super Monkey (if no sacrifices are being made). If you upgrade to Laser Cannon and add Depleted Bloontonium, it allows you to pop any Bloon type at a high rate of fire.
			Path 2 Powerful Darts — Darts move faster and can pop three Bloons each.	Depleted Bloontonium — Shots can now hurt any Bloon type.	Hydra Rocket Pods — Shoots vicious little missiles instead of Darts.	Bloon Area-Denial System — Ability: Shoots missiles toward the nearest 100 Bloons on-screen.	
			Tier 1	Tier 2	Tier 3	Tier 4	
	Spike Factory	19	**Path 1** Bigger Stacks — Generates larger Piles of Spikes per shot.	White-Hot Spikes — Cuts through Lead like a hot spike through…lead.	Spiked-Ball Factory — Produces sharp spiked balls that do extra damage to Ceramics.	Spiked Mines — Spiked balls explode when they lose all their Spikes.	This is one of the least-used towers, next to the Glue Gunner and the Sniper Monkey. However, it's good for stopping any kind of Bloon early on in a game. When possible, place them where their radius overlaps multiple tracks. Spikes are spit out onto all tracks it overlaps. This tower can pop Camo Bloons with no upgrade.
			Path 2 Faster Production — Increases the rate of Spike production.	Even Faster Production — Rate of Spike production increases even more.	MOAB-SHREDR Spikes — Super-Hard-Rending-Engine-Driven-Razors shred MOAB-class Bloons.	Spike Storm — Ability: Lays down a thick carpet of Spikes over the whole track.	
			Tier 1	Tier 2	Tier 3	Tier 4	
	Heli Pilot	17	**Path 1** Quad Darts — Shoots four Darts per volley instead of two.	Pursuit — Superior targeting computers enable a new targeting option to pursue Bloons.	Razor Rotors — Rotor Blades rip up Bloons on contact, including Frozen and Lead.	Apache Dartship — Adds a large missile array and a powerful machine gun.	Set the targeting option to hold a position, Follow Touch, or Patrol, which you need to set two patrol points on the screen. Unlocking Pursuit opens another option: pursuit. This attacks the Bloon farthest along on the track (closest to the exit). It's an expensive tower, but when you get mid to late game, it's worth it for Downdraft or Razor Rotors.
			Path 2 Bigger Jets — More powerful jets enable the Heli to move much faster.	Enhanced IFR Instruments — Allows Heli Pilot to detect and shoot Camo Bloons.	Downdraft — Blows Bloons away from the Heli.	Support Chinook — Ability: Drops med and cash crates, or can pick up and reposition most towers.	

Bloon Appearance Per Level

Based on a normal 85 rounds, this is what you can expect to go up against.

LEVEL	BLOONS THAT ENTER THE LEVEL
01	20 Red
02	30 Red
03	20 Red, 5 Blue
04	30 Red, 15 Blue
05	5 Red, 25 Blue
06	15 Red, 15 Blue, 4 Green
07	20 Red, 25 Blue, 5 Green
08	10 Red, 20 Blue, 14 Green
09	30 Green
10	102 Blue
11	10 Red, 10 Blue, 12 Green, 2 Yellow
12	15 Blue, 10 Green, 5 Yellow
13	100 Red, 23 Green, 4 Yellow
14	49 Red, 15 Blue, 10 Green, 9 Yellow
15	20 Red, 12 Green, 5 Yellow, 3 Pink
16	20 Green, 8 Yellow, 4 Pink
17	8 Yellow Regen
18	80 Green
19	10 Green, 4 Yellow, 5 Yellow Regen, 7 Pink

LEVEL	BLOONS THAT ENTER THE LEVEL
20	6 Black
21	14 Pink
22	8 White
23	5 Black, 4 White
24	1 Green Camo
25	31 Yellow Regen
26	23 Pink, 4 Zebra
27	120 Red, 55 Blue, 45 Green, 45 Yellow
28	4 Lead
29	25 Yellow, 12 Pink Regen
30	9 Lead
31	8 Zebra, 2 Zebra Regen
32	25 Black, 28 White, 8 Lead
33	20 Yellow Camo
34	140 Yellow, 5 Zebra
35	35 Pink, 25 White, 5 Rainbow
36	81 Pink
37	20 Black, 20 White, 7 White Camo, 15 Lead, 10 Zebra
38	42 Pink Regen, 17 White, 14 Lead, 10 Zebra, 4 Rainbow

Bloon Appearance Per Level (cont')

LEVEL	BLOONS THAT ENTER THE LEVEL
39	10 Black, 10 White, 20 Lead, 20 Zebra, 18 Rainbow
40	10 Rainbow, 4 Ceramic
41	60 Black, 60 Zebra
42	6 Regen Rainbow, 6 Camo Rainbow
43	10 Rainbow, 7 Ceramic
44	50 Zebra
45	200 Pink, 8 Lead, 25 Rainbow
46	1 MOAB
47	70 Pink Camo, 12 Ceramic
48	120 Pink Regen, 50 Rainbow
49	343 Green, 20 Zebra, 20 Rainbow, 10 Rainbow Regen, 18 Ceramic
50	20 Red, 8 Lead, 20 Ceramic, 2 MOAB
51	10 Rainbow Regen, 28 Ceramic
52	25 Rainbow, 10 Ceramic, 2 MOAB
53	80 Pink Camo, 3 MOAB
54	35 Ceramic, 2 MOAB
55	45 Ceramic, 1 MOAB
56	40 Rainbow Regen, 1 MOAB
57	40 Rainbow, 4 MOAB
58	29 Ceramic, 5 MOAB
59	28 Lead Camo, 50 Ceramic
60	1 BFB
61	150 Zebra Regen, 5 MOAB
62	300 Camo Pink, 15 Rainbow Camo Regen, 6 MOAB
63	75 Lead, 122 Ceramic
64	9 MOAB
65	100 Zebra, 70 Rainbow, 50 Ceramic, 3 MOAB, 2 BFB
66	12 MOAB
67	15 Ceramic, 10 MOAB
68	4 MOAB, 1 BFB
69	60 Lead, 70 Ceramic Regen
70	200 Rainbow Camo, 4 MOAB
71	30 Ceramic, 10 MOAB
72	38 Ceramic Regen, 2 BFB
73	9 MOAB, 2 BFB
74	200 Ceramic, 1 BFB
75	28 Lead, 4 MOAB, 3 BFB
76	60 Ceramic Regen
77	14 MOAB, 5 BFB
78	150 Rainbow, 75 Ceramic, 72 Ceramic Camo, 1 BFB
79	500 Rainbow Regen, 7 BFB
80	31 MOAB
81	9 BFB
82	400 Rainbow Camo Regen, 10 BFB
83	150 Ceramic, 30 MOAB
84	50 MOAB, 10 BFB
85	1 ZOMG

In-App Purchases

There are several places where you can spend money in Bloons TD 5. You can purchase upgrades, skins, Monkey Money, and Tokens. Tokens are spent in the Monkey Lab, and Monkey Money is used to buy Special Agents and Specialists Buildings. Here's where you part with your hard-earned cash.

Unlock All Upgrades

If you're in a game already and you want a shortcut to unlocking a particular tower's upgrades without waiting to reach the required rank to do so, simply click on the tower that's placed on the board already, and click on the "Unlock All Upgrades" button next to the Settings (gear icon) button. This costs 99 cents, but beware that this is only for that one tower.

Fast Track

Unlocking Fast Track is an option you can select on the Pre-Level menu screen after you choose your difficulty level for single-player games. This option allows you to permanently unlock the Fast Track play mode, where you fast-track past the first 25 rounds. Start at Round 26 with $5000 cash to get up into those high rounds faster. This costs $3000 game cash. If you don't have it, you're taken to a Purchase menu where you can buy a Bundle ($2500 for $2.99), a Pile ($4250 for $4.99), a Vault ($18,000 for $19.99), or a Mountain ($50,000 for $49.99).

Premium Store

In the golden building that is the Premium Store, you can find new skins for your towers for $1.99; these are only visual enhancements, not gameplay ones. You can boost your rank by one point for 99 cents, and then make the same purchases you could from the Fast Track menu, and each bundle type has a similar offer for Tokens. You can also find a Double Cash Mode for $9.99, Healthy Bananas for 99 cents, and Bigger Beacons for 99 cents.

Leveling Up Rank

The fastest way to level up your rank (besides paying for it) is to keep a good game going beyond the required level. No matter what difficulty setting you're using, if you have a good game set up and your Sun Gods and Temple of the Monkey God are annihilating everything, don't give up—keep going as long as you can after Level 65. The higher the level, the quicker XP is earned.

Banana Farms

Create three to six Banana Farms, then sell lower-producing farms when you have two to three Tier 4 farms. This constant and increasingly productive money-making tower is key to remaining stronger than the Bloons in higher levels.

Ability Management

On high levels, when you have several towers with Tier 4 abilities, managing the ability triggers at the bottom of the screen becomes your new priority. A red radar-like dial covers the ability icon. As soon as this is gone, representing a cooldown, trigger it again and keep your eye on all the abilities, so you engage them as soon as they cool down.

Targeting Options

Most towers have targeting options: First, Last, Close, and Strong are the most common. Set these with some thought involved. For instance, if you have two Snipers, and if they're both set to Strong, they could be targeting the same Bloon, so one of them could be missing the majority of their shots.

Tower Upgrades Don't Just Happen with Rank

A tower's tiers of upgrades aren't unlocked when you rank up with XP. The tower has to be placed on the screen and used in the game to earn its own XP. Upgrades become unlocked as towers earn XP for themselves.

Camo Bloons

As described previously in our strategy, Camo Bloons are troublesome, and only Dartling Guns and Spike Factories can see them without upgrades. Camo Leads are even more vicious. Try using Cannon Ships (if there's water on the board), Flash Bomb Ninjas, Monkey Sense Apprentices, White-Hot Spike Factories, Meerkat, or Radar Scanner Village to Bomb Towers to take these out.

CANDY CRUSH SAGA

Developer	King
Publisher	King
Year Released	2012
Platforms	Browser, Android, iOS, Fire OS, Windows Phone, Microsoft Windows, Linux
Type	Puzzle
Suggested Age	4+
Cost	Free

$ IN-GAME PURCHASES
Many

Game Overview

The addiction started on Facebook in 2012, and soon after, *Candy Crush Saga* was available on iOS, Android, Windows Phones, and Windows 10. Levels are completed by swiping three or more matching-color candies together to crush them. Each board has certain objectives, and all boards give you a limited number of moves. *Candy Crush* was the most-played game on Facebook in 2013 and remains in the top-ten grossing mobile apps. As of this publication, there are 3320 levels (15 levels per world on average), with new worlds being added every week!

What You Need to Know

When you start playing *Candy Crush* for the first time, you may feel like it takes no more skill than a Vegas slot machine, and that there's no strategy involved at all since the candy dropping onto the board is completely random. But the more you play, the more you discover that—although luck of the candy drop does play a role—there's plenty here for those who seek strategy. You need a keen eye for recognizing combo opportunities and creating those opportunities. Creating special power-ups that clear large portions of the board is more often than not the key to clearing levels. Once you can see the patterns that lead to special combinations, you begin to control the outcome of all the random candy drops.

Candy Crushing

Following are all the candy-crushing combos available in *Candy Crush Saga*.

Match Three

This core gameplay move consists of swiping a colored candy to create a row or column of at least three matching-color candies. Once performed, the three matched candies are crushed and removed from the board. New randomly colored candies enter the board to replace the spaces created by the three you crushed. This action can cause cascades (chain reactions) as falling candies automatically match three or more candies in other areas of the board. Each candy crushed earns you points, and cascades create point multipliers.

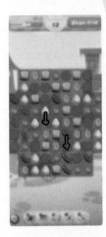

Special Candy

Special Candy is made when you swipe four or more same-color candy in a particular pattern. When used, these Special Candies produce more points. They're often used as moves needed to solve certain puzzle elements. Special Candies are used to destroy Blockers that a normal match-three-candy-crush cannot.

Striped Candy

Striped Candy is formed when you arrange a row or column of four same-color candy in a straight line. The direction in which you create it determines whether the stripes are horizontal or vertical on the candy. When the Striped Candy is activated, the direction of the stripes determines the direction in which the line of destruction moves.

Wrapped Candy

Wrapped Candy is created when you combine five same-color candies in an L or T shape. The shape of the candies can be created at any orientation. The Wrapped Candy can be detonated by combining it with a match of three or more colors, when hit with a Striped Candy shot or exploded with a Color Bomb or another exploding Wrapped Candy. The blast area takes out all adjacent candies in the first blast (eight adjacent candies), and as it moves to the next clear spot, the second explosion takes out another eight surrounding candies.

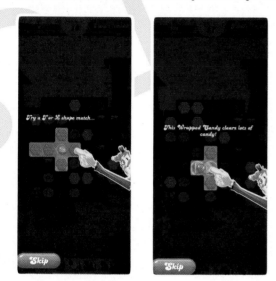

Color Bomb

A Color Bomb looks like a chocolate ball with candy sprinkles. This is the most powerful Special Candy available. Color Bombs are formed when you combine five or more same-color candies in a straight line. When switched with a regular candy, all candies of that same color are eliminated from the entire board with laser precision. See "Special Candy Combinations" for all the amplified effects from using the Color Bomb in combination with other Special Candies.

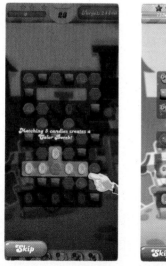

Special Candy / Boosters

There are a few more Special Candies that you encounter on various puzzle boards. These Special Candies cannot be created; rather, they're dispensed or already on the board when you start the level. These are also boosters that can be earned or purchased and become available for selection before the level starts, to be used in the level (depending on the level type). They appear or can be used in Jelly, Ingredient, Mixed Mode, and Candy Order Levels.

Jelly Fish

Swedish Jelly Fish come in as many colors as normal candy. In *Candy Crush* sequels, these Swedish Jelly Fish can be created by combining four candies in a square shape—but unfortunately, *Candy Crush Saga* has not adopted this move. Currently you can only bring it into play as a booster, or it may already exist in the level (maybe stuck in Marmalade or spawned out of Mystery Candy), or it can be generated by striking a Bobber.

Use Jelly Fish by combining one with two other same-color candies (like a normal match-three), or matching three same-color Jelly Fish. Otherwise, Jelly Fish must be used in a combo with other Special Candies, or caught up in the effects of a Special Candy.

When activated, the Jelly Fish swims off-screen and returns as three. Each of the three Jelly Fish swims to a target to destroy it. Jelly Fish cannot be sent to an intended target. You cannot direct them. They have minds of their own and first target Jelly (if multiple layers, then only one layer is destroyed) and Blockers (if Jelly is under some Blocker types, it goes under the Blocker and takes out the Jelly). However, if the Jelly is under a Liquorice swirl or Liquorice Locks, the Jelly Fish only takes out the Blocker and not the Jelly underneath.

Jelly Fish appear during a Sugar Crush if you have remaining lives at the end of a completed Jelly Level. Each remaining life converts to three randomly colored Jelly Fish, which in turn eat candies at random, awarding points—a number dependent on the targets they hit.

Coconut Wheel

This round pink candy is a Coconut Wheel and is a Special Candy that naturally appears only in Ingredient Levels before Level 824. After Level 824, you can find Coconut Wheels in any level type, but the booster version is only available for ingredient-type levels.

The Coconut Wheel cannot be created by any candy combination, but is only spawned by using a booster, or uncovered on the board trapped under Marmalade or Liquorice Locks.

To activate the Coconut Wheel, swipe it with the candy adjacent to it. This destroys the candy and starts the spinning. It eventually moves in the direction it was swiped, turning the next three candies into Striped Candies, which are automatically activated. If you swipe the Coconut Wheel horizontally, it creates vertical Striped Candies, which can bring down ingredients from the top of the board. If you swipe vertically, horizontal Striped Candies are created. All candies must come to a resting place before the Coconut Wheel starts creating Striped Candies.

If the Coconut Wheel is activated by another action (say, exploding candy), it spins and randomly choses a move direction. Even more powerful moves occur when you swipe a Coconut Wheel with a Special Candy (see "Special Candy Combinations" for details).

Lucky Candy

These Special Candies only appear as boosters or in Candy Order Levels, and can come out of a Mystery Candy or be found under Liquorice Locks. These Special Candies cannot be formed by any combination of candy, and can be one of six colors, like normal candy.

Activating Lucky Candies is done the same way as any normal candy—match three or more same-color candies together. Once destroyed, the checkmarked candy becomes the candy type needed to fulfill the order in the board objectives. It could become a regular candy with a specific color, a Special Candy, or in some cases, a Blocker.

Lollipop Hammer

The Lollipop Hammer is a booster-only item. These don't appear on a board, nor are they dispensed. The only way to use a Lollipop Hammer is to have been awarded one or to have purchased them. Lollipop Hammers are rare and should be saved up for the very difficult levels. They allow you to destroy anything on a space. You can remove a candy, a Jelly below a candy, or a Blocker (or one layer of a Multilayered Blocker) without using a single move. You cannot, however, destroy a Chocolate Spawner, ingredient, or a Sugar Chest. You can use it to reveal the contents of a Mystery Candy or a Lucky Candy. When used on a Special Candy, that candy's effect is activated.

You can win these from the Daily Booster Wheel and the Sugar Drop. You can also purchase them while in a level if the booster icon is visible beside the board (if it's an active booster for that level type).

Extra Moves

The Extra Moves Booster is usually first discovered on the Failed Level Attempt menu that pops up at the end of a failed board. Clicking on the Extra Moves Booster automatically takes 10 Gold Bars and puts you back in the game with five more moves. Or, if you don't have the Gold required, the same button takes you to the Candy Shop, where you can purchase more Gold.

Extra Moves on mobile devices also appears on the prize wheel accessed when you click on the Win Moves button on the same Failed Level menu. You earn a free spin every 24 hours, and if that's been used, it costs you seven Gold Bars to spin the wheel. This wheel consists of three +5 Extra Moves and one +15 Extra Moves space. There are also Jelly Fish, a Lollipop Hammer, Color Bombs (x2), and a Wrapped Candy/Striped Candy combo between the Extra Moves spaces.

If you continue to fail the mission after using Extra Moves, the price of Extra Moves increases each time it's accessed. In fact, at the seventh failed attempt, the Extra Moves becomes a +15 move. At the eighth it becomes +50, which means you've used 45 Extra Moves.

On web versions of the game, the Extra Moves Booster can be activated at any time during the game, and each use costs Gold Bars.

Free Switch

The red hand with three fingers is a booster that, when used, allows you to switch any two adjacent candies (even if they don't match) while not using a move. You can also use it as an extra move. Move matching candy to save a move. However, when swiping two Special Candies together with a Free Switch, the Special Candies don't release their combo effect; instead they just switch places.

You can use a Free Switch to move ingredients with another ingredient, candy, or movable Blocker. This is useful if the ingredient gets stuck in a space adjacent to the column where the exit is located.

Free Switches are given as awards from side challenges, such as Star Chaser, or purchased in bundles at the Candy Shop. You can also land on these on the Daily Booster Wheel, or earn them by participating in the Sugar Drop challenge and the Treat Calendar.

Striped & Wrapped

This booster is available on many pre-level menus, and gives you one Wrapped and one Striped Candy at the beginning of the level to use when you please (just make sure to use them wisely and quickly so that a cascade doesn't activate them in an unintended location). This booster can be won from the Daily Booster Wheel, the Treat Calendar, and from the Sugar Drop challenge.

Bomb Cooler

This booster is only available after failing a level that has Candy Bombs (time bombs) in the puzzle. On the Fail screen, you're given a chance to purchase +5 Extra Moves and a +Bomb Cooler for 10 Gold. The +Bomb Cooler allows you back in the game and resets the Candy Bombs that had fewer than five moves on them back up to five moves. So, in other words, if you left the game and some Candy Bombs were on the board with six moves left on them, they would be unaffected.

If you fail the same board again, the next Fail screen offers you a +5 Bomb Cooler (and a +5 Extra Moves and a Striped Candy) for 16 Gold. Now the +5 Bomb Cooler affects all Candy Bombs, adding five moves to every bomb. This continues to grow with each failure. After the seventh failure, you can get a +10 Bomb Cooler. All fails after that allow you to purchase a +15 Bomb Cooler. This is the only way to get these boosters; you cannot get them through features like the Daily Booster Wheel, etc.

UFO

This fun booster usually comes in a group of two or more on a board, locked or out of reach from typical matches. In most cases, you must use Special Candy effects to unlock and then activate a UFO. Once activated, the UFO shoots three Wrapped Candies on the board and typically targets Jelly, Blockers, or Chocolate, or blasts things under ingredients so they fall. If the UFO is free and sitting in a reachable space on the board, you only need to swipe the UFO with any candy to activate it manually.

This booster cannot be won on the Daily Booster Wheel. The only way to receive this booster is if it already exists on a board, or if you purchase one for 20 Gold from the Sweet Supplies Inventory menu. They don't appear in any of the bundles in the Candy Shop.

Striped Brush

This booster lets you paint stripes onto any candy of your choice, and you get to choose the stripe direction. This booster is unlocked at Level 37. The only way to obtain this booster is by purchasing it for 15 Gold through the Sweet Supplies Inventory menu. This is probably the least-purchased booster there is—it isn't all that special since Striped Candy is a common combo created on the boards.

Party Booster

Party Boosters are the newest boosters. When they first appear (you can be anywhere after Level 29), you're given three. Use them wisely; after these three are gone, the only way to get more is to purchase them from the Candy Shop for 30 Gold Bars each. A Party Booster has two stages of attacks. In the first stage, a large star-shaped piñata floats over the board and releases a blast that completely clears a board of unlocked or trapped candy, similar to a Cake Bomb; it only clears one level of Multilayered Blockers. When the dust settles, a Jelly Fish, Striped Candy, Wrapped Candy, and Color Bomb spawn in random areas on the board. If you need to get past a tricky level, this is the booster for you.

Other Special Candy

There are a few other Special Candies that appear in certain level types. These are not available as boosters.

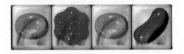

Chameleon Candy

The Chameleon Candy looks like rainbow-colored candy. They're easily identifiable, as they change between two colors with every move you make, and a rainbow effect sweeps across them every few seconds. They cause difficulty in otherwise easy puzzle situations; their color-changing nature causes possible color matches to disintegrate as the color changes to a non-matching one.

Chameleon Candy can be dispensed from Candy Cannons and is destroyed like any normal candy—when color matches of three or more are swiped together, or from the effects of a Special Candy activation.

 Mystery Candy

Mystery Candy behaves and is crushed just like normal candy and comes in as many color variations. They're identified by the question mark painted on them, and they're all egg-shaped. When they're crushed, you have a 50/50 chance of getting a good power-up from within. They produce good outcomes, such as Striped Candy, Wrapped Candy, Color Bombs, Special Booster Candy, and Chameleon Candy. The type of Booster Candy that could be produced depends on the level type, so you could get Jelly Fish, Coconut Wheel, or Lucky Candy.

The possible bad outcomes include Chocolate, Icing, Sachet/Multilayered Icing, Candy Bomb, Liquorice Swirl, Popcorn, and a Chocolate Spawner.

 Candy Frog

The Candy Frog is one of the most complex elements of *Candy Crush Saga*. One frog appears at a time on the board. It feeds on candies that match its current color when matches of three candies or more are swiped. The frog doesn't get crushed when matched with candies. It only moves when swiped to a new position, or when moved to be activated after it reaches its fully charged state. It can also be moved onto conveyor belts. It's fed same-color candy or Special Candy until it becomes a special power-up that acts like a Wrapped Candy.

When fed 12 same-color candies, it reaches its full "Frogtastic!" state. You hear a voice announcing this achievement. Select the Candy Frog, then select a location on the board for the frog to jump to. The frog lands and destroys whatever is on that space, plus the surrounding eight squares (like a Wrapped Candy explosion). After which the frog changes colors and is ready to be fed again. Activating the Candy Frog effect doesn't cost you a move unless it's a Moves Level.

When swiped with Special Candies, the Candy Frog mimics the effects of that candy's abilities. Swipe with a Striped Candy and the frog becomes striped, and with the next frog move it shoots and clears a row or column of candy from the space it moves to. Likewise, when swiped with Wrapped Candy, the Candy Frog becomes wrapped, and with its next move it clears a 3x3 area just like a Wrapped Candy explosion.

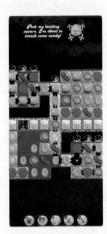

A Color Bomb swiped with a Color Frog turns the frog brown with sprinkles and eliminates all the colors associated with the candy swiped with the frog on its next movement.

Here are a few of the curiosities of the Candy Frog. When a normal colored frog is matched with a Special Candy, the Special Candy is activated, and the frog copies that special effect (Jelly Fish is the exception to this rule). When the colored frog already carries a Special Candy effect and is then matched with another Special Candy, it acts as if it were a normal Special Candy combination (see "Special Candy Combinations").

Candy Frogs can be covered by Chocolate—the frog's eyes are visible through the Chocolate. In this case, the Chocolate must be broken through normal gameplay to release the frog and thus begin feeding it with subsequent moves. You cannot feed a frog that's in Locked Chocolate or inside a Sugar Chest.

Special Candy Combinations

This table reveals all the possible combined effects created by swiping all variations of Special Candies together.

CANDY	CANDY COMBO	RESULTING EFFECT
	Striped Candy + Striped Candy	Both candies detonate in the space swiped into, and from that space a horizontal and vertical line of destruction occurs. This takes out any candy, Jelly, and one layer of Blockers unless an effect Blocker exists in the path.
	Striped Candy + Wrapped Candy	Both candies form a huge, powerful candy in the space swiped into, and a large 3x3 area of destruction moves vertically and horizontally across the board, wiping out every candy, Jelly, and one layer of Blockers in its path (unless an effect Blocker exists in its path).
	Striped Candy + Color Bomb	When this combination is swiped, all same-color candies (that match the color of the Striped Candy combined with the Color Bomb) turn into horizontally and vertically Striped Candies across the entire board and are instantly activated, clearing rows and columns of candy, Jelly, and one level of Blockers unless effect Blockers are present. The Striped Candy originally swiped in the combo doesn't activate; instead it just disappears.
	Striped Candy + Jelly Fish	Combining a Striped Candy with a Jelly Fish creates three Striped Jelly Fish that land on a random space on the board and instantly activate, clearing the row or column (depending on the stripe direction on the Jelly Fish). This clears candy, Jelly, and Blockers in the paths.
	Striped Candy + Coconut Wheel	Combine the Striped Candy with a Coconut Wheel to create a full row or column (depending on the direction you swipe) of Striped Candies that instantly activate, wiping out all candy, Jelly, or (one layer of) Blockers. The wheel goes off-screen and comes back to cross candies it missed on the first trip (say, if you start in the middle of a row or column).
	Wrapped Candy + Wrapped Candy	Combining two Wrapped Candies results in a huge explosion—each creates a 5x5 blast separately, but since they're side by side, a 6x5 blast is the first result. Then both Wrapped Candies individually drop, and each explodes again when they reach a resting space. Again they explode, each creating a blast covering a 5x5 space.
	Wrapped Candy + Color Bomb	This combination results in the Color Bomb selecting all the same-color candies as the Wrapped Candy it's swiped with, then turning them all into Wrapped Candies. They're immediately activated (exploded) from the top of the board to the bottom. Wrapped Candies always deliver two explosions each.
	Wrapped Candy + Jelly Fish	When combined, the Jelly Fish are converted into three Wrapped Jelly Fish that swim across the board and pick three random spaces to explode in, each doing 3x3 space damage. They drop to a resting spot and again explode another 3x3 area.

Special Candy Combinations (continued)

CANDY	CANDY COMBO	RESULTING EFFECT
	Wrapped Candy + Coconut Wheel	This combo behaves the same way it would when combined with a Striped Candy, except Wrapped Candy Bombs are created vertically or horizontally across the entire board, and normal Wrapped Candy Bomb behaviors follow.
	Color Bomb + Color Bomb	When combining two Color Bombs, a large board-wide explosion occurs and acts as a single hit on all spaces, so it destroys all uncovered or non-locked candy, Jelly, Blockers, and a single layer of Multilayered Blockers and Popcorn.
	Color Bomb + Jelly Fish	Creates three Color Bomb Jelly Fish that swim off to three random spaces and eat the candy in those spaces. Next, those three eaten candies convert into fish (a one-to-one ratio) and repeat the process. This happens three times and ultimately destroys 12 random candies.
	Color Bomb + Coconut Wheel	The Color Bomb is activated first, randomly picking a color group to strike, then the Coconut Wheel turns a row or column into Striped Candy. From here it behaves like a Color Bomb crossed with a Striped Candy.
	Coconut Wheel + Coconut Wheel	When two Coconut Wheels are combined, the effect is two continuous lines (vertical and horizontal) of Striped Candy specials created. All the Striped Candies are activated and clear every row or column they face, only stopped by effect Blockers.

Secondary Elements

Secondary Elements are puzzle features to keep the game fresh, fun, and challenging. Secondary Elements can be broken down into two categories: Blockers and Non-Blocker elements. These Blockers can alter the nature of candies with every move, spawn elements and Blockers, and move candies from one place to another. Non-Blocker elements cannot be removed from a board, unlike Blockers, which can be destroyed.

IMAGE	ELEMENT NAME	DESCRIPTION
	Sugar Key	Comes in a variety of colors, and when matched with two other same-color candies, the key is destroyed. All existing Sugar Chests lose one layer. A puzzle with Sugar Keys usually means you must destroy the keys before you can beat the objective.
	Candy Frog	The frog comes in all the colors of normal candy, and when fully fed, it acts like a Wrapped Candy that can be placed almost anywhere on the board to destroy what's on the eight surrounding squares. Feed the frog the same-color candies to fully charge it. The frog is unaffected by gravity and sits in one place until it's swiped or moved for activation. The frog can take on characteristics of Special Candy it's swiped with, and once activated (exploded), the frog changes to another color.
	Teleporter	Teleports candy and Blockers from one space to another. The blue Teleporter is the entry point, and the pink one is the exit portal. You typically have to clear candies below them to make them drop through.
	Candy Cannon	These look like gumball machines and dispense candy onto the board when items below them are removed. The Candy Cannon can release Liquorice Swirls, Candy Bombs, Sugar Keys, Mystery Candy, Chameleon Candy, and Special Candy. Candy Cannons cannot be destroyed, but some may be covered by Blockers.
	Conveyor Belt	Vertical or horizontal belts move any candy or Blocker that falls onto them one space per user move. Objects on a belt move in the direction indicated by the arrows on the belt. Conveyor Belts have portals at each end to transport objects to the next Conveyor Belt. Portals come in three colors: blue, green, and red). Chocolate cannot cover Conveyor Belts.

Blockers

Blockers can prevent levels from being completed, cover up candies, prevent Special Candies from executing their normal functions, prevent candies from taking up a space until cleared, or worst of all, prevent you from accessing candies for matching. A typical Blocker is Chocolate. It starts in one space and covers candies, making them inaccessible. If the Chocolate isn't destroyed in the next move, it multiplies and occupies an adjacent space, covering yet another candy.

Some Blockers can be useful. Marmalade, Icing, and Liquorice Swirls could stop Chocolate from spreading. And sometimes Chocolate covers a Candy Bomb just before it goes off and fails the level.

IMAGE	BLOCKER NAME	DESCRIPTION
	Chocolate	Spawns and covers candies one space every move that it's not destroyed. Destroy Chocolate by crushing candy beside it, or hit it with Special Candy effects. Chocolate can be created by Chocolate Spawners or Magic Mixers, neither of which can be destroyed. When these Chocolate creators are present and a single piece of Chocolate is destroyed, they don't produce another Chocolate for the next two moves.
	Locked Chocolate	The same as Chocolate, but locked down by a Liquorice Lock. This Chocolate doesn't spawn until the lock is broken, which can only be done with a Special Candy effect. Once the lock is broken, you must destroy the Chocolate with the next move, or it begins to spawn more Chocolate.
	Chocolate Spawner	This is a machine that churns out Chocolate in the adjacent spaces around its location. After a certain number of moves, the spawner starts creating one Chocolate per move until you break a piece of Chocolate, at which point the spawner doesn't create another Chocolate until there are two moves with no Chocolates being destroyed. Levels with this element often have more than one Chocolate Spawner, making the spawning location unpredictable.
	Marmalade	A translucent brown Jelly that holds candy, Special Candy, and Blockers. It's a weaker version of the Liquorice Lock; it can be destroyed by normal matches adjacent to its space. A match can even be made using the candy of the same color that's under the Marmalade Blocker. The candy underneath can even be moved to make a match in the next space. These types of matches also destroy the Marmalade. It's the weakest of all Blockers.
	Liquorice Swirl	This swirl of black Liquorice moves with gravity like all other candy, but takes up the much-needed space. It can be selected and moved and matched with other Liquorice but is not destroyed. It's resistant to Special Candy effects and weakens combinations, especially the Striped ones. A hit from a Striped Candy gets rid of only the one swirl and doesn't affect any Blockers or candy beyond it. Break the candy next to it or hit it with a Special Candy effect to destroy it. Jelly Fish cannot destroy a Blocker below a Liquorice Swirl. Wrapped Candy attacks and large candy matches are the best offense.
	Liquorice Lock	Looks like a black-liquorice barn door (a square with an X in it). Anything blocked underneath it cannot be moved or destroyed until the lock is removed, which can only happen with a Special Candy effect. You can also remove it by making a match with the colored candy under the Liquorice Lock.
	Candy Bomb	Also known as the time bomb, this Blocker is the most feared and difficult Blocker in the game. Levels with these can eat through lives in minutes. It appears as a colored sphere with a number in it. The number varies by level and counts down with every move on a one-to-one ratio. When the bomb reaches zero, the level is failed instantly no matter how many moves you have left. The only thing that can stop this is a booster called a Bomb Cooler, which can only be purchased with Gold. Bombs are destroyed by matching three or more same-color bombs just like candy. Or they can be wiped out with Special Candy effects. Bombs can be created from dispensers or Mystery Candy. They can appear under Liquorice Locks, Marmalade, or Sugar Chests, making them difficult to destroy.
	Icing	Icing is a low-level Blocker that looks like a square of white cake icing. It can hide Jelly beneath it, and the Icing must first be cleared to break the Jelly below. Icing can be removed with adjacent matches or Special Candy effects. A Striped Candy effect takes out a vertical or horizontal row of Icing. Color Bomb attacks have no effect on Icing.
	Multilayered Icing	Occupies one space, but there can be multiple instances of it on one board. Multilayered Icing can have two to five layers present. Each layer must be removed to get to the possible Jelly below. Each layer is destroyed by making matches next to it or using Special Candy effects. You must hit it once for every layer there is to completely remove it. Color Bomb effects don't harm the Icing unless it takes out a candy adjacent to it. As pictured, the layers are named as such: Sachet (Layer 1—the bottom layer); Two-Layered Icing; Three-Layered Icing; Four-Layered Icing; Five-Layered Icing.

Blockers (continued)

IMAGE	BLOCKER NAME	DESCRIPTION
	Cake Bomb	This Blocker is large and takes up four spaces in a 2x2 area. The number of times you need to hit it to remove sections of the Blocker depends on the level, but can range from one hit to a maximum of eight. Jelly is often found underneath this Blocker. You can destroy this Blocker by making matches adjacent to it or by hitting it with Special Candy effects and combinations of Special Candy. Once destroyed, a party popper appears and explodes all the candy, uncovered Jelly, and Blockers (one layer of Blockers) from the board. The party popper doesn't remove sections of any other Cake Bombs on the board. A Striped Candy can remove two sections from the Cake Bomb, and a Wrapped Candy can remove four. A Wrapped + Wrapped Candy combo can take out all eight pieces if both explosions are adjacent to the Cake Bomb. Color Bombs have no effect on these Blockers, even if candies adjacent to the Blocker are zapped. A Color Bomb + Color Bomb combo can remove one slice from each of the four quadrants. A Color Bomb + Wrapped Candy (or Striped Candy) combo has a chance to remove several pieces. Jelly Fish target Cake Bomb slices.
	Sugar Chest	These single-space Blockers are immune to any attack and can only be removed from a board by destroying the matching Sugar Key. There can be up to five layers on a Sugar Chest Blocker, which means five keys must be destroyed to take the Sugar Chest off the board. Sugar Chests can cover Jelly or contain ingredients, candy, Special Candy, or Candy Bombs. Jelly Fish cannot eat the Jelly under a Sugar Chest.
	Popcorn	One of the toughest Blockers in the game, Popcorn occupies one space but can have multiple instances on one board. Popcorn has three layers to destroy before it's eliminated. It must be hit with the effects of Special Candy and Special Candy combos—adjacent matches do nothing. Each hit expands the popcorn graphic on the square. Popcorn can be produced by Lucky Candy, be Liquorice Locked, be inside a Sugar Chest, or be covered with Marmalade. Jelly Fish avoid Popcorn even if there's Jelly underneath. Destroying Popcorn can reveal Jelly, Special Candy, or a Color Bomb. Cake Bombs don't affect Popcorn. Popcorn takes damage but stops the effects of a Striped Candy attack and combinations thereof.
	Bobber	The Bobber looks like a floating fishing bobber. It's round with pink, yellow, and blue stripes. When activated with only Special Candy effects, the Bobber produces Jelly Fish. One Jelly Fish is spawned per hit. However, three Jelly Fish are spawned if hit with a Special Candy combination (like Striped Candy + Wrapped Candy), or if a Magic Mixer explodes and the Bobber is within effect range. Multiple Bobbers usually appear on a board at a time and are always indestructible. Jelly Fish spawned from Bobbers are programmed to attack targets in this order if present: Jelly, Blockers, Sugar Keys, Special Candies, and random candies if the other targets aren't present. Bobbers don't block the effects of Striped Candy or Special Candy combos. Activated Cake Bombs have no effect on Bobbers.
	Magic Mixer	These are the most annoying Blockers in the game, next to the Chocolate Spawners. A Magic Mixer takes up one space and looks like a clock with two battery cells on the left and right sides. After two to four turns pass, the Magic Mixer begins spawning Blockers adjacent to the mixer. If these Blockers aren't cleared, the Magic Mixer can spawn Blockers adjacent to the previous Blockers. These Blockers can be locked under Liquorice. They can spawn Popcorn, Sugar Chests, Candy Bombs, Chocolate, Liquorice Locks, and Liquorice Swirls. Unlike Chocolate Spawners, the Magic Mixer is destructible. You can hit it with candy matches adjacent to it, or with Special Candy effects and Special Candy combos. Destroying it takes five hits, and each time you hit it, it delays spawning Blockers for one move. Damage is shown with an immediate spark, battery drainage, and a gradual degradation in the clock graphic. Once destroyed, the blast radius covers a 5x5 space radius around the mixer (equal to a Wrapped Candy + Wrapped Candy combo). The blast can hurt other nearby Magic Mixers and take out candy, Jelly, and a layer of Blockers. Jelly can be hidden under these Blockers.
	Candy Cane	You won't encounter these Blockers until Level 3246. You find these completely encapsulating a square, or just one side of a square (horizontally or vertically). They're indestructible, designed to protect individual spaces on the board. They don't block Special Candy effects, but they can block simple matches. For example, a single horizontal Candy Cane can block a simple three-same-color candy match if it intersects one of three candies in the potential match. It's not possible to swap candy from one side of the Candy Cane to the other. Candy Canes also block candies from falling. They're designed to limit the space on the board for making matches. They can encapsulate Blockers, making them only vulnerable to Special Candy effects.

Level Types

You can find the level type display icons on the Booster Selection menu, reached just before you enter a level. The Level Type button is located to the left of the Play! button that starts the level. Click on the Level Type button to learn the objective details of that particular level.

The numbered space on the world map is color-coded to match the type of level located there.

WORLD LEVEL IMAGE	LEVEL TYPE IMAGE	NAME	DESCRIPTION
3075		Moves Level	Reach the target score in a limited amount of moves.
3306		Jelly Level	Clear all the Jelly, and reach the target score to complete the level.
3307		Ingredients Level	Bring down all ingredients, and reach the target score to complete the level.
3276		Candy Order Level	Collect all orders by removing the wanted items!
3297		Mix Mode Level	A mix between two or more game modes.

Moves Levels

A Moves Level is one that has a target score to reach, with a certain amount of moves available. This is the first level type in *Candy Crush* (Level 1 is a Moves Level). Moves Levels are the easiest level type and are very rare, making up less than 10% of all the existing levels.

The name "Moves Level" is a little confusing, as all level types are restricted to the amount of moves you have. If you always had unlimited moves, none of the level types would be very challenging. This level type should be more accurately named "Target Score Levels."

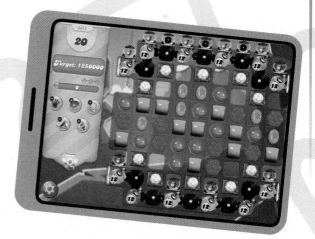

The number of moves needed to reach a score is clearly displayed; as soon as you enter the level, look at the top of the screen. The largest, boldest number displayed is the amount of candy-swiping moves you have, and the target score is to the right or below this number (depending on which way you have your device oriented). All the moves can be used to reach beyond the target score; in fact, you must use all the moves to complete this game type. When all moves are spent, Sugar Crush activates any Special Candies left on the board. Many times, this last action allows you to reach the target score. This is the only level type that never has Bobbers.

Jelly Levels

Jelly Levels make up around 40% of all levels currently in *Candy Crush Saga*. In a Jelly Level, you must clear all the Jelly from the board within a set number of moves. Jelly is removed by eliminating the candy that sits on the same square, with normal matching swipes and Special Candy effects and combinations. Blockers and Locks can keep you from easily removing Jelly. When all Jelly is removed from a board, a Sugar Crush is activated, which releases three Jelly Fish per remaining move. These Jelly Fish then eat random candies on the board, increasing your score. Jelly Levels can be the hardest level type in the game. Jelly Fish are good boosters to use in those hard-to-reach Jelly spaces.

Ingredient Levels

Ingredient Levels make up around 20% of all the boards in *Candy Crush Saga*. The objective is to collect all the indicated ingredients (Hazelnuts and Cherries) by sending them through a green arrow portal. The green portal can be set anywhere but is typically at the bottom of the board. Levels can request varying amounts of Cherries and Hazelnuts, and sometimes it's just one ingredient type. They fall like normal candies but cannot be destroyed or covered by Chocolate. Sometimes the ingredients are on the board at the beginning of the level, and sometimes they drop out of dispensers. When all the ingredients have been collected within the set number of moves, the level is a success. At the end of the level, Sugar Crush creates a Striped Candy out of each remaining move and activates it to rack up more points. You fail the level if you fail to pass all the ingredients through the green arrow portal. Striped Candy, Color Bomb combos, and Coconut Wheels make short work of Ingredient Levels.

Candy Order Levels

These are the second-most-common level type in the game, making up around 25% of the boards. In this level type, you must collect a certain number of candies, candy combinations, or Blockers within a certain number of moves. Once all those orders have been fulfilled, the remaining lives are converted into Striped Candy and activated during the Sugar Crush.

Collecting orders simply means destroying the candy on the order, or creating and destroying the number of candy combos listed. One of the best boosters for this type of game is the Lucky Candy Booster—when broken, it produces one of the candies on the order. This is especially useful when candies on the order are out of reach or trapped under Blockers or Locks.

One of the easiest ways to collect all the orders of candy, Striped Candy, or Wrapped Candy is to use a Color Bomb on that candy type. It either zaps all those colors or creates many Striped or Wrapped Candies and destroys them. Try your best to create Color Bombs during Candy Order Levels (or bring them in as boosters).

When Chocolate is on the order, you must strategize not to destroy Chocolate as soon as it appears, or you risk forcing it not to materialize for a couple of moves. This often causes you to run out of moves to complete the order. Keep Chocolate spawning one after another if possible, then take out large orders of Chocolate with fewer moves or by taking out many Chocolates with Special Candy effects and combos.

Mixed Mode Levels

Mixed Mode Levels are exactly as stated: two or more different objectives in one level. Mixed Mode Levels make up around 10% of all the boards. All Mixed Mode Levels are a combination of Jelly and Ingredient Levels. Previously, there were Jelly and Time Levels, until all Time Levels were taken out of the game. All these that were mixed were turned into Jelly Levels

When you complete a level—and also achieve one of the stages of Sugar Drop collection (24, 60, 84, 120, 180 Sugar Drops collected)—the reward screen pops up and you can claim your reward then and there. Your rewards are: Lollipop Hammer, Jelly Fish, Color Bomb, Coconut Wheel, Free Switch, Striped and Wrapped Candy, Lucky Candy, and Gold Bars. The higher the collection number, the better and more rewards you earn.

When one round has been achieved, there's an eight-hour cooldown period where no Sugar Drops are available for collection.

PRESENT NUMBER	REWARDS
24	Gold (x2)
60	Coconut Wheel, Wrapped and Striped Candy (x2)
84	Coconut Wheel, Lucky Candy
120	Free Switch, Coconut Wheel, Gold
180	Lollipop Hammer (x2), Lucky Candy

Free Boosters: Challenges & Events

If you refuse to spend real-world money and want to earn your way through all the worlds, you can still use boosters, but you have to work harder and wait longer for them—as opposed to forking over some cash at the Candy Shop. Events are challenges that are being constantly created. Partaking in events allows you to earn boosters.

Sugar Drop

Have you seen those levels on the world map with the letter "C" on them? That means that level is a Sugar Drop level. A Sugar Drop is a normal candy but has a white band around it with the letter "C" written in gold. You collect these to obtain rewards. They appear in Sugar Drop levels and in subsequent *newly* unlocked levels. The Sugar Drop only appears on the board during a cascade event, when the announcer says, "Sweet," "Tasty," "Delicious," or "Divine." When this happens, a regular candy is turned into a Sugar Drop. Once on the board, they're collected no differently from a normal candy.

Star Chaser (Misty the Unicorn)

This is the event that features Misty the Unicorn. She needs 10 stars to create a star-shaped constellation. The more stars you earn per level, the quicker you fill up her constellation with gold stars. You can't replay the same level to get more stars; you must complete new levels to add to Misty's constellation chart. You have a limited time (around 24 hours) to complete the challenge. When active, the Star Chaser details appear in the Fun Events menu found on the World Map screen. Here you can see how you rank with others and how much time is left in the challenge.

The idea is to collect a certain number of Sugar Drops to earn prizes. Jumping back into the same level where Sugar Drops appeared doesn't spawn them again. When you click on the Play button on a Sugar Track prompt, a progress bar indicates the number of candies you've collected, as well as the number needed for the next reward.

Denize's Star Dust (Denize the Dragon)

Much like the Star Chaser event, Star Dust features a mystical creature, Denize the Dragon, and you must help her light lanterns by collecting stars. All the same rules apply as Star Chaser; it's just a different host. This event lasts around 30 hours.

Space Dash

When this event is active, finishing levels without losing a life earns you boosters that become active on the first move in the next level. Continue winning levels, and each subsequent level another booster is added to the list of boosters you begin with. The bonuses are over when you fail a level and must restart at the beginning of the challenge to build up stacked boosters again. There are five levels of booster awards.

LEVELS WON IN A ROW	BOOSTER REWARD
1	Color Bomb
2	Color Bomb, Wrapped and Striped Candy
3	Color Bomb, Wrapped and Striped Candy, +3 Extra Moves
4	Color Bomb, Wrapped and Striped Candy (x2), +3 Extra Moves
5	Color Bomb (x2), Wrapped and Striped Candy (x2), +3 Extra Moves

Magic Dash (Mort the Magician)

This event is much like the Space Dash. Once you complete one or two levels, the event kicks in. Continue to pass levels without failing to stack booster prizes that become available on the board on the first move of each next level reached. Helmets fill with boosters after completing a level. The booster rewards are the same as in the Space Dash table in the previous section.

Dexter's Delight Candy Collection (Dexter the Whale)

You get rewards by collecting Orange or Striped Candies, but the level must be completed for these collections to count toward the total. When it's completed, you can earn a group of prizes: Free Switch, Wrapped and Striped Candy, Lollipop, Jelly Fish, Coconut Wheel, and a Color Bomb. The problem with this event is that you must stay in the world to complete the challenge, so many are out of the world before the event ends. There's no way to opt out of the event. While this guide was being written, King announced that they were altering the way this event works.

Candy Pet

This is one of the newest events in the game. Collect candies by winning levels, then bake treats for Rami the Sheep (Thursday through Sunday) or Didi the baby dragon (Monday through Thursday) to earn a sweet reward. You have six stages to earn the big prize. First, you must tap the capsule to hatch the Candy Pet. The first order is 20 (same-color) candies, and the baking time is five seconds. Next, the color of the candy changes, the amount changes to 80, and the baking time greatly increases. This goes on for six stages of increasing orders and baking time. Repeat the process to fill the meter and collect the reward. Candies collected during baking time don't go toward the challenge. Each stage award is one hour of free Color Bomb Boosters, and the final prize includes a Free Switch, Coconut Wheel, Lucky Candy, Color Bomb, and a Lollipop Hammer. These are added to your inventory.

Treat Calendar

Play every day and accept the treats earned every day for seven days in a row. Miss a day, and you start back at Day 1.

DAY	PRIZE
1	Wrapped and Striped Candy combo
2	Color Bomb
3	Coconut Wheel
4	Wrapped and Striped Candy combo, Jelly Fish
5	Wrapped and Striped Candy combo, Color Bomb
6	Coconut Wheel, Jelly Fish
7	Free Switch, Color Bomb, Wrapped and Striped Candy combo

Daily Booster Wheel

This is the best way to get a free booster every day. Give the Booster Wheel a spin every 24 hours to get a free booster. The Jackpot space is rigged; it speeds up or slows down just before reaching it. It's not impossible to land on it but it's very rare. When you do land on it, you earn one of each prize on the wheel. Eventually you learn how many times the wheel goes around so you can try to pick your prize, but the wheel speed and number of revolutions are different on each device.

In-App Purchases

Candy Crush Saga is the pioneer of the freemium model of mobile games; it can be played through entirely without spending money on in-app purchases, but they're available to help you get through the tougher boards that could have you hung up for days or weeks at a time.

Candy Shop

The Candy Shop has multiple bundles available that contain all types of boosters and Gold. The three most expensive bundles also include Free Play hours. The bundles range from $6.99 to $99.99 (there are five bundles). You can also buy bundles of Gold in case you simply need a little something to get you through a tough spot. The lowest Gold package contains 15 Gold and costs $1.99, while the most expensive and largest bundle contains 1000 Gold and costs $79.99.

Feeding Frogs

The fastest way to fill up a hungry frog is to zap a colored candy that matches the color of the frog. This eliminates all the candies of that color on the board and feeds them to the frog. If there are 12 or more, this fills up the frog instantly.

Space Dash Cheat

It's not so much a cheat as a sneaky strategy. Scroll all the way back to the very first level: #1 in Candy Town. Replay this quick and easy introductory level, which only has 6 moves. When you win, jump back in and play again. Continue this for five wins to get the highest Space Dash (or the similar win-with-one-life bonus challenges) bonus. Instead of scrolling all the way back up to the higher level you are stuck on, simply open the Fun Events menu, open Space Dash and press Play. This takes you to the level you are stuck on. If you fail the level, when you exit out of the level you will still be positioned at the first level in Candy Town again. This keeps you from having to scroll all the way back to try to get the easy prizes again, which are: Color Bomb (x2), Wrapped and Striped Candy (x2) and +3 Extra Moves.

Play Low

If you don't have an immediate plan for a board, the go-to strategy is to make combinations low on the board. Playing this way increases the chance to create cascades, which can break Blockers or send down ingredients you otherwise wouldn't expect to destroy or move with your smaller move below.

Multiple Devices

Using multiple devices to play *Candy Crush* gives you a few advantages when it comes to the five-lives limit (with one generated every 30 minutes). Playing on your phone, tablet, and computer allows you five lives on each. You can also ask for lives from the same Facebook friend on each device (each device doesn't know that you've already asked that person for a life). As soon as a life is received, you can turn around and ask that same person for another, and so on (or until they unfriend you).

Color Bomb: Wrapped or Striped Combo?

When you have a Color Bomb adjacent to a Wrapped Candy and a Striped Candy, which one should you choose to combo with? Most of the time it's the Wrapped Candy, since you get double the bang for your buck, so to speak. Since Wrapped Candy explodes twice, you usually do more damage. However, if you're trying for a hard-to-reach Jelly, booster, or Blocker, a Striped Candy combo could be the way to go.

CAT QUEST

Developer	The Gentlebros
Publisher	PQube
Year Released	2017
Platforms	iOS, Android, Steam
Type	Action RPG
ESRB Rating	E
Cost	$4.99

IN-GAME PURCHASES
None

Game Overview

Cat Quest is packed full of action, adventure, and cat puns. An evil overlord challenges the hero to rescue his sister. You must empower the hero with spells and better equipment before he's ready to defeat the evil overlord and his dragons. The cats that populate Felingard provide inns in which to recuperate, improved equipment, and quests that you can undertake to earn gold and gain levels.

What You Need to Know

Don't let the cutesy characters and setting fool you: *Cat Quest* is a game with some depth. The main story is only a small part of what the game has to offer. Beyond the quests that follow the main story, the cats of the land ask for aid constantly. After you wrap up the story, there's still more to do, including a Mew Game mode that allows you to take on the game again with Meow-difiers.

Paws-itively Nyan-Stop Action

The controls and combat in *Cat Quest* are simple. Touch (if you're playing with a mouse, substitute "click" for each instance of "touch") a spot on the screen to move to it. Cats and objects with quests or information to pass along are clearly marked with a chat bubble.

Combat

Touch any enemy to attack it with your equipped weapon. You only need to touch it once to begin auto-attacking. To activate a skill, touch and hold the screen to bring up the skill overlay. Select the skill you want to activate and let it do its thing. The shape on the ground when you select a skill indicates its area of effect.

Watch the ground around enemies for signs of their incoming attack and the area it will affect. Enemies use the same spells as you, so the shapes should look familiar. Enemy skills are generally slower than yours, so you have time to run in for a few hits, or to use a skill, before the enemy attack happens. There's also a brief window to attack enemies immediately after they use their skill. Defeated enemies drop blue (XP) orbs and gold coins.

Cat Gear and Skills

Touch the cat-eared bag in the lower left corner of the screen to bring up the Armor and Skills screen. Use the Armor screen to equip two types of armor (helm and chest piece) and a weapon. Touch any unequipped item to compare it to your current gear.

Weapons and armor are typically found in chests, both those from dungeons and the ones in the blacksmith's shop. Obtaining copies of equipment already in your possession increases the stats of the weapon or armor you own. You can't control what you get from the blacksmith's chest, so only spend gold there once you have more than you can spend on upgrading your skills.

Skills are learned from the temples found around the world, and most are learned from specific temples. To upgrade skills, find a temple and spend the required amount of gold. Spend some time practicing with each new skill as you acquire it to see which ones are best suited to your play style.

Enemy Vulnerability

In combat, the numbers that float over the heads of enemies indicate the damage done to them. The number's color lets you know if the enemy is vulnerable to magic or melee damage. Yellow is the normal color, which means neither resistant nor vulnerable to the type of damage you just inflicted. If the number is white, the enemy is resistant to that type of damage. Red numbers mean the enemy is vulnerable to that type of damage.

Restoring Armor, Health, and Mana

Armor *replenishes automatically when you are out of combat. To restore your* health, *use a healing spell.* Mana *regeneration requires successful melee attacks against enemies. Taking a catnap restores both health and mana to full.*

Quests and Side Quests

The main story line is told through quests offered by characters around the world. **Side quests** pop up on the quest boards located near buildings. Look for circled yellow question marks, then talk to the cat or read the board underneath them. Accepting a side quest puts the main quest line on hold. If you want to drop a side quest, check in at any quest board. The game guides you to the locations you must visit to complete the quests.

Dungeons

One condition for completing many quests is a trip into a **dungeon**. Dungeon entrances are openings cut into a small stone hill. If you leave a dungeon, all the enemies will respawn when you enter it again. If you're in a dungeon for a quest, you must defeat every enemy inside it. Use any of the light shafts you find to return to the surface. Explore dungeons carefully, as some will have hidden paths that you must discover in order to find all of the treasure.

Check Levels Carefully

Few areas are off-limits, even when you're just starting out. If you encounter an enemy with a skull near its health and mana bars, it's probably too dangerous for you to tackle. Check the suggested level for any dungeon before you enter it. If it's many levels higher than you, stay out until you're better equipped to handle the monsters inside. To gain the levels you need, look for side quests that are close to your current level.

Off the Beaten Path

When you're traveling for quests, or just to explore, set your path to pass through stands of **trees**. Gold coins and XP orbs are scattered around the world, and some are hidden behind trees.

Sleep to Save

Catnaps restore your health and mana, as well as save the game. Always take a catnap after you accept a quest if there's a lengthy introduction to it that you'll want to skip if you need to restart it.

Always Open with Flamepurr

You may eventually replace **Flamepurr** when you have access to more skills, but start fights with it as long as it's in your set of skills. Beyond the initial damage that it inflicts, it burns enemies caught in its radius for additional damage over time. Flamepurr also increases the damage enemies take from your attacks and skills. Follow up with other skills to take advantage of Flamepurr's damage boost, then switch to melee attacks to restore mana.

Golden Key for Golden Chests

The large, locked chests that appear in dungeons are all opened with the same key, but obtaining the key won't be easy. The rewards from the quests in Pawt City include the ability to walk on water. Once you can walk on water, go southwest from the Catpital to a wreck. From the wreck, go south until you reach Founder's Island. Check the quest board and accept the quest titled **Golden Key**. The dungeon for the quest is filled with dangerous **mimics** that resemble treasure chests. If possible, tackle the mimics individually. Take out the smaller mimics before you attempt to tackle the big one. After you obtain the key, return to the dungeons with golden chests (the entrances will be marked) and claim your prizes.

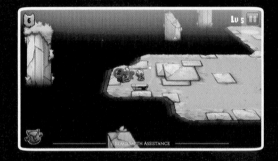

Mew Game and Meow-difiers

For the ultimate *Cat Quest* challenge, you can replay the game with Meow-difiers. Playing with certain Meow-difiers will reward you with special armor after you complete the story mode.

CLASH OF CLANS

Developer	Supercell
Publisher	Supercell
Year Released	2012
Platforms	iOS, Android
Type	Strategy, resource management
Suggested Age	10+
Cost	Free to download

 IN-GAME PURCHASES
Gems, buildings, magic items

Game Overview

One of the premier free-to-play games, *Clash of Clans* is a game of conflict. You spend your time improving your base, training troops, and researching new troops and spells so you can assault the bases of other players while defending your own. You should join a clan (it's in the name, after all) for greater rewards and greater challenges.

What You Need to Know

As with many free-to-play games, you must exercise patience or open your wallet for in-game purchases. Early buildings are constructed quickly. Higher-level improvements take longer to complete, up to many days in some cases. After the tutorial walks you through the first steps of building your base and mustering an army, you are on your own.

Building a Better Base

To stand a chance in battle, you must upgrade your base defenses and the troops you send into fights. Upgrades are limited by your town hall's level. For example, to unlock **goblin units**, you need level **4 barracks**. To upgrade your barracks to level 4, your **town hall** must be at least level 2. Increasing your town hall level also increases how many of each type of building can be added to your base.

Training troops requires elixir. Constructing and upgrading buildings costs **gold** or **elixir** (and **dark elixir** later). To harvest the gold and elixir that fuel everything, you must build additional mines and collectors after completing the tutorial, then drills to collect dark elixir.

Buildings

Three categories of buildings are vital to your base: army, defensive, and resources. Decorations are just that: decorative. They don't assist in the defense of your base in any way.

Army buildings produce your offensive units and spells. **Defensive** buildings protect your base from incoming attacks. **Resources** are the buildings that collect and store gold and elixir.

Workers

There are two more resources to consider when it comes to buildings: **time** and **worker units**. The speed at which worker units complete their tasks is the primary limiting factor when it comes to expanding and upgrading your base.

At the conclusion of the tutorial, you have two workers. When you can pay attention to the game, keep them busy with short tasks, such as clearing obstacles. When you know you'll be unable to check it for longer stretches of time, assign them to projects they can complete while you're away. You can add three additional workers to your base, but they aren't cheap.

Base Layout

The layout of your buildings is an important aspect of the defense of your base and a hotly debated topic by players. Because space behind walls is typically limited, leave low-value targets (the army camp, barracks, spell factory, and laboratory) undefended. Arrange defensive buildings around high-value targets, such as the town hall and resource storage, and put them behind your walls.

Keep in mind that there isn't one perfect arrangement that will stop every incoming assault. Since you're free to move buildings at any time (except when they're mid-upgrade), make adjustments after each incursion.

A Second Base

Once your town hall hits level 4, you're sent on a short boat trip to your builder base *(your original base is identified as "home village"). A short tutorial introduces you to this new base and its purpose. Upgrading the* builder hall, *the main building of the builder base, is done a bit differently. You must improve base defenses before you can upgrade the builder hall to its next level.*

Troops & Spells

Although it will be a while before you can muster them all, there are more than 20 different troops and nearly a dozen spells available in *Clash of Clans*. There are melee and ranged units, units that use magic, hero units, and even flying units.

Your troops train at **barracks** and **dark barracks**, then gather at **army camps**. The troops in army camps will not defend your base, but units sent by clan mates that settle into **clan castles** will. Troops housed in **guard posts** (found in builder bases) will also help on defense.

Spells are produced at the **spell factory** and the **dark spell factory**. You start out with the Lightning Spell but then need to upgrade the spell factory to unlock additional spells.

Upgrades at the Laboratory

The **laboratory** becomes available when your town hall reaches level 3. Spending elixir at the laboratory increases the levels of your troops and spells. Researching these upgrades requires hours or days. With only one laboratory available for building, it's important to minimize its idle time.

Battle Basics

Planning ahead is the most important part of battle. Once the action starts, you have very little control over the actions taken by your troops or defensive buildings. All you can do to protect your base is arrange your defensive buildings and garrison your clan castle before an attack takes place.

When you're acting as the aggressor, you have a bit more control during the battle. You are in complete control of activating and placing spells. While you can't control troops after they're placed, you choose where individual troops begin their advance through the base you're targeting.

Single-Player Campaign

Before you jump into battle against human opponents, check out the single-player missions that pit you against goblin bases. The potential rewards, mainly **resources** and **achievements**, are nice, but the real value in these battles is gaining an understanding of how your troops choose targets during an assault. There is some information available on the Train Troops screen, but you'll learn much more from observing your army in action.

Versus Battle

Initiating a fight from the builder base starts a **versus battle** where you and your opponent attack each other's builder base simultaneously. You must earn more stars than your opponent to win a versus battle. Destruction percentage is used as a tiebreaker if you both earn the same amount of stars.

Purchases

You can purchase gems based on the level of your town or builder hall. Special offers allow you to buy buildings and magic items. These purchases save you the time needed to obtain these materials or construct the buildings, but that's it. There are no items that are exclusive to being purchased.

TIPS

Join a Clan

A clan consists of up to 50 members, which means 49 other players with whom to share experiences and insight. Clan members can provide resources and troops. Being part of a clan also opens up perks, games, and wars. Depending on your clan's performance in games and wars, you can earn rewards that include resources and magic items.

Don't Waste Gems

Save gems for the only building that requires gems: **builder huts**. If you're at five builder huts already (the maximum number allowed), then spend gems to complete upgrades or build units faster. Never use gems to buy gold or elixir.

Earning Additional Gems

The easiest way to earn additional gems is to **remove obstacles** from your bases. Stone removal costs gold, greenery removal consumes elixir. Once a stone is removed, it remains gone. Greenery will grow back every eight hours if you leave a 3x3 area clear inside your base. You won't get gems each time you remove an obstacle, but you will most of the time. On rare occasions, you may find a gem box that is removed like an obstacle and always yields a tidy sum of gems.

Achievements are another reliable source of gems. You earn achievements for completing various tasks or repeating certain tasks a number of times. Scroll through the list of achievements from time to time to see if you are close to meeting the requirements for one and how many gems it is worth.

Base Build Order

When you're in the early stages of setting up your base, add new buildings before upgrading existing ones. That goes for additional copies of buildings already in place. Construction of new buildings is generally faster than completing an upgrade. Save town hall upgrades until you've exhausted the buildings and upgrades available to you at its current level. Check the time required to complete a town hall upgrade. You should time its completion to be shortly before or after you complete all other upgrades.

Secure Your Borders

Arranging the walls around your vital buildings is the key to defense. The arrangement of defenses and other buildings inside the walls is also important (don't leave any gaps where the attacking forces can spawn inside your walls!), but walls give your defenses time to cut down invading units. Set up your defensive buildings so their fields of fire overlap.

Get creative with your wall placement. Set up multiple layers of walls that enemies must breach to reach their targets. Walls can also be more than simple barriers to enemy units. Leave narrow paths that funnel enemies through twists and turns lined with invisible defenses, such as traps and mines.

The Heroes

There are three hero units for your home village: Barbarian King (unlocked at town hall level 7), Archer Queen (unlocked at town hall level 9), and Grand Warden (unlocked at town hall level 11). The sole hero for your builder base army is Battle Machine (unlocked at builder hall level 5).

To gain access to heroes, construct the building associated with the specific hero. These units are immortal, meaning they only need to rest to recover any health lost during battle. Heroes will defend your base against attacks unless you set their mode to Sleep. If you have plans for a hero at a certain time, set them to Sleep so they remain available.

Barbarian King

Barbarian King is the ultimate tanking unit when deployed to attack. Support the Barbarian King with ranged units and healers to get the most out of him. On defense, set up his altar in the middle of important buildings. He won't stray far from his altar, so the attacker can't lure him away from your other defenses. His special ability is Iron Fist, which acts like a personalized Rage Spell (the two won't stack) and summons a temporary force of barbarian troops.

Archer Queen

Just as her name implies, Archer Queen wields a bow with greater power and range than the archer troops produced by the barracks. If you employ her in attacks, she should be in the third row of a coordinated group. The lead group is melee units and tanks, with ranged attack units set up behind them. The Archer Queen's greater range allows her to set up behind the other ranged units, keeping her protected from return fire. She's fantastic on defense due to her range and ability to hit both ground and air units. Keep her altar well behind the walls or she might leave their protection to continue hitting invaders. Royal Cloak, the Archer Queen's special ability, makes her invisible to enemy units and summons archers.

Grand Warden

Grand Warden is a support hero that operates in ground mode or air mode. While he does his part during attacks to deal damage, his true value is in his Life Aura, which is a passive ability that boosts the health of nearby friendly units. His active ability is Eternal Tome, which briefly changes the health bonus to invulnerability. Choose air mode for your Grand Warden if he'll be supported by other air units. If he's the only target for air defenses, he won't survive for long.

Battle Machine

Master Builder outdid himself with Battle Machine, a barrel-themed suit that wields a hammer to great effect. While Battle Machine primarily acts as a tank that allows ranged units to do their work safely, its Electric Hammer ability allows it to join in on base destruction. Each activation boosts the damage for three swings. Save Electric Hammer for buildings that have either high damage output or a large pool of hit points.

CLASH ROYALE

Developer	Supercell
Publisher	Supercell
Year Released	2016
Platforms	iOS, Android
Type	Card collection/tower defense
ESRB Rating	E
Cost	Free to download

$ IN-GAME PURCHASES
Gems (in-game currency)

Game Overview

If you're a fan of the smash hit *Clash of Clans*, the characters you find in *Clash Royale* will be familiar. *Clash Royale*'s simplified gameplay pits two players against each other across an open field bisected by a chasm spanned by two bridges. Players select a number of cards for their deck, then play the cards as they accumulate enough elixir. The goal is to destroy your opponent's towers before they destroy yours.

What You Need to Know

Outside of its introductory tutorial and training matches, *Clash Royale* is strictly a multiplayer game. Between matches, you can purchase items at the shop, upgrade your cards, change up your decks, watch top players on TV Royale, sign up for special events or tournaments, or use the Social tab to keep in touch with friends and clan. Joining a clan isn't required, but it does open up additional gameplay modes.

Elixir-Fueled Battles

The mechanics of battle are simple. You create a **battle deck** of eight cards before you enter an arena. Once the battle begins, you place cards with the goal of either destroying your opponent's towers or protecting your own towers. To win a battle, destroy the opponent's King Tower or destroy more Princess Towers than your opponent. Elixir generation increases for the last minute of a fight. Ties go into overtime, but draws are possible.

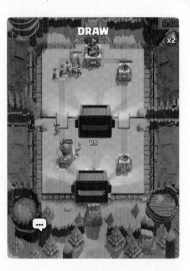

There are restrictions you must deal with during battle. Only four of your eight cards are available for play at a time. Cards that become troops and buildings can be placed anywhere that isn't covered in red (spells and attacks have no restriction on placement). Until you destroy a Princess Tower, that means anywhere on your side of the bridges. You also need enough **elixir** to spawn the unit. If the card is displayed in full color, then it's ready to fight.

The replacement card for the one you place appears to the left of your card selection. There's a short delay before a fresh "Next" card can go into your hand. If you place two cards quickly, your hand may be down an extra card briefly. You must cycle through your deck before a card reappears in your hand. A played card will reappear in the Next slot after you play three cards from your hand.

2v2 Battle

The 2v2 Battle option allows you to join forces with another player and battle two other players. All four players play simultaneously. The King Tower is wider and has two cannons for defense. Trophies are not on the line, but you can still earn chests and gold.

Shop

Touch the chest icon on the bottom of your screen to access the shop. The shop offers **daily deals**, as well as a selection of **royal chests**, **gems**, and **gold**. Nothing is a required purchase, but if you have an abundance of gold or gems, this is where you spend them.

Cards

The Cards screen is where you set up your battle decks, read card info, and upgrade your cards. At first, you can build three distinct battle decks on this screen, but remember to select the one you want to take into battle before you look for a fight. As your king level rises, you open additional battle deck slots.

King Level

The blue starburst in the upper left corner is your king level. Increase your king level to strengthen your King Tower and Princess Towers. Upgrading your cards and donating cards to your clan mates increases your king level.

Earning and Upgrading Cards

To create better battle decks, you must build up your stockpile of cards, then use those cards to advance to the next arena level and unlock better cards. **Chests** are the primary source of cards. Obtaining additional copies of a card you already possess allows you to upgrade it. Upgrading a card also costs gold. If your gold supply is low, upgrade the cards that you use in battle first.

To learn about a unit's preferred targets or special abilities, read its Info page and try it out in training matches. You must have a solid understanding of how your troops will act in battle if you want to reach the next arena level.

Battle

Beyond starting battles and 2v2 matches, the Battle screen also lists quests for you to complete and earn extra rewards. Check daily for your gifts and to see how close you are to completing achievements.

If you're interested in watching other players battle each other, touch the TV Royale button and scroll through your choices. Swipe to the Legendary Arena if you want to see the best players in action.

In-App Purchases

The gems you can purchase for real money have various uses, including faster upgrades for cards, opening chests instantly, paying the entrance fee for challenges, and purchasing gold.

TIPS

Join a Clan

The popularity of *Clash Royale* means that there are always players trying out something new that will defeat what are considered the best current battle decks. Supercell is also keeping the game fresh for players, so there are new cards and events being added regularly. If you want to stay on top of the changes, join a good clan. Share what you have discovered and learn from the experiences of your clan mates.

Completed Quests and Opened Chests

Check for completed quests and opened chests regularly, to avoid the downtime on them. Many chests you earn require a few hours before they'll unlock, and only one countdown can be active at a time. As soon as a chest is ready to open, grab its contents and start the clock on the next chest. Similarly, there's a delay between claiming the reward for completing a quest and a new quest becoming available. You want the countdown to begin as soon as possible.

Deck Building

You can unlock more than 80 total cards that can be used to build a deck of eight. That results in millions of possible battle deck variations, which means there is no single best deck in *Clash Royale*. Your deck should be balanced between attack cards and defense cards and include single-damage attacks and splash-damage attacks.

The first step in building your deck is to determine the card or cards that will be the focus of your **offense**. These cards have a single task: destroy enemy towers.

Next, choose cards to **defend** your towers from enemy attacks. Your choices must include repelling both ground and air attackers. Third, fill out your deck with cards that act as **support** for the selections you made in the first steps.

One thing to watch while building your deck is each card's elixir cost. Loading up on expensive cards is a surefire way to leave your towers vulnerable while waiting for elixir to recharge.

Elixir Use

Let your elixir build up before you make your first move, unless you must counter something your opponent does. Always keep enough elixir on hand to deploy a defensive unit.

Offensive Strategies

There are three offensive common strategies: beatdown, cycle, and siege. There are variations on, and combinations of, these strategies, but they are the three primary offenses.

Beatdown decks are designed to run your tower attackers behind a tank card, like Giants or PEKKA. Beatdown decks often include a cheap spell (to help cycle through cards faster or act as a quick counter to an attack) and a higher cost spell that can either boost your attack team or deal heavy damage to incoming attackers.

Cycle decks focus on quick turnover of the deck and are popular with aggressive players. You select one tower attacker, then fill your deck with cheap cards that you can play quickly, which results in your tower attacker popping up more often in your hand than defensive cards in your opponent's hand. The Hog Rider is a popular card for this type of deck.

Siege decks are built around a powerful weapon, such as the X-Bow or Mortar, that can damage towers from distance. Dedicate the remainder of your deck to defending your towers and weapon of choice.

Aiming Spells

Most spells target a spot on the battlefield, not a unit. That means you must either allow for movement or aim at stationary enemies.

Luring Enemies

Luring is a skill that can help keep your towers standing. If your opponent is using troops that target other troops over towers, you can use cheap units to draw them away. First, you must be able to recognize attacking units that will leave the tower to chase your lure troops. Next, practice spawning your lure units to learn how close they must be in order to get the attention of the attackers. When possible, select lure units that will go after enemy towers. That forces the distracted attackers to chase down your units before engaging them.

CRASHLANDS

Developer	**Butterscotch Shenanigans**
Publisher	**Butterscotch Shenanigans**
Year Released	2016
Platforms	Android, iOS
Type	Adventure
ESRB Rating	T
Cost	$6.99

IN-GAME PURCHASES
None

Game Overview

Crashlands is a top-down action-adventure RPG. Its focal points are combat and crafting. You play as a space delivery driver named Flux and have a trusty companion named JuiceBox. While in your ship you're attacked and crash-land on an alien planet. Your quest is to find a way to get off the planet.

What You Need to Know

General

◆ To **move**, tap where you want to go on your screen or simply hold down on the screen.

◆ To **destroy**, tap on the material you want to harvest.

◆ To **attack**, tap on the thing you want to attack.

◆ To **build**, tap the land you want to build on.

UI

◆ **Inventory** is in the bottom left. This is where you keep all your items that aren't being used in building.

◆ **Quest and data logs** are located above the inventory. This tab displays recently spoken dialogue, current quests, stats, and data on materials and creatures on the planet.

◆ **Building mode** is to the right of the quest and data logs. This tab is where your building structures are located and where you select them for placement.

◆ The **map** is below building mode and to the right of the inventory. This is used to navigate around the planet.

◆ Your **equipped items** are displayed in the four blocks at the bottom of the screen. Tap a block to equip it or use it.

◆ The **menu** is in the bottom right corner. Use it to pause and change settings.

◆ **Time** is located above the menu.

◆ Your **health bar** is on the top right.

◆ Tracked **crafting recipes** are in the top right corner. The recipes show you what materials are needed to craft the item.

Crafting and Building

Crafting is very straightforward. Go to the crafting station required for the type of item you want to build, gather the materials you need, click on the item, and press **Build**. Once you have finished crafting it, it'll show up under the finished section in the Construction tab. Collect it from there to place it in your inventory.

Once you've crafted a structure for building, enter the Building menu and select that item. Place it on the ground in a desired location for the construction. Keep in mind that building wood floors in your structures keeps enemies from spawning up in that area in the future.

Incubators

Eggs drop from certain enemies and can be crafted in one of the crafting stations. Incubators are made to hatch animal eggs. Once an egg is placed in the incubator, you need to wait a certain amount of time before it hatches. When it does hatch, you can name the animal and it becomes your companion. The companion can aid you during battles. If you don't want it to follow you, you can put the animal back in its nest. Other options are available, like milking it.

If you get enough **essence orbs** from your animal companion, then you can upgrade your companion—it takes a lot of orbs but it's worth it. Upgrading your companion makes it stronger in battles.

Farming

To be able to farm you need to make **"furdle durt."** Furdle durt allows you to plant seeds. For one batch of furdle durt (four units) you need eight units of dirt and four of sawdust. Your partner, JuiceBox, gives you the blueprints for this when you collect approximately 30 to 40 seeds.

Craft **armor** as soon as possible. You don't want to be constantly running back to your death location to pick up your loot. After you craft your axe, it won't take too long to farm up some wood to get at least a full set of wooden armor. If you are low on health, take advantage of your companion and let it do the damage while you heal up.

When attacking (or being attacked by) multiple enemies, try to focus on one at a time. It is quite hard to fight more than two enemies at once, because most of the time you'll constantly be doing the attacking instead of having time to deal damage. Take advantage of the **throwable wrench** to stun and deal damage to a target.

You can get a **pickaxe** schematic from Burl. He gives you a mission to return to his house and clear out some **wompits**.

To regain health, keep an eye out for **plants** that can be eaten. Items have a cooldown when consumed/used but they regen your health over time. Wander around the map to look for villages. If you talk to the locals they'll give you more quests, unlocking more schematics for crafting.

Take a little time to just farm materials. When you collect key amounts of materials JuiceBox will give you schematics. You can find **stones** around the map that give you temporary boosts when you tap on them. Keep in mind they have fairly long recharge timers.

It's good to keep ranged weapons like **sticky bombs** on you at all times. It'll make taking on bigger enemies easier so you don't have to risk your health, especially if you are far away from a teleport location. Plant as many **baconweed** plants as you can at your home. It only takes 20 minutes for them to refill. If you have the patience, you could farm off the plant and replant them to get even more. You could leave your phone on while doing something else.

CRYPT OF THE NECRODANCER POCKET EDITION

Developer	Brace Yourself Games
Publisher	Brace Yourself Games
Year Released	2016
Platforms	iOS
Type	Rhythm
Age Range	12+
Cost	$4.99

$ IN-GAME PURCHASES
None

Game Overview

Crypt of the NecroDancer is an action-rhythm dungeon crawler where you must move to the beat of the music to defeat enemies and keep your multiplier going. The game features an award-winning soundtrack by Danny Baranowsky.

What You Need to Know

Control Types

Crypt of the NecroDancer features three types of controls to offer you the experience that best-suited to your playstyle.

Edge

In this control style, the movement buttons are located on the edges of the screen and feature directional buttons in the top, middle, and bottom of the screen on both sides.

Swipe

This control style doesn't have any buttons and instead allows you to swipe on the screen in the direction you wish to travel.

Directional Pads

With this control style, there are two separate directional pads at the bottom of the screen, one on each side. While both directional pads control your movement in the same way, they allow you to find your preference of right-handed or left-handed control.

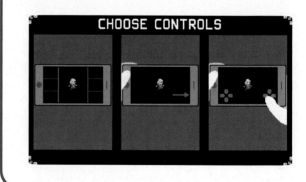

The Interface

Besides movement controls, your interface offers a few other important features. These include the map, items, hearts, gold, diamonds, and the beat indicator.

Map

At the bottom right of your screen is a map that tracks where you've been as you travel through the constantly changing dungeons. A blue blip on the map indicates your character's current location.

Items

The usable items picked up throughout the dungeon are shown in the top left of the screen. This feature shows your currently equipped weapon, as well as usable items—tap to activate them.

Hearts

The number of hearts at the top right of the screen lets you know how much life you have left. Though you start with three hearts, more hearts can be earned throughout the game.

Gold and Diamonds

Crypt of the NecroDancer features two types of in-game currencies: gold and diamonds. Gold is used to purchase helpful items within a dungeon and is lost upon death. Diamonds are permanent and used to purchase permanent upgrades from the lobby shops. However, note that unspent diamonds disappear when you leave the lobby.

Beat Indicator

The beat indicator takes up the bottom of your screen and features several moving dashes that converge toward a heart in the center. The beat of the song lines up with the dashes as they reach the center of the heart. This indicates the time to make your move, so you keep up your gold multiplier. If you stop moving, your gold multiplier resets.

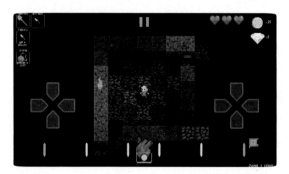

Lobby

The lobby is the main hub room for *Crypt of the NecroDancer*. In here you find staircases that take you to the various zones, allow you to start local co-op, select a character, start your daily challenge, and return to the tutorial. There are also several rooms. Hephaestus and the Dungeon Master both offer permanent dungeon upgrades, purchased with diamonds. The janitor allows you to remove items from the potential dungeon drop list. Codex allows you to try out various advanced techniques to improve your playstyle. There are also a few doors that you unlock by completing other zones.

Making Use of the Shovel

Sometimes an enemy doesn't move on every beat, which can make said enemy difficult to attack. Try digging a hole into a wall and waiting for the enemy to make its way to you before you attack, securing an easy kill.

Ranged Weapons

Fighting from a distance can be a huge help if you're having trouble getting up close. Bows, longswords, and rapiers can give you the edge in combat by allowing you to avoid harm.

Shrines

Shrines appear in the dungeons and provide a level-length buff, but they come with a negative effect. If you're already having a good run at the game, it may be best to avoid the shrine.

DON'T STARVE: POCKET EDITION

Developer	Klei Entertainment
Publisher	505 Games
Year Released	2015
Platforms	iOS, Android
Type	Wilderness survival
ESRB Rating	T
Cost	$4.99

 IN-GAME PURCHASES
None

Game Overview

A German scientist named Wilson caught the attention of a demon and was left on a strange, dark world. He starts with nothing except what he can scavenge from the environment. How long can you keep him alive?

What You Need to Know

Starting with an empty inventory, you must survive as many days as possible while dealing with health, hunger, and sanity.

Expect to stumble out of the gate. While the game provides help with controls, it doesn't lend assistance or explanations about objects or animals. Learn from each interaction and death (there will be plenty of both), with the goal of increasing the number of days you survive with each respawn.

Surviving a World Out to Get You

The majority of your time will be spent collecting materials and food. You begin with the ability to construct a limited number of tools, such as an axe, fire, and traps. These tools allow you to gather additional types of material and food, which should help you survive additional days.

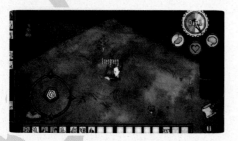

Tracking Time and Health

The top right corner of the screen displays the current day and time of day (**yellow** for daytime, **brown** for dusk, **black** for night). The meters for **hunger** (stomach), **health** (heart), and **sanity** (brain) appear below the day.

Time of Day

Keeping track of the time of day is vitally important. Initially, **daytime** is for exploring and foraging. **Dusk** is for gathering what you need to survive the night and starting a campfire. **Night** is for working near that campfire and keeping it burning. As you start to survive for multiple days and learn more about the world, your day-night routine will start to change.

Hunger

Hunger, represented by the **stomach**, is a constant worry. Despite ways to slow it, the need for food never ends. At first, you forage for seeds and carrots and can set traps for small animals. With the right materials, you can start a farm.

Health

Health, represented by the **heart**, is what determines whether your game continues or ends. When your health goes negative, you're forced to start over from day 1.

Unlike hunger and sanity, health isn't drained by time. There are situations where health goes down over time, but that's typically due to hunger or being on fire or freezing. Eating most kinds of food and consuming certain items, such as healing salve, will restore health.

Sanity

Sanity, represented by the **brain**, tracks mental health. As sanity is lost, your vision changes, strange creatures appear, and you hear voices.

Every action impacts sanity: Being in the dark, wearing certain clothes, eating certain foods, using wormholes, or being close to friendly or aggressive creatures will cause your sanity to improve or decline. Watch the brain icon for an arrow pointing up or down to see how your current activity affects sanity.

Wormholes

Wormholes appear on the ground and serve as a means of rapid transit between areas of the map. Since each use drains your sanity, reserve wormhole use for emergency situations, such as escaping enemies.

Customizing the Map

Before you start up a game, you're given the option to customize every aspect of the map, from weather conditions to how often a type of animal appears. Adjusting these options, in effect, changes the difficulty of the game. You should play a few games with the default settings before you make any changes.

New Characters

Each game you play awards **experience points** (provided you survive the first night). Reaching certain experience point milestones unlocks most new characters. Others become available upon completion of the game or by performing certain tasks.

TIPS

A good start is the key to long-term survival, so these tips focus on steps you can take to ensure early success.

Important Resources

In addition to food, gather **grass**, **twigs**, and **flint** immediately. Twigs and flint are components of axes and pickaxes. Use an **axe** to chop down trees for wood. **Pickaxes** break down boulders into component parts, such as rocks and gold. Without these two early tools, you're stuck relying on luck to find the resources you need to make improved tools and fires.

Spare Your Inventory

Raw materials and cooked food stack, but crafted items don't. Build what you need when you need it, not beforehand.

Don't pick up food you don't need, because you will need it later! Harvested food spoils, but not what you leave on a bush or in the ground.

Handling Food

Cook food to make it a more valuable resource. Roasting it directly on the campfire is fine until you get cooking vessels.

Don't eat it just because it's edible! If there's something new, try it only when you're desperate for food or you have food in your inventory to counter any negative effects. Either way, remember what effect the new item had so you know what to do the next time you encounter it.

No Fighting!

Avoid fights whenever possible, especially in the early days of your games. Your early tools make poor weapons, and trying to hunt with them will leave you frustrated. Run from aggressive enemies, set traps for ground animals, and use a torch to sneak up on sleeping birds at night.

Build the Science Machine Quickly

As soon as you gather one gold nugget, four logs, and four rocks, build the **Science Machine**. Standing near the Science Machine reveals everything that you can build. If you see a light bulb on an icon, you have the parts to build a prototype. Building a prototype unlocks that item so you can build it at any time.

Digging for New Items

Equipping a **shovel** changes how you gather resources. For example, using a shovel on a sapling awards you the typical twig but then adds the sapling itself. You can replant the sapling at a more convenient location for future harvesting.

Digging up graves yields some interesting items that can be traded to the Pig King, but watch your sanity.

Some Things Don't Last Forever

The percentage on top of the icon of an item you create indicates its durability. Each use of the item lowers durability until it reaches zero and the item breaks.

Mushrooms

Mushrooms are different colors based on the time of day you pick them: red for day, green for dusk, blue for night. Eating any type of mushroom (raw or cooked) helps one stat and harms one stat (health, hunger, sanity). **Raw blue caps**, which improve both health and hunger at the cost of sanity, are the exception. Eating combinations of mushrooms will help offset the negative effects. **Red caps** can be used to damage animals and monsters or fed to some animals to produce manure for farming.

Follow the Unnatural

When you encounter a **path** of brick or stone, see where it leads. There's a good chance you'll end up somewhere with different resources (including potential allies) than what's around the rest of the map.

EGG, INC.

Developer	Auxbrain, Inc.
Publisher	Auxbrain, Inc.
Year Released	2016
Platforms	iOS, Android
Type	Idle clicker
ESRB Rating	E
Cost	Free to download

$ IN-GAME PURCHASES
Golden eggs, piggy bank, advanced silo permit

Game Overview

If you've dreamed of starting a virtual egg farm, then this is the game for you. The goals in *Egg, Inc.* are to hatch chickens, sell eggs, and then invest in materials and research to help you hatch more chickens that can lay more eggs, which you can sell and make more money.

What You Need to Know

Your goal is to create an astronomically profitable egg farm. You start with humble buildings and a few chickens but can eventually grow your farm into a space-age facility earning in excess of billions of **bocks** (the in-game currency). One of the game's achievements is reaching one decillion bocks (a one followed by 33 zeroes). In time, your earnings will easily surpass that figure.

Rule the Roost

Tap the red button with the chicken silhouette (the one labeled "Tap this button to make chickens!") to make chickens. The status bar under your available cash indicates how full your hatchery is.

Everything else is done automatically. The chickens head into your buildings and lay eggs. Delivery trucks pull up at your farm to collect the eggs, then take them away to be sold.

Working While You Sleep

Your farm continues to work, even when your device is sleeping. Every time you return to Egg, Inc., you'll have stacks of cash waiting for you.

Your active contributions, beyond tapping the red button, are funding research, selecting upgrades to improve aspects of your egg farm, shooting down drones, and completing missions.

Research

Tap the flask icon or the science station (look for the telescope) to bring up the Research menu. There are two types of research: common and epic. Spend bocks to complete common research. Epic research requires the expenditure of golden eggs.

There are 12 tiers of common research, but many tiers are locked initially. The number next to the flask at the top of each tier indicates how many research upgrades you must purchase to unlock that tier. The number updates with each common research purchase.

Each time you spend bocks on common research, you receive a **golden egg.** Golden eggs are spent in a few different ways, one of which is purchasing epic research advances.

Boosts

The lightning bolt icon next to the research icon brings up the Boosts menu. Boosts provide unlimited chicks for 30 seconds or allow you to skip hours into the future, game-wise, and collect a pile of bocks in a hurry.

Upgrades

There are three non-research upgrades for your farm: **hen housing, shipping depot,** and **silos**. Touch any of the coops to bring up the Hen Housing menu.

You begin with one coop for your hens, with three empty spots for additional buildings. There's no way to increase the number of buildings for hens, but you can upgrade each to a **planet portal** that houses 100,000,000 hens.

The **shipping depot** is the wooden structure next to the road. Your fleet starts out with a single trike and can expand up to four total vehicles. Upgraded vehicles have greater capacity, which must match the output from your chickens.

Silos store the money you earn while you're not actively playing *Egg, Inc.* Each silo stores one hour's worth of money. Adding a second silo costs 10,000 bocks, but adding more beyond that costs actual money.

Drones

Crashed drones leave behind valuables, including **golden eggs**. Whenever you see a drone buzzing your farm, tap on it to shoot it down. If you have trouble tapping the drones, try sliding your finger on the screen until the drone goes down.

Missions

Tap on the check-box icon to bring up your current mission. Completing mission objectives most often awards **money, golden eggs,** or **soul eggs,** which are important when you choose to prestige.

Prestige

The Prestige option in the main menu is similar to upgrading your farm after discovering a new type of egg, but every soul egg in your inventory boosts your income by 10 percent, depending on which epic research you've completed. Of course, you're also starting back with edible eggs, but that's a small sacrifice considering your eggs are far more valuable.

In-App Purchases

Touch the purple house icon near your golden egg count to open the shop. The shop sells golden eggs for real money. To open the piggy bank, which gains one golden egg every time something is upgraded or purchased, you must also pay real money. You can buy an upgraded silo permit, which allows the construction of 10 silos, up from the two allowed by the free permit.

More Fingers = More Chickens

Take advantage of the size of the red button by tapping it with multiple fingers. Use one hand for unleashing chickens from the hatchery and the other to take down drones or collect packages as they're delivered.

Farm Value Is King

If you want to experience everything the game has to offer, you must increase the value of your farm, which in turn unlocks improved eggs. The majority of your farm's value is based on hen housing and the rate your farm earns money.

You can skimp on delivery vehicles (so long as they keep up with your egg production), but always upgrade hen housing when you can afford it. Even if you don't have enough chickens to fill them, the value of the buildings on your farm is considerable.

Early Research Focus

Focus first on boosting your farm's cash production. Increasing egg output with comfortable nests and egg value with nutritional supplements is the best way to accomplish this on fledgling farms. After you unlock tier 2, learn padded packaging and bigger eggs as fast as you can.

Epic research will come much later in your game. When you start, focus on choices that make it easier to increase your farm value: cheaper contractors, lab upgrade, accounting tricks, soul food (once you have soul eggs), and prestige bonus (just before you choose the prestige option for the first time).

A Better Egg Farm

Tap on the egg in the top right corner (or select Upgrade Egg from the main menu) to bring up the Egg menu, which shows your farm's value and the value it must reach to unlock the next egg. Unless you are close to finishing a mission, restart your farm with the improved egg as soon as it's available.

Watch Videos

Use the Watch Video option from the Boosts menu, that is. There's no quiz afterward, so you don't need to pay attention. *Egg, Inc.* limits how many videos you can watch in a certain time frame, so save your views for times when this boost helps you the most.

When to Prestige

Each soul egg boosts your income, so you want at least 10 to get a 100 percent bonus. There's no harm in collecting more than 10 soul eggs first, so any point after 10 would work. Since soul eggs carry over each time you choose to prestige, you should wait until you at least double your stock of soul eggs before going for another prestige reset.

EGGLIA: LEGEND OF THE REDCAP

Developer	DMM.com
Publisher	DMM.com
Year Released	2017
Platforms	iOS, Android
Type	RPG
ESRB Rating	E
Cost	$9.99

$ IN-GAME PURCHASES
None

Game Overview

The land of Egglia was broken apart long ago, and its fragments were sealed inside mysterious eggs. The story opens with a chance meeting between Robin, an elf, and a redcap who is not as violent as the others of his kind. Robin possesses one of the mysterious eggs, and she is shocked to discover that the newcomer can break it open to restore one of the lost lands. Their quest becomes the search for additional eggs and the restoration of all the lands of Egglia.

What You Need to Know

At its heart, *Egglia* is a game of rediscovery. You search for the mysterious eggs that restore the lands of the world. Along the way, you fight dangerous enemies and find new friends. If you increase their level of friendship with you, they may hand over a mysterious egg.

While you're recreating the world and making friends, you're also building a village and populating it. As new citizens appear, some open businesses that sell items to help you during your adventure.

Restoring the World

Each time you get a new egg, go to the world map and choose a location for it. Each new land introduces additional enemies, items, and characters to the adventure.

Secret Areas

Some lands unlock secret areas when placed next to each other. The good news is that land placement isn't permanent. You can rearrange lands for the cost of a single eggshell. Look for the full list of lands that have secret areas in the Tips section.

Companions and Other Residents

The characters who populate your town serve a variety of functions. Some open shops, while others will travel with you to the other lands. Anyone with an exclamation point (!) overhead has a quest for you. If there are three dots (...), then they have a request for a certain item. A heart indicates they want to talk, and they will often reward you for listening.

One of the goals in *Egglia* is to increase your friendship level with everyone. Give them gifts daily (check the Eggpedia for more information on the residents), then construct and furnish homes for them. Dunkel and Yergan are your sources for homes and furnishings, so get to their quests as quickly as you can.

Gardening with Tao Xin

The green sign in the back of the village leads to Tao Xin. Plant buds in the three plots, then wait for them to grow into the taters fed to spirits.

Companions are the characters who will travel with you to lands outside the town. While you move and fight, they pick up items based on their field skill. The icons next to the field skill tell you what items they gather. The better your friendship with potential companions, the higher their field skill becomes. Before you select a companion, check their morale score. Anyone with a morale score under 10 won't be available to accompany you unless you wait for their morale score to replenish itself, or have the proper elixir.

Spirits

Spirits provide occasional conversation while you're home and special abilities (known as **runes**) while you're exploring. While exploring, assign two spirits to assault roles and the third to support. The runes available for use depend on their current role. The link rune is a passive ability that is active each time the linked spirits are on the active team. Spirits need **mana** to use runes. One mana is replenished each turn, to a maximum of 10.

To find new spirits, travel under the well and place food items on the three flowers. If you repeat an item that was used previously, you may get a tater instead. Evolving spirits requires a visit to Tekko, at the sign with purple crystals. He converts seeds into jewels that will evolve spirits.

Explore the Lands

Touch the world icon to leave your home. Touch one of the available lands, then the Area Info button to learn more about the selected land. The Area Info screen displays mission requirements, rewards, and attainable items that are collected by your chosen companions or from chests. The Companion button allows you to set your companions and spirit formation. When everything is set, touch Confirm.

Each turn begins with a dice roll. Move to one of the highlighted spaces and take an action (attack an enemy, chop down a tree, use a rune, or collect an item) by double-tapping the screen. Your goal is to reach the space marked Next or Clear before you run out of turns. On your way to the Next or Clear space, try to gather items and defeat the enemies that get in your way. Failure to reach that space, or losing all of your health, returns you to the world map. Clearing a stage opens up slightly more difficult versions of that stage with new missions and enemies.

Following Friends

Use the Friends option in the menu to search for other players. Players who follow each other can send two lottery tickets per day. The tickets max out at 20 total per day (from following 10 friends), and the prizes you earn could be furniture or keys for Event Isle.

Robin's Friendship

The most important relationship in the game is the one with Robin. Do her quests when they come up and give her a gift daily. Her favorite is a Spirit Vial, so make that her daily gift when possible.

Check In Daily

The game provides bonus items every day you start the game. Even if you don't have time to play, at least start up the game and check your mail.

No Sale

Other than gold logs, don't sell any items that you collect. They're worth more as gifts to improve your relationships with your companions.

Runes in Combat

When you get new spirits, check their link runes. Place spirits with the same link rune together to activate its effect. For your support run, especially early in the game when you're still learning, choose Thalia for healing.

Egglia uses five attributes for affinities: shadow, fire, light, water, wind. Shadow and light are vulnerable to each other. Wind is vulnerable to fire, fire is vulnerable to water, and water is vulnerable to wind. Choose assault runes that work best against the more powerful enemies in each area.

The Role of the Dice

Think of the number that appears when you roll the die as action points. Moving a space takes one action point. When you're finished moving, the remaining points become the number of regular attacks available to you. If you plan on attacking a creature, you want that remaining number to be as high as possible. When the number on the die is low, but you are in a situation where you must do significant damage, use an assault rune.

Event Isle

One of the first eggs you receive opens the Event Isle, which is open briefly every day. What you find on it depends on the day of the week. Because your time is limited, focus on fast runs that maximize item gathering and avoid fights. Choose runes that boost dice rolls, such as Flying Start and Re-Torte.

Map Bonus Stages

LAND	CONNECT TO
Bamboo Grove	The Floating Gardens
Coral Coast	Himmel Peaks
Desolare Sands	Elysian Meadows
Elysian Meadows	Desolare Sands
The Floating Gardens	Sela Swamp, The Rusla, Bamboo Grove
Forest of Fungi	The Willowwacks
Hailstone Caves	Luciferous Labyrinth
Himmel Peaks	Coral Coast
Luciferous Labyrinth	Hailstone Caves, The Rusla
Patisserie Palace	Quazo Forest
Quazo Forest	Patisserie Palace, Waylost Woods
The Rusla	The Floating Gardens, Luciferous Labyrinth
Sela Swamp	The Willowwacks, The Floating Gardens, The Rusla, Waylost Woods
Waylost Woods	Sela Swamp, Quazo Forest
The Willowwacks	Sela Swamp, Forest of Fungi

ETERNIUM

Developer	DreamPrimer
Publisher	Making Fun, Inc.
Year Released	2014
Platforms	iOS, Android
Type	Action RPG
ESRB Rating	T
Cost	Free to download

$ IN-GAME PURCHASES
Gems, special buys

Game Overview

Once known as Mage and Minions, *Eternium* is an action-filled adventure. There are three hero classes available to play, and you're joined by computer-controlled companions as you combat evil forces threatening the world.

What You Need to Know

Eternium is not a complicated game, and that's part of its appeal. You explore new areas, defeat the enemies you encounter, and open any treasure chests you find. Some enemies drop gold, while others drop items that go into your inventory. When you find or craft better weapons or armor than what your character is using, equip it.

Treasure Chests

Treasure chests appear gold when you zoom out on the level map. Most chests open after you defeat all the enemies guarding it. Treasure chests bound in chains are opened with gems. When you find a bound chest, you should ignore it unless you're at max level. Equipment from these chests won't last long, so don't waste gems on them.

Fight, Loot, Equip, Repeat

Eternium's controls are all touch-based. **Touch** a spot on the screen to move your hero. Touch enemies to **target** them with auto-attacks. **Swipe** simple shapes on the screen to activate spells and abilities.

The majority of gameplay takes place in villages, forests, caves, and dungeons infested with the undead, dragons, and a multitude of other aggressive creatures. Between battles you can improve your gear, upgrade your abilities, buy and sell items, and loot treasure chests.

Your Hero in Action

Your first task is creating a hero, which can be a **bounty hunter**, a **mage**, or a **warrior**. Bounty hunters and mages are ranged characters, while warriors like to fight up close.

After you create your hero, your adventure begins with a search for companions at The Shores of Hope. **Abilities** appear on the left side of the screen, next to the commands needed to activate them. The **top of the screen** displays your hero's health, the health of your target, and the level map button. When shapes appear on the ground (in this shot, it's the arrows), it's a warning about an enemy ability about to be activated.

The level doesn't end automatically after you defeat the final enemy. You must press a button, which allows you to collect any remaining treasure or explore any side areas you may have missed. Subsequent trips through levels are often speed runs in which your only concern is high-value targets. If you find their locations on your first trip, you won't waste valuable time hunting for them later.

Heroic Improvements

As you progress through the adventure, you face more powerful and dangerous enemies. Your hero levels up as you collect XP, but gaining levels isn't enough. You need to improve your abilities, gear, and companions.

Better Gear

Tap the **helmet icon** to bring up the Gear screen. Tap any item in inventory to compare it to what's currently equipped. Icons with holes in the center indicate room for the addition of a **gemstone**, which are not the same as the gems you use for purchases.

Stats

The + icon under damage reveals more of your hero's stats. Touch and hold any box to learn what each stat does. The ellipses (...) icon brings up all of your hero's attributes.

You are also given options to add a socket and to reforge gear. **Reforging** changes the gear's current stat bonus to a different one in exchange for some gold. **Adding a socket** adds a gemstone socket to the gear, with the number of sockets limited by the gear's quality. Adding a socket costs gems, so don't bother with it until you're at max level. Detaching a socketed gemstone costs gold and doesn't destroy the gemstone, so there's no harm in it.

Crafting Gear

Most of your gear comes from enemies and treasure chests. There's a **Store tab**, but don't buy gear from it until you're at max level. The **hammer and anvil icon** brings up the Craft screen, where you can create new gear, which consumes three pieces of gear, some gold, and a little time.

The exception is **jewelry**. The Jewelry tab is where you obtain rings and necklaces. Crafting a single ring or necklace with a random attribute costs gold. You could spend gems to force specific stats, but that's something to avoid unless you're at max level and drowning in gems. The **fuse option** combines three rings or necklaces of the same quality lined up in your inventory into a single necklace or ring of the next quality tier.

Better Abilities

Heroes unlock new abilities and ability slots as they gain levels. Abilities come in three varieties: primary, secondary, and passive, each with a distinct shape. **Primary abilities** are activated by tapping the screen with one or two fingers. **Secondary abilities** are activated with simple swiping motions. **Passive abilities** are always active, but a rare few require input from you.

Use the Abilities tab to exchange abilities from All Abilities (which lists unused abilities) and Current Abilities. Tap on an ability icon to learn more about it. To upgrade an ability, drag it to an Ability Upgrade slot and pay the gold. All abilities can be upgraded to level 10. The higher the level, the longer it takes to complete the upgrade, so keep the upgrade slot busy at all times.

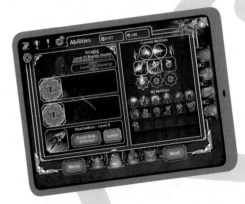

Better Companions

A big part of Act I: Elderath is finding three **companions**: Marcus the Warrior, Eileen the Healer, and Robin the Marksman. You can add four more companions from the store for 500 gems each: Norgrim the Warrior, Maggie the Potioncaster, Endar the Headhunter, and Xagan the Blue Wizard.

Companions learn new abilities as they gain levels, but only one is under your active control. You begin with a single companion slot. Use the **Team screen** to change active companions and spend gems to unlock up to two more slots.

Tanks

Marcus and **Norgrim** share the same abilities. They are tanks, with high armor and health. Their job is to keep enemies focused on them, allowing you to inflict damage in relative safety. Their active ability is charging into enemies, leaving them damaged and briefly stunned.

Ranged Damage

Robin and **Endar** have identical abilities. They shoot arrows at enemies from a safe distance. Their job is to inflict as much damage as they can. Their active ability, Multishot, is a spread of arrows directed at enemies.

Xagan fills the same role as Robin and Endar but uses magic instead of arrows. His active ability damages and freezes enemies.

Healers

Eileen and **Maggie** have the same auto-abilities but a different active ability. They keep your hero and companions alive in combat with healing and a magical shield. Eileen's active ability, Vortex, traps enemies in a single location, leaving them unable to act. Maggie's active ability is Silence.

In-App Purchases

The game's premium currency is gems, which have a variety of uses, including speeding up in-game events, unlocking inventory and ability slots, and purchasing gold. Gems are always available for purchase in various quantities.

Eternium also offers special buys that combine gems with items normally purchased with gems. The premium purchase that every long-time player would urge you to buy appears in your mailbox shortly after you begin playing and during special events. Do not miss out on purchasing a living weapon (Stormblade, Stormgun, or Skybreaker) if you believe you'll be playing Eternium after you hit max level.

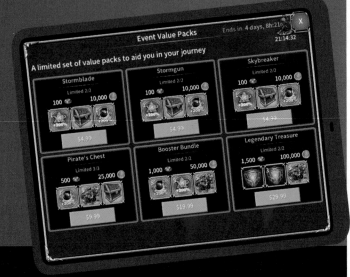

Gear

The golden rule of gear: Until you're max level or have obtained living gear, your gear won't last long. Don't spend much time or gold on it, and do not spend a single gem on it.

When your primary goal is to reach max level, mix in some gear that boosts your **experience gained** attribute. Don't overdo it, of course. You still need stats that allow you to kill enemies quickly. After level 70, your hero gains **champion** levels and points, which allow you to boost hero stats. Create a set of gear that boosts experience gain and use it when you're trying to boost your champion level.

If you receive a chest with a set item (typically through the Reward Calendar), open it only with a max-level character.

Companions

Keep companions alive in battle. If companions die, they won't revive until after combat ends, meaning you lose out on the support or damage they provide. When your goal is to get through levels as quickly as possible, you must avoid anything that causes delays.

Select companions that complement your hero. While you're leveling up, take a healer and a tank. That changes when you start speed runs; your companions should change to those that help you kill enemies the fastest.

If you like a certain companion from the store, you can purchase multiple copies, but only after you have unlocked everything else you need with gems. Duplicate companions are a luxury!

Legendary Jewelry

To make the legendary jewelry for your max-level heroes, craft 27 rings or necklaces, then **fuse** them into nine rare items, then three epic items, and finally one legendary-quality item.

You have some control over the items created via fusion, so choose jewelry that gives the best possible stats for your class. The stats on crafted jewelry are random, so be prepared to burn through gold while producing rings and necklaces before you get the 27 you want.

Earning Gems

Gems are the premium currency in *Eternium*, so spend them carefully unless you plan on buying them in bulk. Easy ways to earn gems include completing levels multiple times, adding friends, completing achievements, and turning on Rewarded Videos under Advanced Options.

Daily quests are another consistent source of gems. Each character you have that is at least level 9 is eligible for daily quests. Unlock those extra hero slots and get them to level 9.

Where to Spend Gems

The actual spending priority depends on how much max-level game-playing you plan on doing, but the following are necessary gem purchases:

- Additional hero ability slots
- Additional hero slots
- Additional minion slots
- Minions from the store
- Additional inventory slots (on individual heroes and the shared stash)
- Reforged gear at max level

Max-Level Hero...What's Next?

Once your first hero hits level 70, there's still plenty to do, such as earn all the story mode stars. If it's your first max-level hero, level the other two hero types. If you want to focus on your level 70 hero, get that hero's set gear and legendary jewelry.

Reforge your gear and try out different gemstones to see which stats help maximize damage. Use the training grounds on Elderath to measure the damage output of your hero and companions.

Run trials of valor, then compare your progress against the best players on the leaderboard and participate in special and seasonal events.

FRUIT NINJA

Developer	Halfbrick
Publisher	Halfbrick
Year Released	2010
Platforms	Android, iOS, Windows Phone, Symbian, Bada, Xbox 360, Facebook, PlayStation Vita, and Xbox One
Type	Arcade
ESRB Rating	E
Cost	Free to download

$ IN-GAME PURCHASES

Starter pack, golden apples, starfruit

Game Overview

In *Fruit Ninja*, you must slice fruit that is tossed up onto your screen. The many game modes change some features of gameplay. You also earn in-game currencies to buy vanity items like looks for the blade and backgrounds for the "dojo." You also earn XP to level up and unlock the new modes and vanity items—with an option to buy the items.

What You Need to Know

Classic Fruit Ninja Mode

The objective of Classic Fruit Ninja mode is to slice as many fruits you can to increase your score before you lose. You lose by missing too many fruits.

You **slice** by touching and holding the screen and then sliding toward fruit that is tossed onto the screen. Hitting multiple fruits with one slice rewards extra points, depending on how many were hit. You lose when you get three strikes. You get a **strike** when a piece of fruit falls off the screen. You can take one strike away for every 100 fruits sliced. If you hit a **bomb** (one occasionally comes up) you instantly lose.

Zen Mode

Zen mode adds a **time limit** to the game, and you must try to beat your high score before time runs out. There are no bombs and no strikes in this mode. Zen mode is unlocked at level 2.

Arcade Mode

Arcade mode is unlocked at level 4. In Arcade mode, you only have one minute to beat your high score. Special **bananas** are also tossed into the dojo. They have unique **bonuses**, such as tossing more fruit on the screen, doubling your earned points for a limited time, slowing down the speed of all fruit for a limited time, or stopping the countdown. Slicing a bomb in this mode deducts 10 points from your score instead of ending the game. However, hitting the bomb clears the screen. There are no strikes for missing fruits.

Mini Games

Mini games are unlocked at level 6. It costs you **starfruit** to play mini games. Completing these mini games gives you **golden apples**, which are used to compete in Event mode.

Challenges

Challenges are unlocked at level 8. Spend golden apples to play these challenges. Challenges have you pitted against AI opponents, and you must beat their score. Only one challenge can be played daily.

Event Mode

Event mode is unlocked at level 9. In Event mode, you can play for tokens to spend at the store. To enter the matches, you must spend golden apples. Fruit ninjas in each arena grant you special powers to help you fill a meter to gain more tokens.

In-App Purchases

You can purchase the starter pack, golden apples, and starfruit. The starter pack costs 99 cents and gives you 100 golden apples, 2,000 starfruit, and a chainsaw blade.

There are multiple bundles for both golden apples and starfruit. Watch an ad to receive five apples for free, or purchase bundles of 50 (for 99 cents) to 3,000 (for $34.99). Receive 100 starfruit for free for watching an ad, or purchase starfruit bundles ranging from 2,000 (for 99 cents) to 120,000 (for $34.99).

Buying starfruit and golden apples with real money obviously speeds up the process over earning them through normal gameplay but is completely optional; you do not need to purchase these items to get through the game or enjoy it more.

Missions

Complete the missions to earn more starfruit and XP.

No More than 2

You can use multiple fingers to slice fruit. We suggest using **only two fingers**, because most of the time using more than two locks up the screen and you can't slice until you take your fingers off the screen.

Pomegranate

Use two fingers when the **pomegranate** comes up. The pomegranate allows you to slice it unlimited times until the time runs out and it explodes everything on the screen. Slice as fast as possible to get more points.

Go Bananas

When a **frozen banana** is activated, take your time to line up the fruits so you can get the point multipliers. This is even better when paired with the **frenzy banana** or **point multiplier** banana.

GALAXY OF PEN & PAPER

Developer	Behold Studios
Publisher	Behold Studios
Year Released	2017
Platforms	iOS, Android, Steam
Type	Space RPG
Suggested Age	12+
Cost	$3.99 app/$14.99 Steam

$ IN-GAME PURCHASES
None

Game Overview

Galaxy of Pen & Paper is a nostalgic trip two decades into the past and an adventure two centuries in the future. A game master (GM) guides a group of gamers through a daring, space-themed adventure via a computer and its blazing-fast (28.8 kbps? Nah, gotta be 56k!) modem. It's an adventure with everything: Advanced weaponry? Check! Laser battles in space? Check! Praying no one picks up the telephone? Double-check!

What You Need to Know

You are in control of the gamers playing a game. During the adventure, you explore planets and space stations and do battle on alien planets and in gleaming starships. You design the GM, then customize the gamers and their characters. Every choice you make impacts the adventure, so choose wisely.

Party Like It's 1999 (and 2999)

The game kicks off with the creation of your first characters, and part of that creation is selecting the **personality type** of the gamer. There are eight gamer types. Each one adds two total bonus points to either one or two of the four stats used in this game, and each type has a passive ability. Choice of **race** works similarly, distributing eight attribute points between the four stats and adding another passive ability. **Class choice** has the biggest impact on stats but does not include a passive ability. You can't double up on gamer personalities or classes in the party.

Attribute Points by Gamer Type

GAMER TYPE	POWER	BODY	MIND	SENSES
Achiever	1			1
Buddy	1	1		
Showoff			1	1
Slayer	2			
Socializer		1	1	
Storyteller				2
Thinker			2	
Romantic		2		

Attribute Points by Race

RACE	POWER	BODY	MIND	SENSES
Human	2	2	2	2
Green	1	1	3	3
Simian	3	3	1	1

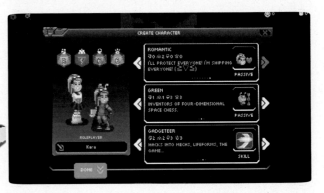

Movement

You move between nodes on a planet's surface. In outer space, you travel to planets, space stations, and other celestial bodies. The icons that appear on the map indicate possible actions at a location. Some examples are **exclamation points** for missions, **word bubbles** for NPCs that will talk to you, and a **skull on a red background** for a random battle. While flying through space, you may have random encounters with pirate ships.

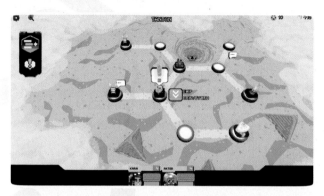

Combat

There are two types of combat: party and spaceship. Both are turn-based, which means one character or ship performs an action, then the next character or ship acts.

In **party combat**, the order of turns is displayed at the top of the screen. When it's a character's turn, select an available ability or action. The chess piece knight icon opens up non-combat options, such as waiting to take your turn or attempting to flee the encounter.

Set the difficulty of encounters by adding enemies to the fight. While you must defeat a certain number of enemies for most missions, you can break them down into manageable numbers over multiple battles.

Item Use

Using an item before your character acts does not use up that character's action.

For **ship-to-ship fights in space**, you begin each turn with a number of **action points (AP)**. Your ship's AP score grows as you discover more powerful DICE engines. Available actions appear below your ship's health. The cost for performing actions changes as you act. Repeating an action costs twice the AP you just spent to perform that action. Unused AP carries over to your next turn.

Gaining Levels

Earning **XP** raises your character's level; however, only characters that are alive at the end of a battle earn XP. Gaining levels adds to the points used to purchase new abilities and boosts the character's stats. Your points don't expire, allowing you to save up for the more expensive (and powerful) abilities.

Party Composition

The typical RPG group consists of a tank, two characters focused on dealing damage, and a healer. While that setup works well in this game, you do have some flexibility. Since item use doesn't use up a character's action, healing with items is limited only by your stash of credits. Use the advantages of front- or back-line placement, and don't forget you can swap rows as an action.

As your characters gain levels and can purchase new abilities, always choose complementary abilities. If something works better when a certain status is in effect (such as Burn or Poison), then choose abilities for other characters that inflict that status effect. Only four abilities can be active at a time.

More Classes & Cryochambers

Special side quests pop up during the adventure that unlock four additional classes. Each class unlocks only after you complete the quest, meaning you must turn it in and get the achievement. Classes are unlocked for all future games, even the ones you start from scratch.

You can switch classes mid-game after **cryochambers** are added to your ship. Place a character in a cryochamber (remember to remove any equipped items first!) to open a character slot. Your newly created character starts out at the same level as the current lowest-level character in your party. You can swap characters from the cryochambers at any time.

Bonus Missions

Bonus missions are available shortly after you begin the game. Select these missions from the Mission Creation menu. You earn **reputation** for completing these missions. Mix up the missions you do since the amount of reputation awarded decreases if you repeat the same style of mission.

Treasure & Artifacts

Take note of any changes to the map after you finish a fight. **Treasure chests** may appear, and what you find inside is always a nice bonus.

When you're supremely confident in your party, set up fights against the largest possible groups. The game may warn you about the difficulty of the encounter, but a win could net you an **artifact**.

Class Tips

Use the following tips to help create your adventuring party. The optimal stats choice uses raw numbers and does not take into account passive abilities granted by the choices of gamer personality or character race.

Bounty Hunter

With all of their abilities that increase the Critical Chance stat, bounty hunters can deal damage in big chunks. That's great against rank-and-file enemies that drop after one or two hits but can cause problems against bosses. If your tank can't keep up with your bounty hunter's threat generation, invest in gadgets that reduce threat.

Optimal stats choice: Achiever and Human

Engineer

Whether designed to tank or deal damage, keep your engineer on the front line. Tanking engineers may not need much in the way of healing because they have abilities that restore their shielding and health. If you're using an engineer to deal damage, you can't go wrong with the Breach ability.

Optimal stats choice (tank): Romantic and Simian

Optimal stats choice (damage): Thinker and Green

Gadgeteer

Depending on how they're set up, gadgeteers can be damage focused or act as support. Gadgeteers have passive and active abilities that boost Critical Chance, which means they must equip items to combat threat generation. To be at their best, another character in your party should be able to inflict the Poison status on enemies.

Optimal stats choice: Showoff and Green

Heavy

The ultimate front-line combatant, the heavy exists to draw and hold the attention of enemy forces so your other characters can do their jobs safely. If you're considering High Threat abilities, either select all of them or take none of them.

Optimal stats choice: Romantic and Simian

Medtech

Stash medtechs in the back line so they can keep everyone else alive and functioning. Get the First Aid ability quickly. Any health restored over the target's maximum is used to restore their shield. If you like a healer who can chip in damage during battles, you should build a party around inflicting the Poison status.

Optimal stats choice: Thinker and Green

Negotiator

Negotiators are setup characters. They can deal damage, but many of their abilities either boost Critical Chance for allies or inflict negative effects on enemies. More so than any other class, negotiator ability choices rely heavily on what you choose for other characters.

Optimal stats choice: Showoff and Green

Savage

Savages are front-line damage dealers with a few abilities that affect multiple enemies in one attack. If you include a savage in your party, keep in mind that more powerful enemies are generally immune to Stun. If you know a big fight is coming up, change out any Stun-based abilities for others that are more effective.

Optimal stats choice: Slayer and Simian

Trooper

Troopers can pull double duty, functioning as either tanks (front line) or damage dealers (back line). They excel against enemies with the Mark status on them and possess multiple abilities to inflict it. Use Scan Targets against large groups and Get Over Here! or Combat Sovereignty when tanking.

Optimal stats choice (tank): Romantic and Simian

Optimal stats choice (damage): Slayer and Simian

GANGSTAR VEGAS

Developer	Gameloft Montreal
Publisher	Gameloft
Year Released	2013
Platforms	Android, iOS, Windows 10
Type	Action-adventure
Suggested Age	13+
Cost	Free to download

 IN-GAME PURCHASES
In-game currency, diamonds

Game Overview

Gangstar Vegas is the fifth installment of the *Gangstar* series, released in 2013. Set in a modern-day Las Vegas, *Gangstar Vegas*'s story revolves around protagonist Jason "The Kid" Malone, a skilled MMA fighter with a price on his head. The mafia's Frank Veliano is after him after Jason wins a rigged fighting match that Veliano wanted to go the other way. *Gangstar Vegas* is an open-world experience where you can rob banks, partake in street races, and enter underground fighting tournaments. You can earn money through property management and Vegas-related activities, such as video poker, blackjack, and slot machines.

What You Need to Know

Skill Points

You begin the game with five skill points (SP). Skill points are used to upgrade your abilities, weapons, and vehicles. The SP upgrades can be found in your Profile menu—Skills is the first menu option. When you run out of SP you need to convert diamonds into SP, and if you don't have any to convert, in-app purchases come into play. You can buy bundles that contain varying amounts of diamonds (50 to 1,560) for up to $99.99! Ouch. It's best to be patient and find ways in-game to earn diamonds and cash.

Cash and Diamonds

Most everything in the game that is purchasable is paid for with diamonds. You earn cash and diamonds through normal game progression. Cash can be converted to diamonds in the shop.

Upgrades

Weapons and vehicles have three upgrade levels. A weapon becomes more powerful (does more damage, carries more ammo, has a faster reload time, holds more ammo, and has a faster rate of fire) each time it's upgraded to the next level. Melee weapon upgrades do nothing but improve the aesthetic value; they do not affect performance. Vehicle upgrades improve top speed, acceleration, and durability and give you more paint-job options.

Diversions

Call them side missions, distractions, or diversions, these missions fall outside task-driven missions. These challenges range from races to gambling. They appear as orange icons in the mission list in Quick Play and on the map.

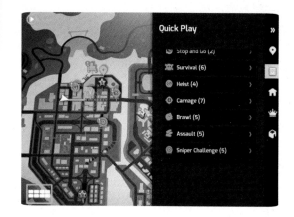

Survival

This is a capture-the-flag-type challenge. You're required to defeat waves of enemies while being restricted to a preset zone, marked with a large yellow glowing ribbon. Step outside the zone and you have 10 seconds to return or fail. At times you need to step out to pick up dropped ammo from the fallen. You can purchase ammo and med-kits during the challenge.

Heist

Similar to when you robbed the casino with Karen in the beginning of the game, heists involve finding and killing the building manager to get the keys to the register, safe, or vault and then defending the location of the money from waves of enemies trying to stop the heist. Once out, you need to lose the cops and return to your stash location to complete the job.

Carnage

Eliminate as many targets as possible in the given amount of time. Typically, you are given three minutes and have a choice of weapons to start with before the challenge begins. During the challenge you can obtain a vehicle to make you more resistant to the enemies shooting back at you. You can run over targets and perform drive-bys to take out a greater number of targets.

Delivery

Pick up a vehicle and deliver illegal packages to drop locations in a set amount of time. You must exit your vehicle at the drop locations to successfully deliver the goods.

Mission Types

To earn cash and diamonds, you should partake in all the mission types. Keep in mind there are level restrictions as you progress, so completing various mission types is necessary—it's not possible to stick to just one mission type and see it to the end without playing the other types.

Assassination

Fight your way to a well-defended target and either intimidate or kill your prey. You typically have to fight through many guards to get to the target and to get away from the area to complete the mission.

Assault

This mission type involves completely ridding an area of all enemies. There are many stages to this kind of mission, and more enemies will spawn or roll in to challenge you in the next stage. Once all the stages of battle are complete the mission is won.

Fight to a Target

This mission style is very similar to the assault mission type, except once you've battled your way to the target you need to plant a bomb or interact with something in the environment to finish the job.

Chase

A chase mission involves you pursuing a vehicle while maintaining a certain distance from the vehicle. If you get too far away, you are given 15 seconds to reenter the zone to continue the mission. Get outside of the zone for too long and you fail. Depending on the mission objective, chase missions require you to either stay with the vehicle to the end and fight the enemy after exiting vehicles or to just destroy the vehicle during the pursuit.

Time Attack

These are street races involving a certain number of laps around a predetermined course around Vegas. Come in first to win.

Ring Challenge

This race-type challenge involves driving through all the yellow rings on the course while leaving as much time as possible on the clock at the end of the challenge. The faster you drive through all the rings the better your score. The red rings make the challenge more difficult, as they take five seconds off your time for each one you pass through. Yellow rings add five seconds.

Freefall

This is a skydiving challenge where you jump from a plane and maneuver through the target rings, which are floating in the sky and arranged in a descending path to the ground. You can choose to pull your parachute when you feel it necessary to slow down, but you have to purchase parachutes (in this game nothing seems to be free), and using one slows you down to the point where you may fail the challenge. The idea is to get through as many rings as you can in a small amount of time for the high score. Tilt up to slow down and tilt down to speed up (with or without the parachute).

Racing

Race around a preset course around Vegas and beat the competition to the finish line. You must also beat the target time to win; even if you come in first, you could end up losing the challenge. On the flip side, you could come in second and still pass the mission—it's all about beating the different stages of time to win the associated prize and not so much beating the competitors.

Brawl

This is a hand-to-hand fight with a number of opponents. Take out waves of opponents as quickly as possible. This diversion is similar to Frank's mission, Eye for an Eye.

TIPS

Keys

A certain number of diamonds or keys will unlock those special chests you see in the shop, which contain rare items. You can get keys to these chests by gambling in the Vegas casinos. The only other way to get keys is to use diamonds or to actually purchase them with real money. These chests contain awesome items, but to many, it's not worth spending real money to open them. Spend time at the casinos to try to win keys.

Early Weapon Purchase

Since everything in the game is so expensive relative to the amount of money you make in the beginning of the game, we suggest you save up for (or buy with real money) a good assault rifle. This allows you to breeze through the early missions faster and much more easily, and you aren't wasting money on a steady upgrade of pistols and Uzis that won't get you very far in the harder missions. Save and spend wisely.

Upgrading

With just a little bit of time spent on the game, you'll realize that skill points are hard to come by and expensive to purchase, with both in-game and real money. So, be smart about what you upgrade. If you have purchased an assault rifle as recommended, you should upgrade assault rifle skills first. Otherwise, focus on damage and the rate of fire of the handgun class, and don't worry about all those other categories until you are much farther along in the game.

Run-and-Gun

The option to take cover behind walls and obstacles is a little wonky at best, so we suggest you run-and-gun in most situations. Of course, there are some hairy situations where covering will save your life, but there are just as many that can get you killed as you struggle to get out of cover to attack your assailant. Keep moving; running-and-gunning is going to win out over taking cover most of the time.

Fast Travel

Every mission and diversion has a Start option accessed from the Map menu. Save time and warp; don't waste time driving to all the mission start locations.

Never Lose

If you have plenty of money saved up, you should never die during a mission, because med-kits, armor, and ammo are always available for purchase in the shop via the Map screen during a mission. Or simply click on the icons on the screen below the map in the top left corner during gameplay.

Lose Your Wanted Status

The easiest way to lose a wanted status when not on a particular mission is to start a new mission; there are no restrictions on starting a mission while being wanted. If you are just causing general chaos while trying to make some extra dough, then start a mission and finish it or fail it. When you return to the map your wanted status will be clear.

Chop Shop & Making Money

Head to the nice residential area in the southeast part of Vegas and steal a level 2 Störer (try to do so without alerting the cops). Drive it to the Chop Shop and sell it for $270,000. You have to wait 20 minutes for the shop to cool down before you can bring another, but the wait is worth it. Also, play solo events or watch videos to earn diamonds, which can be converted to SP to upgrade your skills.

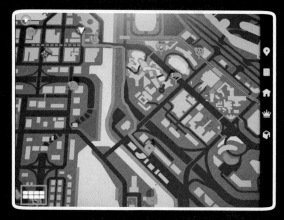

In-App Purchases

There's no shortage of places to spend real money in Gangstar Vegas. If you're short on lives, ammo, armor,

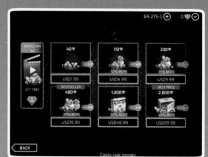

or parachutes, the game will automatically take you to the shop if you have game money or diamonds. If you don't have the funds, you are prompted to spend real money to get the diamonds needed to buy the items required to complete a mission. In the shop, tap the money or diamond display at the top of the screen to access bundles of $300,000 to $15,000,000 in game cash (for $1.99 to $99.99 of real money!). Choosing the View More option takes you to a window where you can see all the diamond bundle options. Save your money and use our tips to get what you need.

GEMS OF WAR

Developer	Infinite Interactive
Publisher	505 Games
Year Released	2014
Platforms	iOS, Android, Steam
Type	Gem matching, team building
ESRB Rating	T
Cost	Free to download

$ IN-GAME PURCHASES
In-game currency, stat boosters, equipment, VIP bonuses

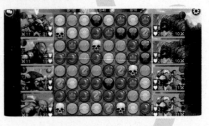

In-Game Collectibles and Currency

At the end of battles and after completing quests, you often receive rewards of various types. Some collectibles come and go with special events, but the following are available at all times.

ITEM	USES
Gold	Unlock and level kingdoms. Play the Arena minigame. Unlock gold chests.
Souls	Level up troops and hero classes. Can be obtained by disenchanting extra cards.
Gems	Purchase hero armor, or trade for gold and souls (in the shop). Unlock event chests. Crafting material.
Glory	Buy new troops, souls, treasure maps, and spoils of war (in the shop). Unlock glory chests.
Traitstones	Unlock traits for troops and hero classes. Crafting material.
Keys	Open chests. Key types will match the chests they open.
Treasure Map	Play Treasure Hunt minigame.

Game Overview

Gems of War is an incredibly deep gaming experience built on relatively basic game mechanics. At its core, *Gems of War* is a gem-matching game. Layered on top of that is building the best team to defeat computer and human opponents.

What You Need to Know

The complexity of *Gems of War* really shines through in its customization; you can customize everything, including your hero (unlocking classes, earning weapons), troops (recruiting, upgrading), team bonuses (kingdom, mana, team, type), various currencies (where to obtain, where to spend), and kingdoms (quest line, challenges, powering up, leveling up).

If this sounds overwhelming, don't worry! You can tackle *Gems of War* at your own pace. Use the information in these pages as a solid foundation from which to start your journey. When you're ready to push into the most challenging aspects of the game, find and join a guild. *Gems of War* has regular updates, and the best resource for staying on top of these changes is the players in a good guild.

In-App Purchases

Gems of War offers a wide variety of in-app purchases. There's nothing for sale that you couldn't earn through playing the game. You're spending money to skip the grind of acquiring gold, gems, souls, traitstones, and so forth. Even the VIP points you earn from purchases reward you the same items you get from playing the game, just in far less time.

Gem-Matching Maestro

The game begins in the land known as Broken Spire, where you learn the ropes of battle, the basics of team building, and how to complete quest chains in kingdoms, which in turn opens additional game modes within the kingdom.

From that point onward, the focus of the game is building up your hero and assembling teams of troops that work well together.

Clear Zhul'Khari First

Complete the quest chain in Zhul'Khari to add Tyri to your forces and unlock the Treasure Hunt minigame. The Treasure Hunt minigame is an excellent way to build up your resources without leveling up your hero. You don't want to level up early because your level determines who you face in PvP and makes Arena (unlocked in Broken Spire) more difficult.

PvP

If your goal is PvP, join a guild after you do a bit of research on it. PvP tactics change as new troops are added and the game is updated. Joining a guild has many other benefits, but a shared pool of knowledge and experience is the most important one.

Gem Matching

Leave Puzzle Hints (in the settings) turned on. It doesn't always point out the best move, but it will show you the best type of move available (four or more gems, skulls, etc.). It's easy to overlook gem matches since you're staring at a field of gems, so you may miss a match of four gems until the game suggests it.

Your normal priority (exceptions will happen!) for matching gems should be: any match that grants an extra turn, match three skulls, match three gems that grant mana to your troops, match three gems that deny opponents mana for their best troop.

Gain an understanding of how gems fall after being destroyed. You can really control the board (as much as the board can be controlled) by anticipating the fallout from matching different sets of gems. Is there a match near the top of the board? Check lower on the board in the same columns to see if there's another match that, when completed, will cause the gems you're eyeing to fall into place. Don't match gems, no matter how tempting they are, that will give opponents an easy four-plus gem match. Unfortunately, there's nothing you can do about the gems that fall in from the top to replace those destroyed by matches.

Spells and Gems

Understanding the verbiage used in the descriptions of spells is important. **Removing** gems/rows/columns does not destroy them, so no one gains mana and no opponents are damaged by removed skulls. **Destroying** gems/rows/columns blows up only the gems as described in the text, which means your team gains any mana coming from the destruction and skulls do damage. **Exploding** gems takes out the gem you select, plus any surrounding gems, resulting in incoming mana and outgoing damage.

Team Building

Building a great team isn't as simple as choosing your four best fighters and jumping into combat. However, it does begin with making the best hero and troops possible, and then you can explore other ways to improve your team.

Hero Customization

Your hero levels up and increases skills by acquiring XP in battles and challenges. With each increase in level, you're given a point to assign to one of two masteries (masteries are tied to mana colors). New weapons are unlocked as you increase each type of mastery. Changing your hero's weapon is done on the Troops & Teams screen, not the Hero screen.

The final way to customize your hero is by choosing a class. Completing the training quest in a kingdom unlocks the hero class linked to it. You spend souls to increase class level and traitstones to unlock traits.

Select the class info to view class bonuses. Additional class bonuses are unlocked at 50, 100, 150, and 250 wins in battle as that class, as well as when the class reaches level 10.

Upgrading Troops

Use souls to increase levels; that in turn raises skills values. Each card has three traits that are unlocked by expending traitstones, but they must be unlocked in order. Sacrificing a specific number of cards allows you to change the rarity of a troop. Troops higher on the ascension path (common, rare, ultra-rare, epic, legendary, mythic) have higher stats and a higher maximum level.

You won't earn orbs often. They can be used in place of souls or traitstones, or when sacrificing multiple cards for ascension.

Team Bonuses

Three categories of team bonuses come from troop selection: same mana, same type, and same kingdom. Your team needs two, three, or four troops from the same kingdom for a gradually better bonus. Type bonuses are awarded for three or four of the same type of units (split types count). For a mana bonus, your team must include four unique units that use the same color of mana (split colors count). The color of the weapon wielded by your hero counts toward the mana bonus. Your hero's class (if sufficiently upgraded) impacts kingdom and type bonuses.

Kingdoms also convey team bonuses. Unlocking a kingdom opens a new banner. Banners provide mana bonuses when you match gems. Spending gold to level a kingdom up to 10 provides a skill bonus (attack, defense, magic, or health). Increasing a kingdom's power (level and unlock traits on troops native to the kingdom to increase power) increases the skill bonus. Only one banner is active at a time, but kingdom bonuses are cumulative.

Team Composition

Use a variety of colors. The bonuses for selecting troops with the same mana aren't worth the frustration of waiting for one color of gem to appear so you can gain mana from matches.

Order your team carefully. Mana goes to characters closer to the top of your team first. Anyone lower on the list must wait for surges or the top characters to fill.

Select troops that have spells that work well with each other. Pair a troop that creates gems of a certain color with another troop that uses the same color of gem to boost damage output. If you have someone that does greater damage against opponents suffering from a status (e.g., hunter's mark, webbed, burning) then add someone who inflicts that status.

Team bonuses are not percentage-based, so your low-level teams benefit disproportionately. They're nice additions at higher levels but early on they're extremely powerful.

Look for traits that add attack, defense, health, or magic, and load up your team with troops that meet the criteria for the bonus stats. There's a good chance many of your selections will have traits that benefit the rest of the team.

Hero Armor

Armor provides gold, soul, and XP boosts, depending on what armor is equipped. Armor choice does not help out during battles.

GODFIRE: RISE OF PROMETHEUS

Developer	Vivid Games
Publisher	Vivid Games
Year Released	2014
Platforms	Android, iOS, Google Play, Windows
Type	Action-adventure
Suggested Age	12+
Cost	$2.99

 IN-GAME PURCHASES
Coins, Fury Pack, Judgment Pack, Olympus Pack, Pandora's Box, Hera's Mystery, and Horn of Plenty

Game Overview

Godfire: Rise of Prometheus is a third-person action-adventure game that has console-style gameplay. You play as Prometheus, a Titan whose mission is to recover the spark of fire and give it to the people. To complete your task you must fight hundreds of different enemies, solve puzzles, and upgrade your armory to help you defeat your enemies.

What You Need to Know

Coins

Coins are earned by collecting treasure, breaking pots, completing missions, or purchasing them from the in-game store. Coins can be used to upgrade your weapons and armor or to purchase perks.

Upgrade Points

Upgrade points are earned by completing levels or can be bought with coins. They are used to upgrade your Health, Wrath, Attack, and Defense stats.

Treasure

Treasure is hidden throughout missions and can contain coins, health, wrath, or armory items. You can use "Ariadne's Thread" to help you locate these more easily. If you choose not to use Ariadne's Thread, you'll know you are near treasure when an icon with a blue hand appears on screen.

Health

You regain health by killing enemies and breaking pots, or you can find health power-ups in chests. Keep in mind that blocking does not completely stop all damage inflicted.

Wrath

Wrath is the yellow bar below your health. Wrath is gained from killing enemies and performing executions. Wrath makes your heavy attacks more effective. If your wrath bar is full you can hold down the heavy attack button to unleash an area-of-effect attack.

Puzzles

Puzzles need to be completed to open pathways, continue story objectives, and open treasures. **Grayscale puzzles** are completed by turning the gray panels back to their original position to remake the original picture. You'll know it's in the right spot when color returns to the panel.

Block puzzles are completed by moving the blue blocks out of the way for the orange block to reach the other side of the puzzle.

Movement

When not in combat you can walk or run using the analog button on the left of the screen or by tapping the screen in the direction you want to go. While in combat, the left analog button allows you to dodge-roll.

Combat

Attacking

Do not use heavy attacks as your main method of inflicting damage. Instead, you can do more damage by performing a chain of light attacks and then a heavy attack.

Executing

While fighting minions, there's a chance to execute them (usually when they are low on health). This is ready when a red skull marker appears around your attack buttons. You take almost no damage from the enemies around you while executing.

When Surrounded

There are multiple ways to get out while being surrounded by enemies. One way is to perform heavy attacks; this contradicts the general attacking advice, but heavy attacks have a wider radius, so you can hit more than one enemy, which is especially useful when surrounded. If the opportunity arises, execute one of the enemies surrounding you to gain wrath or health.

Enemy Blocking

When your opponents are blocking, your attacks do less damage. You could try to take them out with the little amount of damage you do against them while they're blocking, but it's better to wait for them to attack and then go in for a light attack yourself to break their guard. Then start chaining hits together.

Blocking

Blocking ends an enemy's chain (excluding bosses), allowing you to go in for an attack. After the second act, blocking is a little more important because enemies start to do considerably more damage. When blocking, you can still take damage, but you can decrease the amount by using skill points to increase defense.

Dodging

Dodging isn't necessary when fighting minions, but when fighting bosses, you take more damage than normal while blocking because of their damage output. Dodging out of the way of their attacks is the better strategy.

Armory

Upgrades

Upgrading all your stats (Health, Wrath, Attack, Defense) equally is important. Don't leave any of them in the dust—having your stats balanced is key.

Buying Skill Points

Coins are hard to come by if you choose not to purchase any from the store. Don't buy skill points with coins. Save them for upgrading your armor and weapons.

Perks

Be sure to equip your earned perks to further enhance yourself with small boosts to your stats.

Miscellaneous

Coin Farming

If you need to get coins, go into Survival mode and collect the chests with the white auras.

Survival

Play Survival mode to collect feathers to get the best perk in the game: The Wings of Icarus. In Survival mode, you'll go up against waves of minions. Killing minions does not grant health.

Kill the Healer

If you don't kill your enemies' healer, you'll be wasting a lot of time hitting a foe who'll just regain the lost health. You'll know where the healers are because blue orbs fly out of them toward the other minions.

Extra Life

Every time you die you can get one resurrection chance. Dying after this forces you to restart from the last checkpoint. After you have restarted, you get another resurrection chance if you die again.

HADES' STAR

Developer	Parallel Space Inc.
Publisher	Parallel Space Inc.
Year Released	2017
Platforms	iOS, Android
Type	Strategy, resource management
ESRB Rating	E
Cost	Free to download

$ IN-GAME PURCHASES
Crystals (in-game currency)

Game Overview

The newly discovered Hades Galaxy is filled with star systems and valuable minerals. Corporations are scrambling to colonize planets and the potential riches that come with them. Hazards in this new galaxy include an aggressive, space-faring race, unstable red stars, and competitors from your home planet, but none of that will keep you from claiming your share of the prize.

What You Need to Know

Continual improvement is the focus of *Hades' Star*. You build colonies on planets and extract raw materials from them. The raw materials become a fleet of spaceships and space stations, powered by hydrogen. Upgrading your ships, planets, and stations takes time and consumes resources.

Profit-Driven Galactic Exploration

The opening tutorial begins with establishing a colony, then covers the construction of space stations and spaceships. Ignore the tutorial when it insists on using crystals to speed up research or production.

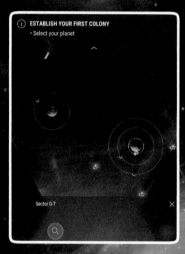

Planets

There are six types of planets you can colonize: desert, fire, water, terran, gas, and ice. Depending on the type of planet, it will produce a combination of shipments, credits, and hydrogen. Upgrading a planet costs credits but increases its production output and storage capacity.

Resources

The top right corner of your screen shows three resource trackers: credits, hydrogen, and crystals. Colonized planets and transports ferrying goods between planets and natural satellites increase your credits. **Hydrogen** is produced by some colonized planets and is also harvested by miners working asteroid fields. **Crystals** are a premium currency purchased with real money or earned through completing achievements.

Credits are spent to build and upgrade planets, stations, and ships, and to conduct research. Hydrogen fuels ship and station movement. Without hydrogen, your fleet can't go anywhere. Crystals are a wildcard. You can trade crystals for artifacts, credits, and hydrogen, or spend them to finish upgrades or research instantly.

Space Stations

Space stations act as your production and research facilities. There are eight space stations that you can build and upgrade:

- Shipyards build and upgrade your fleet. The size of your fleet is limited by the level of your shipyard.

- Short range scanners reveal adjacent sectors. You must scan the surrounding sectors before you can travel to them.

- Red star scanners detect stars on the verge of supernova and transport ships adjacent to the scanner to that star's system.

Brenwyn	✕
Colonized by MoronOx	

PLANET LEVEL	1 + 1 / 15
SHIPMENT YIELD	87 + 7/h
SHIPMENTS PER HOUR	0.8
MAX SHIPMENTS	10
CREDIT YIELD	0 + 1/h
CREDIT STORAGE	1 000 + 400
HYDROGEN YIELD	8/h
HYDROGEN STORAGE	200 + 60

UPGRADE	⟨ 50	⏱ 10s

- Research stations reverse-engineer the artifacts brought back from the red star trips into the modules that improve your starships.

- Diplomacy stations link your system with one owned by another player, allowing for shipments and defensive aid.

- White star scanners are gateways used for battles between corporations.

- Warp lane hubs are linked together to allow travel between two points without consuming hydrogen.

- Trade stations generate and receive shipments like a planet or natural satellite; however, they do not increase your overall credit and hydrogen storage capability.

Your Fleet

The spaceships under your command come in three types: battleship, miner, and transport. **Miners** extract hydrogen from asteroid fields, **transports** carry shipments, and **battleships** protect all of your interests.

The shipyard assembles your fleet, where you can also spend credits to upgrade the blueprints used to build the ships. The modules derived from artifacts are used to customize your ships.

Back	TECHNOLOGY	✕

🔋	**BATTERY**	
	LOCKED	

Does damage to a single target at a time.

TYPE	Passive
DAMAGE PER SECOND	100
ATTACK RANGE	120AU
ADDITIONAL HYDROGEN USE	0.4/100 AU
INSTALL PRICE	⟨ 1 000

Blueprint progress for next upgrade:
2/1

UNLOCK	⟨ 2 500	⏱ 1h

Opposing Forces

Computer-controlled Cerberus ships are always hostile and are typically encountered around red stars, but some will also pop up in yellow star systems. While you are competing with other players for artifacts, combat between players must be prearranged.

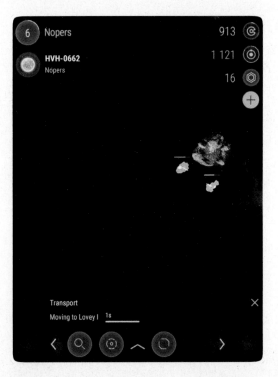

In-App Purchases

Crystals are available for purchase in lump amounts or as scheduled deliveries. The Starter Pack *special purchase provides both crystals and a 10 percent reduction in the prices for ships and upgrades to ships.*

TIPS

Personalize Your Possessions

If you want to rename your planets or ships, touch the magnifying glass icon and scroll down to Rename. The option to disband a ship to free up a spot in your fleet appears here as well.

Space Station Placement

Place your **research station** near your **red star scanner** to cut down on travel time for transports. If you need to spend hydrogen to move it after the tutorial, it's worth it.

Short range scanners should be built to maximize the number of sectors they can scan without overlap. Since they can't move outside the sector in which they're built, there's no way to squeeze extra life out of them once all neighboring sectors have been scanned.

Artifacts

Check your hydrogen level before starting a red star run for artifacts. You don't want to exhaust your fuel halfway through and lose ships or spend crystals.

Always target the highest level artifacts first, and always lead with your battleship. Without upgrades, your transports are destroyed with a single hit.

It's possible to store artifacts on colonies, but they'll suspend shipments until the artifact is removed.

Keep your research station working on artifacts as much as possible. That's its only job, and that's how you get better modules for your fleet.

Ship Upgrades

Don't rush to add upgrades to your ships simply because they're available. Wait until the additions and upgrades are necessary before you spend credits that could go to upgrading planets or space stations.

Battleships need only enough upgrades to safely handle the Cerberus ships guarding the red star systems you find. Transports should be upgraded so their transport capacity (cargo bays and overall weight) can handle artifacts coming from the red stars you discover. Miners should be upgraded only when they're unable to keep up with the hydrogen demands of your fleet.

The **Sanctuary** upgrade module is a great contingency for your ships. Any ship you were about to lose in combat or to a supernova jumps back home instead.

Cerberus Forces

Despite impressive firepower, **Sentinels** are lightly armored and are easy fights when you encounter them solo. When they are paired with **Guardians**, maneuver your battleships so they fire on the Sentinels first.

When you start discovering level 4 red stars, Cerberus ships become more dangerous. **Interceptors** are aggressive. When your ships enter the same sector as an Interceptor, it comes alive and starts hunting them. It will even pursue ships into different sectors of the map. The remaining ship types (Colossus, Destroyer, and Phoenix) require multiple battleships with many upgrades in place. The best way to take them out is to eliminate any smaller vessels first, then focus on the capital ships.

KNIGHTMARE TOWER

Developer	Gameloft
Publisher	Gameloft
Year Released	2016
Platforms	Android, iOS, Windows
Type	Off-road rally racing
Suggested Age	6+
Cost	Free to download

 IN-GAME PURCHASES
None

Game Overview

Knightmare Tower is an arcade-style game where you travel up a tower defeating monsters and enhancing your knight with upgrades that help you complete your mission: saving the captured princesses.

What You Need to Know

Four **armory** stats are upgradeable: Armor, Sword, Boots, and Rocket. Upgrading increases your chances of getting farther up the tower. When upgraded, Armor increases health, Sword increases damage inflicted, Boots increase your attack speed, and Rocket allows you to launch faster and lose less speed when falling. The Sword stat is the first thing you should upgrade in the armory.

The **accessories** upgrades increase your chances of finding more (and better) loot, help you gain more speed when defeating monsters and lose less speed when falling, and help with speed boost generation.

Potions are unlocked once you rescue the third princess. Monsters may drop potions when defeated. Every upgrade to the potion adds another very specific stat to it—instead of increasing one particular stats number like you find with armory and accessories.

Each princess you rescue unlocks new items, which from then on are dropped by defeated monsters.

Maximize Launch Speed with a Speed Boost

The **speed boost meter** is at the top left corner of the screen. To maximize launch speed, try to tap right before the bar hits the top of the meter. You need to kill multiple monsters to fill this booster. Once you use the booster, the meter empties. Avoid taking damage while trying to fill the meter or the meter will decrease.

Deal Damage to Boost Speed

Dealing damage is important, because killing enemies gives boost, and boost gives speed. It's also important because the farther up the tower you go, the more your enemies evolve. Evolving means that they have more health and better weapons.

Relax & Concentrate

It's crucial to be patient and line up your shot. You don't want to mistakenly miss your target and go plummeting off-screen, making the lava rise faster. Also, don't forget that you don't have to dash-attack a monster. Take it easy sometimes and just slowly descend onto an enemy to hit it.

Lava Hazard

Falling out of the screen's view won't damage you, but it will slow you down. If you become too slow, lava catches up with you and you will lose.

Attack Warning

You'll know when an enemy is about to unleash its attack because it'll blink white just before it attacks. Keep an eye out for this.

Blue Spike Balls

One of the enemies is a blue spike ball. If you do not kill this enemy in time, spikes come out of its body. You can still kill the monster while it's in this spiked state, but you'll take damage, so kill it early.

Spitting Brown Monsters

The spitting brown monster has a projectile attack. This is the first monster you encounter that takes more than one hit to kill. Take them out as soon as possible. To effectively kill this monster without taking damage, wait for it to shoot, then rapidly tap while above it to take it out or at least deal a lot of damage before it shoots you again.

Upgrading the Sword stat in the armory strengthens your attack, reducing the amount of tapping you have to do to kill monsters, which helps when attacking monsters with projectiles, such as the spitter.

Tiny Bats

Unless you are confident in your attacking and aiming skills, it's probably better for you to avoid the tiny bats. They are fast and you don't want to waste speed trying to hit them.

Dragons

The dragons are very simple to take out, but take them out relatively quickly if you don't want your area covered in fireballs. They stick to either the left or right of the screen, so just get above them and rapidly tap to attack.

Giant Purple Spike Worm

The giant purple spike worm needs to die. This beast fills a fair portion of your screen, and its whole body is covered in spikes. Focus your attacks on its head above all other enemies in the area.

Skeletons

When fighting the skeleton, do not attempt to dash-attack him while he's firing his laser gun—it won't damage him.

Boss Battle

Be sure to complete quests to earn extra gold for upgrades. In the Quests tab, you can purchase quests if they are too hard or if you just want to speed past them. Once you complete all the quests you'll get the **key** to open the locked ceiling where "the evil being resides."

The boss has many weapons at his disposal; they can be destroyed, but to damage the boss you need to watch for his head to peek through an opening. This is when you hit his head to dole out damage. The number of times you must hit him to defeat him depends on the sword you wield.

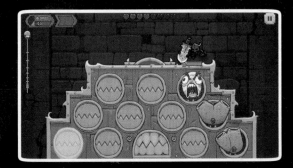

LEGEND OF GRIMROCK

Developer	Almost Human
Publisher	Almost Human
Year Released	2012
Platforms	Windows, macOS, Linux, iOS
Type	Action role-playing
Suggested Age	9+
Cost	$4.99

 IN-GAME PURCHASES
None

Game Overview

Legend of Grimrock is an action role-playing game with a real-time, 3-D grid-based interface, with dungeon-crawler-style gameplay and a Dungeon Master feel. You control a party of one to four characters with an expansive inventory and equipping interface. As in any RPG, experience is earned and skills are enhanced. Gameplay is a mixture of exploration, solving puzzles, and combat. For a serious challenge, you can choose the Old School option at the beginning of the game to give you the Dungeons and Dragons feel, where you must chart your own progress through the dungeons using pencil and grid paper. The digital tutorial allows you to print your own grid sheet.

What You Need to Know

Stats

Understanding the stats of your party is key to your success.

Health

Each character has red and blue bars next to their portrait on the marching order menu at the bottom of the screen. The red bar is your health while the blue bar represents energy. If the red bar drains, you die. Health is the ability to resist pain and withstand injuries. Character class and Vitality affect the number of health points gained at first and at subsequent character levels.

Feed your characters so that they regain health and energy when they rest. Rest when you need to regain health. The Rest option is on the tab on the left side of the screen. Improving the Vitality attribute makes this bar (and stat) grow much faster during level-ups.

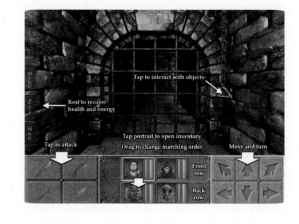

Energy

Energy is the ability to act. Strenuous activity—such as special attacks and spellcasting—consumes energy, and running out of energy prevents these actions. Willpower affects the number of energy points gained at first and at subsequent character levels.

Mages' spells depend on energy, so it's very important to manage this. Ranged weapons (missile type or thrown) are unaffected by the status of energy; these are not special attacks.

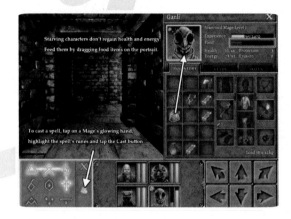

Protection

Protection is the combined protection value of all equipped armor, clothes, and other defensive gear. Protection decreases the physical damage of attacks against characters during melee attacks. To raise this stat, your frontline characters must wear heavy armor, which means you need to assign points to Strength, but the rub is that this is one of the last attributes you want to increase early in the game. You probably won't max out this stat your first time through without a serious amount of grinding—continually defeating respawning monsters. Instead, spend your points on Dexterity or Vitality early on.

Evasion

Evasion affects the character's chance of evading physical attacks. The damage from an evaded attack is completely negated. Evasion is determined by Dexterity, equipped shields, and other gear. This stat increases the chance that you'll completely dodge an enemy's melee attack. Keep in mind that elemental attacks do not count as melee attacks and that resistance to shock is the stat associated with those types of attacks. Don't put all your faith into this stat; you can move and dodge while fighting to avoid enemy attacks, and it's highly recommended that you do.

Damage

This is the amount of damage you deal with a physical attack. Damage is based on your Strength for melee and throwing weapons and your Dexterity for missile weapons. Skills and equipment give you additional bonuses to damage. Increasing this stat strengthens the damage from all non-magical attacks.

Accuracy

Accuracy affects your character's chance of hitting a target in melee combat. It determines how many times you successfully hit a monster during the confrontation. Every point of a selected weapon skill adds one point to your Accuracy with that weapon, which is why you should use all the points earned at level-up on your favorite weapon. Accuracy is determined by Dexterity skills and equipped weapons. Keep in mind that the battles are live and that the moment you press the attack button matters. Learn the timing of the monsters' attacks so you can interrupt them during their animations, creating a counterattack while canceling their attack.

Resistances

Resistance is the amount of a certain type of attack you are resilient to: fire, cold, poison, or shock. This is percentage based, so if you're 50 percent resistant to fire then you will receive 50 percent less damage from a fire attack. Mages can reach 100 percent resistance to an element, which makes them completely invulnerable to that element. You can raise your resistance by using items that add more resistance as well as by upgrading Dexterity and Vitality to the max.

Max Load

Load affects the movement speed of the party. If one or more prisoners are burdened (yellow bar), movement speed is diminished. If one or more prisoners are overloaded (red bar), the party can't move. Things that will weigh you down: food, torches, weapons, armor, treasures, skulls, rocks (and other nonessential items used for pressure floors). Increasing your Strength to improve your carrying capacity is not advised, as this is the least of your worries. Distribute the loads across your party members and give the heavy load to your minotaur (if you have one in your party).

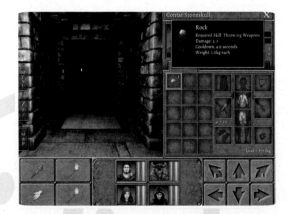

Attributes

When creating characters at the beginning of a game, you have 10 extra points to distribute to one of these four attributes: Strength, Dexterity, Vitality, and Willpower. This is the best time to shape your character; it's difficult to make big changes to this once on the adventure. Think about what kind of character you want to build and think about the weapons they'll carry so you know what attributes do or do not need to be raised (since a weapon may raise the skill enough to be plenty effective in battle).

Strength

This affects your carrying capacity and damage with melee and throwing weapons. Increasing this stat with level-ups raises your carrying capacity by 3 kilograms per point and +1 Attack Power for every two points of Strength. You need around 15 Strength to carry the heaviest set of armor in the game. A minotaur carries 15 kilograms more than all the other characters.

Dexterity

Dexterity affects your accuracy, evasion, and damage with missile weapons. Increasing this stat with level-ups raises your accuracy, evasion, and resistance to shock and fire. Dexterity helps you survive melee combat, so your frontline attackers, especially, need to focus on increasing it. The more you add to Vitality and Dexterity, the better your resistance gain per point invested.

Vitality

Vitality represents the overall health and stamina of your character. It affects the number of health points gained at first and at subsequent levels and helps to get rid of harmful conditions. Boosting Vitality lowers the duration of poison and sickness, which means you wouldn't have to carry around potions. The more Vitality you stack in the beginning the more health you gain over the course of your adventure. Invest a lot here when you are creating a character.

Willpower

Willpower is the force of the mind and the ability to manipulate arcane powers. It affects the number of energy points gained at the first level and at subsequent levels. Do not have less than 10 Willpower while using axes, maces, and swords; they consume a lot of energy, which is directly related to Willpower. Willpower increases your max energy gains at level-ups. However, if you plan to use a dagger or any thrown or missile weapon, don't bother with Willpower, as they do not need energy to be used. Mages can use Willpower to cast more spells per encounter, since they do require a minimum amount of energy to fire.

Manual Evade

Don't just stand there and take monster attacks straight on; instead side-step and attack when a monster misses its attack attempt. Keep a torch burning so you don't get cornered or step into a trap while you are evading the monster. Evading is especially important when fighting trolls and wardens. You should also dodge ranged attacks from enemies such as wyvems, uggardians, and goromorgs.

Share the Fight to Spread XP

Make sure that all the party members get in at least one hit when you fight a monster. Otherwise, those who were not involved only get 50 percent of the XP for the battle. Make those mages cast spells from the back of the party even when up against easy monsters. If their magic is ineffective against a monster with a similar element, make them throw rocks or shuriken.

Pressure Plates

You can use rocks, arrows, your party, or monsters to stand on pressure plates to open doors. The most common kind of plate has no weight requirement, which makes broadhead arrows (weighing only 0.1 kilogram each) and burned-out torches excellent choices for activating these while keeping your limited capacity available for items more important than rocks.

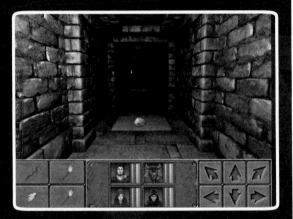

Investigate Every Bracket, Sconce, and Torch

Inspect everything interactive on the walls—many times adding or removing a torch triggers a secret wall.

Skull Puzzle

There's a late-game puzzle element that requires you to have a skull. When you find one, keep it in your inventory until you reach this puzzle to avoid having to backtrack so far to retrieve it.

Watch Your Back

If a wall drops, trapping you in with enemies, often more enemies will be coming up behind you from the direction you just came.

Drop Items Logically

Make piles of items near stairs that lead to the next level so that if you need them later you not only know where they are, you also don't need to backtrack as far to get to them.

Everything Has a Purpose

Try to hang onto one of each item; everything has a purpose—if not on the current level, possibly the next one. Thrown items are often used to solve puzzles.

Teleport Puzzle

A puzzle on the fourth floor requires you to stand on the pressure plate to make a teleport square appear four seconds afterward. Then you must throw an object through it. The only way to solve this puzzle is to equip a throwing weapon or stone and throw it like you would for a thrown weapon attack and not like lobbing a stone; you need the added momentum.

Pits Do Not Equal Instant Death

Pits never mean instant death, so don't be afraid to fall into them to explore them; they often contain secrets. Most pits also have monsters, so rest up before you take the leap of faith.

Health Potions Are the Best

Don't bother carrying any potions except health potions. As your Vitality increases you no longer need antidote potions. Energy potions are useless since only your mages need them and you rarely fight long enough that they'll need more energy. Health potions also counter the effects of disease, so you don't need antivenom or antidote potions; the effects are annoying, but they won't kill you if you have health potions.

Boxes or Bags

Food, spell scrolls, skulls, torches, and treasures are the things you'll want to keep up with, and the best way to store them is in bags, not boxes (which bring an element of difficult inventory maintenance to them). Bags weigh a lot less and have close to the same amount of storage (six spaces to a box's 10).

Iron Doors

There's usually high quality loot behind iron doors, and there are iron doors on every floor except the one with the final boss. Look for clues on how to open them. Some require keys and others special actions. It's worth the extra effort to open iron doors.

LINELIGHT

Developer	My Dog Zorro
Publisher	My Dog Zorro
Year Released	2016
Platforms	iOS, Android, Steam
Type	Puzzle
ESRB Rating	E
Cost	$1.99 mobile/$9.99 Steam

IN-GAME PURCHASES
None

Game Overview

In *Linelight*, you solve puzzles in a universe composed of light. The controls are simple, and the puzzles will become simple after they've infuriated you a dozen times.

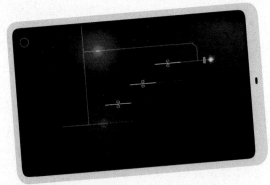

What You Need to Know

Linelight doesn't limit the number of tries you have to clear a puzzle. You have unlimited lives, and when you restart the game, you return to the last puzzle you attempted to solve.

There are three sets of achievements in Linelight: reaching the end of a world, finding all yellow diamonds, and finding all green diamonds. **Yellow diamonds** are on the main track through each world.

Green diamonds are off the main track, at the end of an (initially invisible) purple path. For a hint about the locations of green diamonds, touch the circle in the top left to bring up a map, then look for white dots.

The large **white circles** that appear on the map when you touch Level Select act as checkpoints you can move to instantly. They're unlocked as you complete puzzles and advance through the map. Use these checkpoints to reach green diamonds more quickly.

Playability

Linelight was originally released on Steam, then ported to mobile devices. The content for this guide was created for the mobile version, so some things may not work the same if you're using a keyboard and mouse.

Two-Dimensional Puzzle Solutions

If you're using a touchscreen device, then that is your controller. Keep a finger or thumb on the screen and your cursor (the bright line) moves with it. If the controls feel too touchy, or not responsive enough, you can adjust that in the settings.

Guide your cursor along the track until a puzzle stops your progress. Two types of complications make up the puzzles: computer-controlled cursors of various colors ("enemies") and obstacles built into the environment. Initial puzzles will have one or maybe two of these complications. As you progress deeper into each world, the game combines multiple mechanics into complex puzzles.

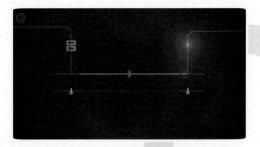

Enemies

These colored cursors are tagged as enemies because if they touch your cursor, you are sent back to the start of the puzzle. Of course, you can't simply avoid them. The solutions to many puzzles involve tricking these colored cursors into opening locks or toggling lines to open a path you couldn't otherwise create. Enemy cursors come in four colors: red, orange, purple, and pink.

Red cursors move in set patterns. When you encounter them, observe the path they follow a few times before you get too close. Getting past red enemies generally requires quick reflexes and precise timing.

Orange cursors also move in set patterns, but they generally don't move unless your cursor is in motion. To view their patterns and judge their speed safely, double tap the screen and hold your finger steady. Your cursor won't move, but the orange cursors will.

Purple cursors are magnetic. They move when you double tap and hold down your finger. They attempt to reach your cursor but can only follow the existing lines. They are often limited by boundary lines.

Pink cursors are mimics. You spawn them by entering a narrow rectangle that briefly turns your cursor pink. Any action you take while your cursor is pink (a quick flash lets you know when the time is about to expire) is repeated by the pink cursor that emerges from the rectangle. After the pink cursor completes its task for you and it's in the way, double-tap and hold until it dissipates.

Boundary Lines

If you're wondering why a cursor is stopping short of what seems to be a clear path, check the thickness of the track. Thicker parts of the track act as barriers for colored cursors, but not for yours.

Obstacles

An obstacle is anything that impedes a cursor's progress, either completely stopping it or altering the way it moves. Obstacles affect all cursors equally, even those controlled by the computer.

When you encounter **moving dashed lines** that are the same color as the track, note the speed at which they move. When any cursor is on them, the cursor speeds up or slows down to match the lines.

Solid lines of various colors are controlled by a nearby toggle or toggles. With multiple lines and toggles, the colors of each indicate the toggle(s) that controls a given line. Moving through the toggle changes the location or size of the corresponding line. The line switches location or size each time a cursor passes through the toggle, regardless of the direction it enters

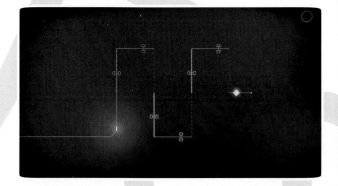

A common obstacle you encounter is a **rectangle** that blocks the path. There are a few varieties, and each requires a different action to remove it and open the path ahead.

For rectangles with a **key shape** in them, there will be a key nearby that unlocks it. If you are struck by an enemy after obtaining the key but before opening the lock, the key resets to its original position.

To open rectangles with **colored outlines,** guide a cursor into a patch of track outlined in the same color as the rectangle. The number of lights inside the rectangle indicates how many patches of track must be activated at the same time to open the rectangle. For any number of lights greater than one, you must enlist the help of other cursors.

Rectangles **filled with a color** are removed upon contact with a cursor that matches the fill color. The challenge with these rectangles is guiding the enemy cursor to it without getting your cursor caught in between.

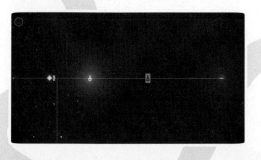

A Smaller You

The final tool you employ in solving puzzles is a curled line that crosses over the path. Going through the curls in the proper direction generates a smaller version of the cursor that passed through it. The smaller cursor follows whatever it has copied and will leave traces of itself in certain intersections.

Only a lit up curl will generate the smaller version, so if you encounter one that looks empty, you must locate another curl and move its smaller cursor to fill it by going through backward. Colored cursors will also gain a tail if one passes through a lit up curl.

Change Your View

You can play the game in portrait or landscape view, and the puzzles themselves will adjust. Stick with whatever feels more comfortable; however, if there's a puzzle where you know the solution but timing the movements to complete the solution is causing problems, change your device's orientation. That slight alteration may be all you need to get past the puzzle.

Scrutinize Easy Puzzles

Linelight introduces new enemies and obstacles with fairly simple puzzles. Take this time to study the basics of how each enemy acts and how they can be used to get past obstacles. To reach the end of each world, you must solve complex puzzles that involve multiple types of enemies and obstacles. If you don't understand how one obstacle works, you'll have a tough time coordinating a few at once.

Timing Is Vital

Moving past many red and orange enemies requires precise timing. In many instances, you must be almost touching one to reach an objective, then make a tight turn into a branching line outside of its path before it doubles back and takes you out.

Dead End or Safe Spot?

While you're watching red and orange cursors to learn their patterns, take note of any short segments that don't lead anywhere. They may serve as safe spots for you to duck into if the colored cursor moves faster than yours, or if there are multiple enemies using the same track.

Use Reset Level if You're Stuck

If you backtracked to get a green diamond and can't get past a puzzle you solved earlier, you may need to reset the level to return obstructions to their original locations. Hold down on the words Reset Level until the bar at the top of the screen fills. This affects only the local puzzle, not the entire world.

MAKE HEXA PUZZLE

Developer	BitMango Corporation
Publisher	BitMango Corporation
Year Released	2016
Platforms	Android, iOS
Type	Puzzle
Suggested Age	4+
Cost	Free

IN-GAME PURCHASES
Coins, ad removal

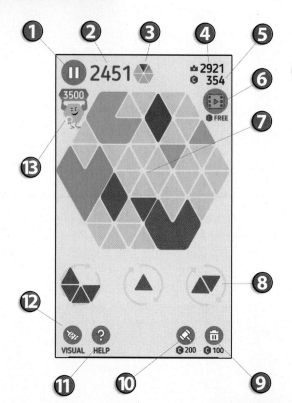

Game Overview

Make Hexa Puzzle is a challenging yet fun puzzle game where you drag colored triangles—and more complex shapes made from triangles—onto a board to create hexagon shapes with matching colors. When a full hexagon is built, that shape is removed from the board and points are awarded. There are both timed and non-timed levels, so you can play at a speed at which you are comfortable.

What You Need to Know

The Game Board Interface

1. Pause Menu

The **pause button** brings up the Pause menu, where you can return to the main menu, restart the board, resume your game, or enter the Settings menu.

2. Score

This displays your current score. Each time you place a shape on the board and and each time you complete a hexagon, **points** are added here.

3. Rainbow Block Display

Each time you create a double-hexa, two of the six sections of the hexagon fill. You earn a **rainbow block** once all six sections are filled. The larger the special hexagon you make, the more quickly you fill the rainbow block display.

4. High Score

This displays your all-time high score. The main goal in the game is to continually strive to try to beat your own high score.

5. Coins

This is your **coin total**. You earn coins by watching ads. You use coins to hammer shapes on the board or trash pieces in queue. You can also purchase bundles of coins from the store.

6. Watch Ads (Free Coins)

Click on this **movie clip icon** to see an ad. Each ad earns you 40 coins. You can watch four ads back-to-back until the option to watch ads no longer appears for a period of time.

7. Hexagon Puzzle Board

This is where you place pieces (which appear in the queue at the bottom of the screen) to create hexagons. This is the **game board**.

8. Game Pieces

Three game pieces (**triangles** and shapes formed from triangles) appear in play at the bottom of the screen. When you drag one to the board it is immediately replaced with a new game piece. There are always three pieces to choose from.

9. Bin

Click on the **trash can icon** to delete a game piece from the selection of three at the bottom of the screen. Using the bin costs coins. Each time you use it the cost increases. Using the bin allows you take out a piece that is causing you problems, and that piece is then replaced by a new piece.

10. Hammer

The **hammer** is similar to the trash can, only this allows you to smash any one triangle piece that has been placed on the board already to make room for a piece that otherwise would not fit on the board. This also costs coins, and once used the price to use it again increases.

11. Help

Pressing **help** opens a short, interactive **tutorial** on the basic moves in the game. Here you can learn about making hexagons with pieces of the same color; making doubles to get rainbow blocks and bonuses; how to use the rainbow block to remove pieces; and how to use the hammer and the bin.

12. Visual

Press the **paintbrush icon** to bring up visual options. Press the **triangle icon** that comes up to paint color-specific graphics on each piece. Press it again to turn this off. Press the **sun icon** to put the screen in a night-mode color scheme. Touch it again to turn this feature off.

13. Hexti

The Make Hexa character, Hexti, jumps out to show you intervals of scores to remind you what the next number goal is. This breaks gameplay up into stages and earns you **achievements** when each stage of points is reached.

The Main Menu Interface

14. Time (Mode)

If the game isn't challenging enough, click on this option to play a similar game with a **time limit**. In this mode, you have 100 seconds to get as many points as possible. They make it manageable by only giving you one color to deal with, but the caveat is that you cannot freely rotate your pieces. If you wish to rotate a piece it costs you coins, and each time you use the rotate option it becomes increasingly expensive. Create specials (doubles, triples, quadras, etc.) to add a little more time to the clock.

15. Make Hexa Puzzle Mode

Tap on this icon to enter the normal Make Hexa Puzzle mode.

16. Big Size Board

To unlock the **big size board**, you must first earn and save up 2,000 coins. Once it is unlocked you get to play on a board that is larger than normal. The board is two rows taller and two rows wider, but the top and bottom rows are the same width as the old board. Gameplay is the same but could last longer because you have more room to work with.

17. Game Center

This is where you go to check your **achievements** and **leaderboard**. Both links take you to the same screen, where you can toggle back and forth between these two menus.

18. Shop

Click here to enter the **shop**, where you can purchase a Remove Ads option and multiple bundles that include increasing amounts of coins (from 400 to 10,000 coins for $0.99 to $16.99).

19. BitMango

This will take you directly to BitMango in the App Store or Google Play store depending on your device. Here you can download their library of games.

20. BitMango Help

This will take you directly to BitMango's **help page** on their website.

21. Settings

Click here to adjust **sound effects volume** and **background music (BGM) volume**, to toggle on and off the **notifications**, and to play the **tutorial** (which earns you an achievement).

In-App Purchases

You do not need to make any purchases from the store to enjoy this game, but purchases allow you to keep your high score streak going if you are out of hammer or bin options. At the store, you can purchase bundles of coins that will keep your streak going.

Double

The most common special move is combining 10 triangles (two merged hexagons) into a long shape (2 x 4). This fills two of the six rainbow block display sections. A double-hexa is worth 240 points.

Triple

This special move combines 12 triangles (three merged hexagons) into a rounded triangle shape. This fills three of the six rainbow block display sections. A triple is worth 540 points.

Quadra

A quadra move is one that combines 16 triangles (four merged hexagons) into one very large triangle. Achieving this shape is equal to two doubles and fills four of the six rainbow block display sections. This special is worth 960 points.

Hepta

The message "Invincible" appears when you make this move, and you earn the **Out of This World** achievement. This is seven hexagons in one shape. It combines 24 triangles into one very large triangle. Achieving this feat fills up the rainbow block display from nothing to completely full as soon as you make the move, giving you a rainbow block immediately. This is worth 2,940 points!

Rainbow Block

All the above specials have one thing in common: They're made to create rainbow blocks by filling the rainbow block display at the top of the screen. Once it's full, a **rainbow block** is created. The rainbow block enters play with the rest of the shapes at the bottom of the screen and occupies one of the shape's spaces. So, you have two shapes and one rainbow block in play until you use the rainbow block and free up room for the third shape to enter play. Drag the rainbow block on the board to eliminate a full hexagon radius from the board while earning 60 points. This clears six spaces on the board so you can keep playing, but with a little bit more room.

Overall Move Strategy

The AI deals eight different colors of pieces to you (three at a time), and these eight colors have multiple shape configurations. What the AI deals you is random to a degree. It seems like the AI could be more difficult more often by lengthening the time between same color deals—but it doesn't. When you get on a roll, there appears to be the hint of a systematic method to what the AI deals to you (your selection of three shapes at the bottom of the screen).

To control the madness of the deal, place colors on the board a full hexagon shape away from other colors so that the shapes that are offered have a pre-chosen area where color matches (hexagons) can be made. In other words, keep different colors as far away from each other as possible always. This also means beginning on the outer edges.

When you place larger shapes on the board, make sure that the openings (where more shapes can be added) face the inner open board so you don't limit the types of shapes you can use to complete the hexagon. For instance, in this screenshot, if you placed a hexagon shape that was only missing one triangle on the edge of the board—with the missing space facing the outer edge—then you'd be limiting the shapes needed to complete the hexagon (you'd need a single triangle and that's all that would fit there). When you need a specific color and shape, it seems to take forever to receive that order. Try to keep as many options open as possible.

Continuously strategize to create big combos, doubles, and quadras to earn rainbow blocks, but know that it's not as easy as it seems. There will always be remnants of hexagons left on the board. These fragments and odd shapes force you to shift the areas you set aside for that color. If the AI is kind and gives you the shapes you need, you can manage the chaos and continue to make matches.

When you get a rainbow block, use it to clean up the messy areas so you can continue to make more hexagons. And if you have a good streak going (reaching new high scores), then don't forget to use the hammer and the bin to keep you going. Watch ads when offered to collect coins. You don't have to purchase them if you play enough and watch ads.

When you break it down, limited space is the enemy. If you had unlimited space to play, then one round would last forever. So, save up 2,000 coins and unlock the bigger board, and that'll give you two more rows and two more columns to play in. This means you can achieve longer rounds and higher scores. This also means there's more room to try to build bigger hexagons right from the start, with at least four colors in their own sections.

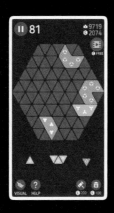

Achievements

NAME	DESCRIPTION	PTS
Beginner's Luck	Make two same colored hexas with one piece.	5
Between Luck & Skill	Make three same colored hexas with one piece.	5
Lucky Cover	Make four same colored hexas with one piece.	5
Mission Impossible	Make five same colored hexas with one piece.	5
Super-Human	Make six same colored hexas with one piece.	5
Out of This World	Make seven same colored hexas with one piece.	5
Start of Temptation	Use a hammer.	5
Miner	Use a hammer three times in one round	10
Thorn	Use a hammer 10 times in one round.	10
Double-Red	Make red double-hexas twice in a round.	10
Double-Orange	Make orange double-hexas twice in a round.	10
Double-Yellow	Make yellow double-hexas twice in a round.	10
Double-Green	Make green double-hexas twice in a round.	10
Double-Mint	Make mint double-hexas twice in a round.	10
Double-Blue	Make blue double-hexas twice in a round.	10
Double-Purple	Make purple double-hexas twice in a round.	10
Double-Ivory	Make brown double-hexas twice in a round.	10
Piece of Cake	Collect 200 coins.	5
Work Like a Dog	Collect 1,000 coins.	5
Smell of Wealth	Collect 10,000 coins.	10
A Feather in Your Cap	Collect 100,000 coins.	10
Rebel	Make zero hexas in a round.	5
Birth	Make only one hexa in a round.	5
Well Begun Is Half Done	Complete the tutorial.	5
Curious Folks	Tap the locked (big size board) icon.	5
Beaten Baby Hexti	Score over 1,200 points.	5
Beaten Bronze Hexti	Score over 2,010 points.	5
Beaten Silver Hexti	Score over 3,500 points.	5
Beat Gold Hexti	Score over 5,000 points.	10
Beat Top Hexti	Score over 9,000 points.	15
Beaten King Hexti	Score over 12,000 points.	20
Don't Stop Me Now	Play for 30 minutes (one board).	5
Longrun	Play a round for 10 minutes.	5
Rolling Piece	Rotate a block 10 times.	5
Man of Combo	Make two combos.	5
God of Combo	Make five combos.	30
Good Manager	Make two combos with multiple hexagons.	15
Hiddencard	Make a rainbow block.	5
Multi-Hexa Meister	Make seven rainbow blocks.	20
Thrilling	Fill up 80% of the board.	5
New Way of Play	Fill up 100% of the board.	30
Can't Stand It	Use a bin in one round.	5
Trash Collector	Use a bin three times in one round.	10
Night	Play 10 times in night theme.	5
Day	Play 10 times in day theme.	5
What's New	Download update version.	15
An Addict	Revisit the game within an hour.	30
New World	Play big mode.	15

MINECRAFT

Developer	Mojang
Publisher	Mojang
Year Released	2009 (2011 for Pocket Edition/ mobile version)
Platforms	Android, iOS, Windows Phone, PC, Xbox 360, Xbox one, PS3, PS4, PS Vita, Nintendo Switch, Wii U
Type	Sandbox, survival
Suggested Age	8+
Cost	Paid download

$ IN-GAME PURCHASES

Skin Packs, Mash-up Packs, Worlds, Texture Packs, and multiplayer downloadable content

Game Overview

Minecraft is a sandbox survival open-world game where you build whatever structures you want by harvesting raw materials to craft tools and building materials.

Minecraft Pocket Edition features a "Survival" and a "Creative" mode. Each mode offers a range of difficulty settings (Peaceful, Easy, Normal, and Hard). Peaceful difficulty gets rid of the requirement to eat and also gets rid of monsters. The harder the difficulty, the faster you starve, and the more damage you take from starvation. Monsters (who from now on will be called mobs) spawn more frequently and are stronger.

Survival Mode

Survival mode requires you to survive the world you've been placed into. If you choose any other difficulty than Peaceful, you need to harvest or hunt for food, collect resources, and survive or sleep through the night to escape the threat of mobs such as Spiders, Skeletons, Zombies, and more. Other settings can be altered before you load into your world, like the option to spawn a starter chest with random materials when you load in for the first time, the option for friendly fire—if you choose to play multiplayer—keeping inventory after death, and more.

Creative Mode

Creative mode allows you to build whatever you want without the struggle of having to survive, and you get to fly! You don't take damage, and you have access to every item in the game.

Multiplayer

Multiplayer worlds offer a wide range of game modes, both PvE and PvP, or simply playing Survival with friends in your own world. Many worlds are created by other players; you'll have plenty to explore on that front.

What You Need to Know

This guide primarily focuses on the mobile edition of *Minecraft*. Some features in other versions may not be present in every version.

Basic Controls

- To walk around, locate the arrows on the left side of the screen. Once you have hold of the arrows, drag and hold in the direction you want to go.

- To sprint, double-tap the Up arrow and hold.

- To look around, place your finger on the screen and turn it in the direction you wish to look.

- To jump, tap the button in the bottom right of the screen.

- To place/attack/harvest, tap the screen on the block you wish to interact with.

- To mine/break, hold the screen on the block you wish to interact with.

- To crouch, double-tap the button in the middle of the moving arrows. Crouching prevents you from falling off the block you're currently standing on.

Inventory and Crafting

Your inventory is where you store the goods you collect. To enter the inventory, tap the square with the three dots on the far right of the toolbar.

The toolbar is where you keep the items from the inventory that are currently equipped. You can have nine items equipped at a time.

You need to make a Crafting Table to craft more complex items. To do this, you must chop down one Wood, go into the inventory, place the Wood block into the crafting recipe blocks, and collect the four Wooden Planks. Use those four Wooden Planks, place them into the four empty squares, and collect the Crafting Table. The Crafting Table is one of the most essential items in the game.

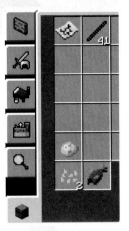

In the inventory, the Quick Craft tabs are on the left side of the screen. These tabs show you what you can make with the items you have. Items are automatically filed into the correct slots on the Crafting Table, so you don't have to memorize the crafting recipes. To craft the items in these tabs, tap the item you want crafted, then take it out of the crafted square under the Crafting Table.

Tools

All tools must be crafted from a Crafting Table. All tools require Wooden Sticks and the main resource you want the tier of the tool to be made from. The order (from lowest to highest) of tiered tools that can be made is: Wooden Planks, Cobblestone, Iron Ingots, Gold Ingots, Diamonds. The higher the tier of resources used to craft the tool, the more efficient it is. Gold is sometimes better than iron but has a significantly lower durability. If you can, avoid using Gold tools.

Pickaxe

Pickaxes are required to harvest ore. If you try to mine a Stone material without a Pickaxe, it won't be added to the inventory. Pickaxes' tiers allow certain ores to be harvested and mined at a faster rate. Some blocks mined are destroyed no matter the Pickaxe used (like Monster Spawners).

- Wooden Pickaxes can harvest Stone blocks, Brick blocks, Coal blocks, and Netherrack.
- Stone Pickaxes can harvest all previously mentioned blocks, plus Iron blocks and Lapis Lazuli blocks.
- Iron Pickaxes can harvest all previously mentioned blocks, plus Gold blocks, Diamond blocks, and Redstone blocks.
- Gold Pickaxes can only harvest Stone blocks, Brick blocks, Netherrack blocks, and Coal blocks, but mines some of them faster than other Pickaxes.
- Diamond Pickaxes can harvest all previously mentioned blocks, plus Obsidian.

Axe

Axes are used to harvest Wood faster than using your hand. All Wood blocks can be harvested using your hand, but it's faster to use an Axe. Axes deal more damage than Swords, but using them for anything other than a Wood chopper has downsides.

An Axe takes double durability damage and has a slower cooldown between hits than a Sword. Since all Axes can harvest the same blocks, they're sorted by durability and speed (with the exception of Gold):

Gold Axe (lowest durability but faster than a Diamond Axe), Wood Axe, Stone Axe, Iron Axe, Diamond Axe.

Shovel

Shovels allow you to dig up Dirt, Snow, Sand, and Gravel faster. Using a Shovel to dig up Snow also allows you to harvest Snowballs. Again, the only difference in Shovel tiers is durability and how fast they dig. They're organized accordingly (with the exception of Gold):

Gold Shovel (lowest durability but faster than a Diamond Shovel), Wood Shovel, Stone Shovel, Iron Shovel, Diamond Shovel.

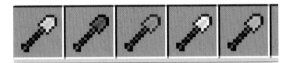

Hoe

Hoes are used for farming. When you tap on Dirt while holding the Hoe, it plows the land, allowing you to plant seeds or Wheat. The only difference in Hoe tiers is the durability of the tool. Hoes are so easy to make that using any rare resource would be a waste. This list orders Hoes from lowest durability to highest:

Gold Hoe, Wooden Hoe, Stone Hoe, Iron Hoe, Diamond Hoe.

Equipment

These items are miscellaneous tools that don't follow the crafting rules of those mentioned so far (not made with mostly Wood, Cobblestone, Iron, Gold, or Diamond). These items have no tiers.

Fishing Rod/Carrot on a Stick

The Fishing Rod can be used to catch fish, but can also be used to pull Minecarts and mobs closer to you. To fish, tap on a source of Water. When you see bubbles moving toward the bobber at the end of the rod, this means a fish is coming. Once the bobber sinks under the Water, tap to reel the fish in. The fish lands somewhere near you, at which point you simply need to pick it up.

The Carrot on a Stick version can be used to lead pigs while you're riding them.

Flint and Steel

Flint and Steel is used to light blocks on fire. Only Wood and Wool blocks burn away. Flint and Steel is also used to activate Nether Portals and ignite TNT. You can use Flint and Steel to burn mobs, players, or animals. If you burn an animal, it eliminates the need to cook their meat later—if they drop any.

Shears

Shears are used to collect leaves, Wool from sheep, String from cobwebs, ferns, dead bushes, and vines.

Compass

The Compass points you in the direction of your spawn point. When the red needle points straight up, that means going forward is the way to the spawn point.

Map

Maps allow you to see an overhead view of the world. You're displayed on the Map and shown the direction you're facing—if you add a Compass to the map on an Anvil. To make the Map bigger, add more paper to it on an Anvil. To get more coverage on a Map, have it in your hands and move toward an undiscovered location. The new portion appears on the Map.

Clock

The Clock shows you the sun and the moon and where they are relative to the horizon. This mostly comes in handy if you're mining and want to know whether it's day or night.

Lead

The Lead holds any animal or mob it can grab and keeps them from moving—if you attach it to a fence—or causes them to follow you while you're holding it. This is primarily used for horses.

Saddle

The Saddle is used on pigs, mules, donkeys, and horses so you can ride them. Simply tap on the animal with the Saddle and hop on (by tapping it again).

Bucket

The Bucket is used to hold Water, Milk, and Lava. To fill or empty the Bucket, tap on the liquid you want to obtain. To get Milk, tap on a cow while holding the Bucket.

Water Buckets can be used for farming or to eliminate a patch of Lava while mining. Milk can be used to make a Cake, or drunk to get rid of status effects. Lava Buckets can be used to make Cobblestone or traps.

Totem of Undying

If you take fatal damage while it's equipped in your hand, the Totem of Undying prevents you from dying. If you don't want it in your right hand, it can be equipped in your left. To do this, go to the armor slots and place it in the fifth slot. When the totem activates, it's consumed from the inventory and leaves you with half a Heart remaining with some status effects for Regeneration II, 40 seconds of Fire Resistance II, and five seconds of Absorption II.

Weapons

Weapons are for killing mobs, animals, or players. Swords and Bows and Arrows are the best items to use for the job.

Sword

The Sword is more efficient in dealing damage than tools like the Pickaxe, Hoe, Shovel, or your bare hands. Swords can also be used to chop some blocks down faster, like vines. Swords can be made from the same items used to craft tools such as the Pickaxe. This list is organized so the Swords are arranged from least to most damage and durability:

The damage output varies depending on whether the target is armored and the strength of said armor.

- ◆ Gold Swords deal 2 Hearts of damage per hit.
- ◆ Wood Swords deal 2 Hearts of damage per hit.
- ◆ Stone Swords deal 2 1/2 Hearts of damage per hit.
- ◆ Iron Swords deal 3 Hearts of damage per hit.
- ◆ Diamond Swords deal 3 1/2 Hearts of damage per hit.

Bow (and Arrows)

The Bow is a ranged weapon used to fire off Arrows. Where there used to be only one type of Arrow, there are many types in *Minecraft* now. You can put a potion effect on them. If you have more than one type of Arrow, to ensure you're using the right type, equip it in the fifth armor slot.

Armor

- ◆ Leather Armor: Leather armor absorbs 28% of damage in a full set. Leather armor is also the only set of armor that can be dyed.

- ◆ Gold Armor: Gold armor is slightly more durable than Leather armor and absorbs 44% of damage in a full set.

- ◆ Chainmail Armor: Chainmail armor can only be obtained by killing Skeletons or Zombies wearing it, trading with Villagers, or by getting it in Creative mode. This armor absorbs slightly more damage than Gold.

- ◆ Iron Armor: Iron armor absorbs 60% of damage in a full set.

- ◆ Diamond Armor: Diamond armor absorbs a whopping 80% of damage in a full set.

- ◆ Elytra: This piece of armor gives no actual armor protection and is equipped in the chestpiece slot. It allows you to glide by pressing and holding the Jump button in the air.

Horse Armor

Horse armor is found in chests around the world, or you can trade items to obtain it. Put horse armor on your horse by mounting the horse and equipping it. Horse armor cannot break.

- ◆ Leather Horse Armor: 12% damage resistance.
- ◆ Iron Horse Armor: 20% damage resistance.
- ◆ Gold Horse Armor: 28% damage resistance.
- ◆ Diamond Horse Armor: 44% damage resistance.

Food

Most food in *Minecraft* is only used to relieve hunger. Some foods grant additional benefits like extra temporary Hearts, or negative effects like food poisoning. To get food, you can kill animals for meat or grow it from seeds. Meat can be cooked to fill more hunger bars per consumption. Food can also be used to restore Hearts of tamable animals like dogs and horses. Some foods can be used to make animals breed.

Farming

To farm, use a Hoe to plow a block of Dirt. To allow the seed grow, the Dirt block must be touching a Water source, whether beside it or below it. Plants need time to grow, but the process can be sped up with Bone Meal. Sugar Cane is an exception to the Hoe rule—it can be planted beside Water on either Dirt or Sand blocks. Pumpkins and Melons need one adjacent block available to grow over on.

- ◆ Wheat: Wheat is harvested after growing seeds.

- ◆ Beetroot: Beetroot is harvested after growing Beetroot Seeds.

- ◆ Potato: Potatoes are harvested from Potato crops.

- ◆ Carrot: Carrots are harvested from Carrot crops.

- ◆ Apple: Apples fall from destroyed Oak and Dark Oak Leaves.

- ◆ Melon: Melons are harvested by destroying a full Melon after Melon Seeds have grown.

- ◆ Pumpkin: Pumpkins are harvested by destroying a full Pumpkin after Pumpkin Seeds have grown.

- ◆ Sugar: Sugar is made from Sugar Cane.

Meat/Fish

Cooked meat and fish are some of the best—or THE best—food sources, if you don't count Golden Carrots and Apples. Raw meat can be obtained from killing pigs, cows, chickens, sheep, and rabbits. This meat can be cooked in a Furnace, or you can use a flame to kill the animal and have it cooked on drop, whether you use a Flame Sword Enchantment or Flint and Steel. Caught fish can also be cooked. Rotten Flesh and Raw Chicken cause negative hunger effects, making the hunger bar deplete faster.

- Cooked Chicken: Cooked from Raw Chicken (dropped by chickens).
- Cooked Porkchop: Cooked from Raw Porkchop (dropped by pigs).
- Cooked Beef: Cooked from Raw Beef (dropped by cows).
- Cooked Mutton: Cooked from Raw Mutton (dropped by sheep).
- Cooked Rabbit: Cooked from Raw Rabbit (dropped by rabbits).
- Cooked Fish: Cooked from Raw Fish (fished for).
- Cooked Salmon: Cooked from Raw Salmon (fished for)

Miscellaneous Foods

Golden Food

Golden Apples and Carrots are made by surrounding either an Apple or a Carrot with Golden Nuggets in the Crafting Table. A Golden Carrot simply fills six hunger bars, while a Golden Apple fills four hunger bars and also grants Regeneration II for five seconds and Absorption for two minutes.

Stew/ Soup

- Mushrooms can be used to make Mushroom Stew. Combine Mushrooms with a Bowl on a Crafting Table (fills six hunger bars).
- Rabbit Stew is made from one Carrot, one Cooked Rabbit, one Baked Potato, one Mushroom, and a Bowl (fills 10 hunger bars).
- Beetroot Soup is made with six Beetroots and a Bowl (fills six hunger bars).

Cake

When Cake is made, place it down and eat it by clicking on it. It cannot be eaten from the inventory; it's a good idea to place it in your home and eat it then to refill hunger. One bite of Cake refills two hunger bars. You can take a total of seven bites from the Cake. Cake is made from 3 Milk Buckets, 3 Wheat, 2 Sugar, and 1 Egg.

Mobs

Mobs are monsters and creatures. Animals and Villagers roam the Overworld day and night. At night (or in enough darkness), monsters start to spawn. Following is a detailed list of the more commonly seen animals and monsters, and what they do.

- ◆ Cows: Cows can be bred with Wheat and milked. When killed, cows drop Beef and Leather.

- ◆ Pigs: Pigs can be bred with Carrots. When killed, they drop Porkchops. You can put a Saddle on a pig to ride it, but the only way to control the direction is with a Carrot on a Stick.

- ◆ Sheep: Sheep can be bred with Wheat. When killed, a sheep drops one Wool of its color and Mutton.

- ◆ Rabbits: Rabbits can be bred with flowers, Carrots, or Golden Carrots. When killed, they drop Rabbit Hide and Rabbit Meat.

- ◆ Chickens: Chickens can be bred with seeds. Chickens drop Feathers and Raw Chicken when killed. A chicken can drop Eggs within 5-10 minutes.

- ◆ Wolves: Wolves can be bred with most meats when tamed with a Bone. A tamed wolf can become your companion. If you don't want the wolf to follow you, tap it to make it sit still. If you travel far enough with a non-sitting wolf and it isn't with you, eventually it teleports to you if it hasn't been killed. You can dye your wolf's collar different colors. Untamed wolves can be hostile if you attack them.

- ◆ Squid: Squid drop Ink Sacs when killed.

- ◆ Ocelots: Ocelots spawn in Jungle biomes. When tamed, they become cats. They can be tamed and bred with Raw Fish. Ocelots have no drops. Ocelots and cats scare Creepers away.

- ◆ Horses: Horses, mules, and donkeys drop Leather when killed. Horses can be equipped with horse armor, and with Saddles to be ridden. Donkeys can be equipped with Saddles, and they offer extra inventory space. Breed horses with Golden Apples and Golden Carrots.

Non-Hostile

Most non-hostile animals can be bred or killed for food. Where they spawn depends on the biome.

- ◆ Villagers: Villagers can be found in villages. Villages can typically be found in Savannas, Taigas, and Deserts. Villagers can trade items with you. The prime currency is Emeralds.

Hostile

Hostile mobs attack you and spawn at night or in large, dark areas like caves. If your home has no light, they can spawn inside. To avoid monsters aboveground, sleep through the night in a Bed. Beds are also your spawn point after you sleep in them, as long as they aren't destroyed.

- Spiders: Spiders in the daytime are not automatically hostile. Spiders drop String and Spider Eyes when killed.

- Zombies: Zombies in the day start to burn unless they're in a Water source or shade. When killed, zombies drop Rotten Flesh. Zombies also have a low chance of dropping Carrots, Potatoes, and Iron Ingots.

- Skeletons: Skeletons in the day start to burn unless they're in a Water source or shade. Skeletons have Bows, so they attack from a distance. When killed, Skeletons drop Arrows, Bones, and possibly a Bow, but it'll be damaged.

- Creepers: Creepers can linger a bit in the day without burning. They blow up if they get too close to you. If a Creeper blows up in a Water source, it doesn't destroy the surrounding blocks. Creepers drop Gunpowder when killed. If a Creeper is killed by a Skeleton, it drops a random Music Disc that can be played in Jukeboxes.

- Slimes: Slimes, when killed, split into smaller Slimes. They go from Big, to Small, to Tiny Slimes. Tiny Slimes drop Slimeballs.

- Endermen: Endermen don't attack you unless you look into their eyes. Endermen hate Water. They can pick up blocks and teleport. When killed, Endermen have a chance of dropping Ender Pearls, which can be used to teleport you to where you throw them.

- Witches: Witches throw negative Potions at you. When killed, Witches drop either a Glass Bottle, a Stick, Redstone, Sugar, a Spider Eye, Gunpowder, or Glowstone Dust.

Gaining Experience

Almost every activity in *Minecraft* earns you experience. This comes in the form of glowing orbs that appear when you do something important: kill monsters, breed animals, mine special items, smelt ore, etc. Collect these orbs by walking close to them; they reach you on their own if you go anywhere near them!

Levels Require Different Amounts of Experience

Getting from Level 1 to 2 takes much less experience than going from Level 39 to 40. As you progress higher and higher in level, the amount of experience you need to go higher increases. Don't stockpile levels beyond whatever point you currently need. In general, Level 30 (for Enchanting Table work) or Level 39 (for Anvil work) is the highest you ever need to go. Pushing for levels beyond this yields diminishing returns. You're much better off spending your levels to enchant something and then progressing in levels again.

Losing Experience

Death causes your character to lose a huge amount of experience. Some of your experience falls to the ground, and you can retrieve it if you make your way back to your corpse in time, but the rest is gone forever.

Enchanting

Minecraft isn't a run-of-the-mill RPG or game where levels give you more health, damage, and other basic stats. You're a farmer, a miner, and a survivor. These stats aren't really going to change. Instead, you use levels to enchant your weapons, armor, and tools, to make them better at performing various tasks. We'll discuss how you can get the most out of the enchanting system.

Making an Enchanting Table

When you're ready to spend some experience levels, make an Enchanting Table. You need Diamonds, Obsidian, and a Book to do this. Make a Diamond Pick to mine the Obsidian, gather more Diamonds as needed, and use Leather and Paper to make your Book. When you're done, you have an Enchanting Table ready to go, but it can't handle major Enchantments. Basic Enchanting Tables only add low-cost Enchantments to items. These are nice, but the really incredible stuff requires more effort.

More Power for the Table

To give your Enchanting Table more options, place Bookshelves around it. It takes 15 Bookshelves to fully power an Enchanting Table. Arrange these Bookshelves two blocks away from the table, either in a "U" shape around the table or wedged into a nearby corner. Bookshelves only count if they're two spaces away—they can't be adjacent to the Enchanting Table. Stack the shelves two high but not three high. Diagonal spaces count just fine. Given these double stacks, you can have 18 Bookshelves in your "U," which is more than you need.

Anvils

Anvils let you combine items, including their Enchantments. The primary item is saved and the secondary item is destroyed, with all of its pertinent Enchantments transferred to the primary item. Enchantments that aren't allowed to affect a specific item aren't transferred, so they're simply lost. Thus, you can't put armor Enchantments on a Bow, even if you combine a Bow with an Enchanted Book that has multiple armor Enchantments. Anvils can also combine two regular items, as long as they're of the same type. Two Diamond Picks with the same Enchantments can be used on the Anvil together. The second is destroyed to repair the primary.

Brewing

Brewing is a fun way to make Potions. Potions help you endure tough fights, survive in dangerous areas, and damage some of your enemies. You can't brew early in the game because you need a number of tricky ingredients to get anywhere with this art. We'll tell you what to do!

Collect Ingredients to Make a Brewing Stand

The first step is to gather the primary ingredients you need. Nether Wart and Blaze Rods are two of the toughest (and most important) items on the list, so let's focus on these. Both materials are found in the Nether. Make a Nether Portal and bring ample supplies through to the other side. Seek out a Nether Fortress, then scour the place for chests and stairways with Soul Sand nearby. These are the only two places in the game where Nether Wart is available. Not all chests contain Nether Wart, and not all Nether Fortresses feature the stair gardens. Finding these items is luck of the draw. Blazes, on the other hand, are found frequently in Nether Fortresses. Fight them with ranged attacks, or retreat to draw them forward. Kill as many as you can to get Blaze Rods.

Once you have a few of these goodies, make a Nether Wart garden. You don't want to search Nether Fortresses every time you need more Nether Wart, so don't do any brewing just yet. Wait until you have an adequate Nether Wart garden. Sadly, you can't use Bone Meal to speed up your

garden; getting a large garden going is a fairly time-intensive process, but it's well worth your investment. Break all of your initial Nether Wart into seeds, and plant all of them. Do the same thing with the yields from your initial planting, and continue to increase the garden from there, taking only one or two Nether Wart at first to play with, and then more as your garden reaches a substantial size.

Now craft a Brewing Stand, a Cauldron, and some Glass Bottles. Fill your Cauldron with Water. This is useful for filling Water Bottles, and they look cool in your brewing area anyway. Having an infinite Water source (four holes with two Water sources in two blocks diagonal from each other) nearby isn't a bad thing, either. Place all of your crafted items in one room with a chest or two, and grab your Nether Wart. With these and a number of other odds and ends, you're ready to start brewing. Blaze Powder acts as a fuel source for your brewing work. Every piece of this powder lets you brew 20 ingredients' worth of Potions, so it lasts fairly well!

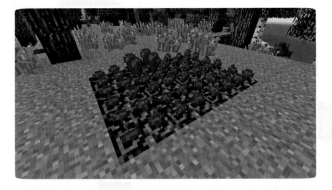

Types of Potions

Potions come in two stages. You make the first stage by interacting with the Brewing Stand and adding a Water Bottle with some ingredients. After adding your ingredients, wait for the brewing to finish, and collect your finished Potion.

There are five basic Potions, as follows:

Base Potions

POTION NAME	INGREDIENTS	EFFECT
Awkward Potion	Water Bottle + Nether Wart	Builds into much more powerful Potions
Mundane Potion (Extended)	Water Bottle + Redstone	Used to make a Potion of Weakness (Extended)
Mundane Potion	Water Bottle + one of the following: Blaze Powder, Ghast Tear, Glistering Melon, Magma Cream, Spider Eye, Sugar	Used to make a Potion of Weakness
Potion of Weakness	Water Bottle + Fermented Spider Eye	Reduces melee attacks by 0.5 damage
Thick Potion	Water Bottle + Glowstone Dust	Used to make a Potion of Weakness

So far, it doesn't look like brewing is very useful. You can make a Potion that reduces your own melee damage—yay? But trust us, this gets much better.

After you have a primary Potion, use the Brewing Stand again. This time, you add one of the primary Potions instead of a Water Bottle. Now you start having fun!

Secondary Potions

POTION NAME	INGREDIENTS	EFFECT
Potion of Fire Resistance	Awkward Potion + Magma Cream	Three minutes of fire immunity
Potion of Healing	Awkward Potion + Glistering Melon	Restores 4 damage
Potion of Leaping	Awkward Potion + Rabbit's Foot	Boosts jumping height and reduces falling damage for three minutes
Potion of Night Vision	Awkward Potion + Golden Carrot	Lets you see as if the area is perfectly lit for three minutes
Potion of Poison	Awkward Potion + Spider Eye	Poisons a target for 1 damage every 1.5 seconds (for 45 seconds)
Potion of Regeneration	Awkward Potion + Ghast Tear	Restores 2 damage every 2.4 seconds (for 45 seconds)
Potion of Strength	Awkward Potion + Blaze Powder	Adds 130% to your melee damage for three minutes
Potion of Swiftness	Awkward Potion + Sugar	Increases speed and jumping distance by 20% for three minutes
Potion of Water Breathing	Awkward Potion + Pufferfish	You don't need to breathe underwater for three minutes
Potion of Weakness (Extended)	Awkward Potion + Fermented Spider Eye	Reduces melee damage by 0.5 for four minutes

Now you start to see a lot of possibilities. Potions of Healing let you restore health instantly, unlike food. Fire Resistance is useful when you fight Blazes and Ghasts in the Nether. Regeneration is critical to your survival in boss fights, against Withers or the Ender Dragon.

Nether Wart and a few key ingredients allow you to make extremely useful Potions, and you can brew even more powerful versions if you're willing to spend a bit more time and effort. Read on!

Tertiary Potions

POTION NAME	INGREDIENTS	EFFECT
Potion of Fire Resistance (Extended)	Potion of Fire Resistance + Redstone	Eight minutes of fire immunity
Potion of Harming	Potion of Healing or Poison + Fermented Spider Eye	Inflicts 6 damage
Potion of Harming II	Potion of Healing II or Poison II + Fermented Spider Eye or Glowstone Dust	Inflicts 12 damage
Potion of Healing II	Potion of Healing + Glowstone Dust	Restores 8 damage
Potion of Invisibility	Potion of Night Vision + Fermented Spider Eye	Turns you invisible (but not your weapon or armor) for three minutes
Potion of Invisibility (Extended)	Potion of Night Vision (Extended) + Fermented Spider Eye	Turns you invisible (but not your weapon or armor) for eight minutes
Potion of Leaping (Extended)	Potion of Leaping + Redstone	Lets you jump higher for eight minutes
Potion of Leaping II	Potion of Leaping + Glowstone Dust	You can jump even higher
Potion of Night Vision (Extended)	Potion of Night Vision + Redstone	Lets you see as if the area is perfectly lit for eight minutes
Potion of Poison (Extended)	Potion of Poison + Redstone	Poisons a target for 1 damage every two seconds (for two minutes)
Potion of Poison II	Potion of Poison + Glowstone Dust	Poisons a target for 1 damage every second (for 22 seconds)
Potion of Regeneration (Extended)	Potion of Regeneration + Redstone	Restores 2 damage every 2.4 seconds (for two minutes)
Potion of Regeneration II	Potion of Regeneration + Glowstone Dust	Restores 2 damage every 1.2 seconds (for 16 seconds)
Potion of Slowness	Potion of Fire Resistance or Swiftness + Fermented Spider Eye	Slows movement for 1.5 minutes
Potion of Slowness (Extended)	Potion of Fire Resistance (Extended) or Swiftness (Extended) + Redstone or Fermented Spider Eye	Slows movement for three minutes
Potion of Strength (Extended)	Potion of Strength + Redstone	Adds 130% to your melee damage for eight minutes
Potion of Strength II	Potion of Strength + Glowstone Dust	Adds 260% to your melee damage for 1.5 minutes
Potion of Swiftness (Extended)	Potion of Swiftness + Redstone	Increases speed and jumping distance by 20% for eight minutes
Potion of Swiftness II	Potion of Swiftness + Glowstone Dust	Increases speed and jumping distance by 40% for 1.5 minutes
Potion of Water Breathing (Extended)	Potion of Water Breathing + Redstone	You don't need to breathe underwater for eight minutes

There are a few simple ways to remember how the Potion system works. Everything starts with Nether Wart. Your initial Potion should almost always be made by adding Nether Wart to a Water Bottle. Done.

For Tier 2 Potions, use your Awkward Potion from the first stage and add an ingredient to get whatever base effect you need. Look at our Secondary Potion table to figure out what you need/want.

To make Potions last longer, add Redstone to a Secondary Potion.

To make Potions stronger, add Glowstone Dust to a Secondary Potion.

To make Potions work when thrown, use Gunpowder.

Gunpowder turns normal Potions into Splash Potions. This makes Potions of Weakness and Potions of Poison useful against specific enemies. Potions of Poison II really add damage over time.

If you want a Potion to have effects that target an area and last longer, try to craft Lingering Potions. Start with a Splash Potion of the type you want, and then brew it with Dragon's Breath to create a Lingering version of the effect. When thrown, this spreads out on the ground and delivers its effects over time against anything that stands in the affected spot.

Poison Doesn't Always Work

Don't try to poison Spiders, Cave Spiders, or the Ender Dragon. They don't take any damage from Poison.

Skeletons, Wither Skeletons, Withers, Zombies, and Zombie Pigmen are immune to Poison and don't take damage from Potions of Harm, either. In fact, they heal from them instead! However, they take damage from Splash Potions of Healing.

Witches take reduced Poison damage, so it's not worth your time to use Poison against them.

People often brew Splash Potions of Healing so they can heal themselves as quickly as possible. Tossing the Potion into the ground at your feet gives you health much faster than just about any other option. It's way faster than food and considerably faster than drinking a Potion of Healing in a normal way.

The Nether

The Nether is a world of Redstone, fire, and strange beasts. It's possible to enter this dimension after gathering several special materials from the Overworld. After you make a Nether Portal, it's possible to travel back and forth between these dimensions at will.

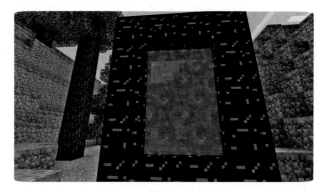

Creating a Nether Portal

To access the Nether, you need to construct a Nether Portal. To do this, your character must have access to a source of fire (Flint and Steel), Diamonds (for a Diamond Pick), and Obsidian. Once you have access to all of these materials, mine 14 blocks of Obsidian and bring them to your base. Construct a Nether Portal by placing four blocks of Obsidian in a line on the ground. Build the two ends into pillars of Obsidian that are five blocks high, and then fill in the gap on top with two connecting blocks. Light the inner hollow space of this Obsidian frame—use your Flint and Steel to do this.

Now that the Nether Portal is active, you can jump into it and wait for the teleportation spell to zip you between worlds. Don't jump out from the Portal on the other side until you make sure you won't fall into Lava or suffer any other ill effects.

What to Bring into the Nether

The Nether is one of the most dangerous places in Minecraft. Light is dim, Lava is plentiful and flows faster than usual, and monsters are deadlier than in the Overworld. It's easy to die, so take only what you need to survive. Don't bring items you can't afford to lose.

Diamond tools are not required in the Nether. You don't need to cut through any hard materials, so Iron Pickaxes are sufficient. Bring those, some Swords, a Bow, Arrows, Wood and Cobblestone (neither of which is found naturally in the Nether), food, Torches, Flint and Steel, and anything else that might seem useful. The weapons are necessary to fight the Nether's monsters, and some items are standard equipment for any mining or exploration trip. Bring Flint and Steel on any Nether trip; if your Nether Portal gets snuffed out over there (for example, by getting hit by a Ghast's fireball), you have to relight it.

Monsters from the Nether	Resources in the Nether
◆ Blazes	◆ Glowstone
◆ Ghasts	◆ Nether Quartz
◆ Magma Cubes	◆ Nether Wart
◆ Wither Skeletons	◆ Netherrack
◆ Zombie Pigmen	◆ Soul Sand

When you arrive, make a central base as close to your Portal as possible. Wall it off with Cobblestone from back home. Cobblestone doesn't burn; Netherrack, the natural stone of this area, does! Any long-term structure you build in the Nether should be made from heavier, non-flammable materials. Your base needs to have a Crafting Table, Furnace, Chests, and preferably an Ender Chest once you can craft those. Put your best loot into the Chests each time you take a break to ensure you don't lose anything if your character falls or tunnels into Lava. In the Nether, this is not a rare occurrence.

New Rules Compared to the Overworld

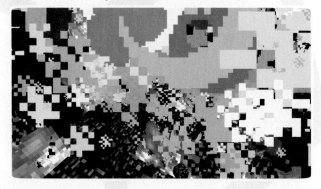

You can't use water in the Nether. It boils away instantly, so that's pretty useless.

Beds aren't great to bring, either, unless you plan to use them as makeshift TNT. When you try to sleep in a Bed, the whole thing explodes. It's better to avoid the situation entirely unless you're interested in blowing things up with a piece of bedroom furniture.

What to Do in the Nether

Besides fun and exploration, you can accomplish several goals when you get to the Nether. Harvest Netherrack, Nether Quartz, Soul Sand, and Glowstone as soon as possible. These are fairly common materials, and you can't find them anywhere back home. Collect an ample supply of each.

Netherrack is the least useful. It burns forever, so you can make cool fire pits and fireplaces with it, but that's about it. The stone is way too ugly to be useful for nice bases or homes.

Nether Quartz is lovely. The blocks you make with it are really cool-looking, though it takes a good while to farm enough Nether Quartz to make large buildings. We recommend making a wizard's tower out of Nether Quartz. So cool!

Glowstone is a bright material used to create blocks that are better than Torches; they work underwater and shine quite clearly even from long distances. Glowstone breaks into chunks when you mine it, so a Pickaxe with Silk Touch is useful, though not required.

Soul Sand is hard to walk on. It's fun for making traps, slowing other players and monsters, and for a few specific tasks, like summoning the Wither. Look for Soul Sand when you travel, and get at least a partial stack of it.

Locating and Assaulting Nether Fortresses

Nether Fortresses contain even more valuable materials than the Nether itself. Blaze Rods and Nether Wart are both amazingly useful, and you won't find either of these without going to a Nether Fortress.

Search for Nether Fortresses by walking east or west from your starting point. Nether Fortresses are aligned north to south and are built along lines that run the entire length of the Nether. Once you bump into a Nether Fortress, you're set! Additional forts are located north and south from there, so exploration isn't as challenging.

Additionally, Nether Fortresses are large enough that you won't usually wander past them. They're made of compressed Netherrack, called Nether Brick. Their Fences, Stairs, and sundry monsters make them major landmarks.

Fight carefully through Nether Fortresses to snag Nether Wart from small growing areas near some of the Stairs, and collect material from slain enemies. Wither Skeletons drop Wither Skeleton Skulls if you're especially lucky. You need three of them to summon a special boss monster, and it takes a long time to gather them.

Ranged weapons are a must in these forts. Blazes have ranged attacks, and Wither Skeletons can too if they pick up a Bow. Also, some regular Skeletons spawn in Nether Fortresses, so be on the lookout for them.

You'll find Magma Cubes near the base of these areas, and they too drop useful items. Fight them at range to avoid damage, or go in for melee attacks if you're well-armored and feeling lucky.

Not all Nether Fortresses have gardens of Nether Wart, but even the ones that don't often contain Chests of loot. These can yield Diamonds, pieces of metal, Gold equipment, more Nether Wart (yay!), Saddles, and Horse Armor. Because of this, you can collect your first Nether Wart and start a garden of your own by searching carefully for Chests and growing areas along the steps.

Grinding

Getting three skulls from Wither Skeletons takes more time than almost any other gathering task in Minecraft. It's tough, so do everything you can to improve your chances of finding these rare items.

Use enchanted Swords to deal maximum damage versus undead. It's even better if these weapons have Looting III on them. It doesn't quite double the rate of skull drops, but it's still a 60% improvement! Not bad.

If too few Wither Skeletons appear in your current Nether Fortress, don't be afraid to search for a new one. Thanks to differences in their layouts, some forts spawn more Wither Skeletons than others.

Destroying a Wither

Once you hunt enough Wither Skeletons to get the three Wither Skeleton Skulls you need, bring them back to the Overworld with a supply of Soul Sand.

Choose a spot for battle in advance. Don't do this near your base, because the Wither's explosive attacks will wreck the whole area. Underground areas are a bit easier, because you won't have to navigate massive Dirt chasms and such while racing back toward the Wither.

Use a Potion of Night Vision before the battle. Torches don't survive the Wither's explosions, and you won't want to fight in pitch-darkness.

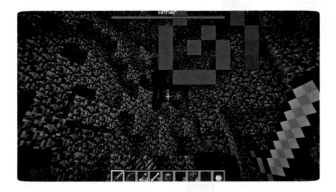

Also, bring the following useful items: a Diamond Sword (with Smite), Splash Potions of Healing, Strength Potions, an enchanted Bow (with Power), Diamond armor (Protection IV is almost a must), and an Enchanted Golden Apple.

To summon your Wither, build a small altar of Soul Sand—one block on the bottom, three horizontal blocks stacked above it. Then place the three skulls on top of the altar. This brings the Wither into being. Run! Immediately!

The Wither charges to full health and detonates the area around the altar when it reaches full power. You don't want to be around for this blast.

After you hear the strange explosion, return for battle. Use your Bow to reduce the Wither to half health. This isn't too hard, because the Wither's ranged attacks take a moment to reach you, so ranged combat gives you an advantage. Dodge the explosive skulls the Wither sends your way, and fire back as often as you can.

Drink potions to restore health if you get behind, and then use your Enchanted Golden Apple and Strength Potions when it's time to go for melee attacks. Withers become immune to ranged damage at half health, so you have to finish them with your blade.

Once you're buffed with the Enchanted Golden Apple's and Strength Potions' positive effects, charge toward the Wither and go for broke. Attack aggressively and kill it while the Apple's regenerative effects are still working.

The Nether Star that drops is required to make Beacons, and these offer really neat bonuses for your character and any friends. Plus, you can get multiple achievements by going to the Nether, farming materials, summoning a Wither, and killing it. It's all worthwhile!

Light a Beacon

Once you have a Nether Star, return to your base and craft a huge pyramid of blocks. The largest effective pyramid has to contain 164 blocks of Iron, Gold, or Diamond. Each block costs nine Ingots of the material in question, so it's quite a daunting amount of resources to gather.

You can always construct your pyramid in tiers. The first level only needs to have the Beacon on top and then nine blocks in a square beneath it.

That's 81 Ingots of material, so it isn't too bad. Once you have that, save up more resources until you can craft the second stage. Go on from there so you don't have to wait until you have the entire thing ready before you get the perks of an active Beacon.

You can cluster multiple Beacons together by placing them on a large pyramid. In the end, this saves on space and materials by quite a large margin. A 2x2 top with four Beacons, with a 4x4 tier beneath it, is much more useful than a single large pyramid with one Beacon.

What Do Beacons Do?

Completed Beacons light the sky and look wonderful, but that's the least of their effects. Once they're constructed, you turn on Beacons by adding a single piece of Iron, Gold, Emerald, or Diamond. This activates a buff that influences your character and any friends within a certain range.

Range of Each Pyramid

Tier I	20 Blocks
Tier II	30 Blocks
Tier III	40 Blocks
Tier IV	50 Blocks

A Beacon's range reaches horizontally by the number of blocks listed in the preceding table. However, the Beacon's powers reach upward (vertically) by 250 blocks. This is why many players construct Beacons near the bottom of the Overworld. Note that your Beacon has to have open access to the sky to work properly, so you have to dig a hole down toward the bedrock to let the Beacon shine free.

Normally, Beacons give you one power each. As you make larger pyramids, you get more choices for powers, but you don't get any secondary powers until Tier IV. These maximum-sized pyramids let you make strong primary powers or get a free secondary Regeneration effect.

Some of the primary effects are locked until you make a certain pyramid size. The initial choices are Speed and Haste. Resistance and Jump Boost require a Tier II pyramid. Strength requires a Tier III pyramid.

Positive Effects from Each Beacon (Choose One)

Haste	Faster mining
Jump Boost	Higher and longer jumps
Resistance	Improved armor rating
Speed	Faster walking and sprinting
Strength	Increased melee damage

For the best effect, craft four Beacons and use the wider pyramids to get almost all of these buffs. A Tier II pyramid built in this fashion needs to have "only" 52 blocks but gets you four primary powers. That's less than one-third the cost of a single-Beacon Tier IV pyramid.

If you ever get enough material together for a four-Beacon Tier IV pyramid, life is great. The increased range really helps, and your total number of effects makes it a joy to mine, work, or farm near the pyramid.

The End

The End is another special dimension in *Minecraft*. You cannot get there at first, but Endermen help you reach it eventually.

Endermen and Eyes of Ender

Endermen are rare monsters, but you find them here and there throughout the Overworld. Large, dark areas that are at least three blocks high have a chance to spawn Endermen at any time.

Fight these enemies by attacking their feet. This prevents them from teleporting. Don't use ranged attacks, and don't look them in the eyes, because that makes them aggressive before you're ready to fight.

Kill enough Endermen, and you start to accrue Ender Pearls. These items are useful for instant teleportation. Throw them at your target, and bam!—you're there. This causes damage to your character, but it's still fun.

That said, you're best off saving most of your Ender Pearls; they're crafted into Eyes of Ender. These items help you find Strongholds and then activate Portals located only within those Strongholds.

Craft more than 12 Eyes of Ender when you want to reach the End. Use the Eyes to locate the nearest Stronghold, attack that base, and look for the room with the End Portal. This is where Silverfish spawn. Track them back to that room, destroy their Monster Spawner, and then fill in the 12 slots around the End Portal with your Eyes of Ender. Doing so opens the way—you can now get to the End.

Note that you can't get back, so don't step through the Portal until you stash your best items at home.

Going to the End

End Portals stay activated once you've found them and used your Eyes of Ender. That's good news, because your trip to the End won't always go well. We recommend not taking all of your good equipment for your first trip there. You should get your bearings, make sure your spawn location is "safe," and try to build a starting base with your first life there.

The game's final boss is here; it's called the Ender Dragon. This thing is so powerful that it breaks most blocks by flying through them. Obsidian and the End Stone that dominate this dimension are both exceptions. Bring enough Obsidian to quickly create a small room beside the Portal where you spawn (not on it). Form this room and drop an Ender Chest there, if you have one. This lets you harvest End Stone and transport it back to the Overworld even before you're able to kill the Ender Dragon. We'll discuss strategies for fighting this boss in a moment.

Dragon's Breath

Dragon's Breath is a shimmering material left behind after the Ender Dragon breathes at you. Look on the ground for it! If you see any, rush over and use Glass Bottles to harvest as much of the Dragon's Breath as you can. It's a primary ingredient for making Lingering Potions (these turn your Splash Potions into area-of-effect items that last over time).

The Outer Islands

There are outer islands in the End. You can't get to these islands by flying or throwing Ender Pearls. The distance to reach them is way too far for that. Instead, you reach the islands by taking an End Gateway. These spawn near the central Portal every time you kill an Ender Dragon. This is one of the reasons it's sometimes worth respawning the boss so that you can fight it again. Given enough time and effort, you can cause up to 20 of these Gateways to appear, each leading to different areas on the periphery of the End.

To go through a Gateway, throw an Ender Pearl into it. There isn't enough room for you to get in between the blocks on your own, and this method is a quick way to go through.

End Cities

The outer islands can be explored after you've defeated the Ender Dragon, when it's relatively safe. A prominent feature on the islands is the End City. Look for these structures and explore them carefully when you discover one of them. They're filled with Chests of loot, which makes them quite valuable. However, they're guarded. Expect to encounter Shulkers, disguised as Purpur blocks.

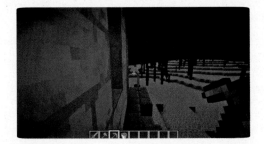

Chorus Plants

The outer islands have Chorus Plants and Chorus Flowers. These are like Cacti in the regular Overworld. Destroy the bottom of the plant to bring down the entire formation. The Chorus Flowers can be replanted onto End Stone to make them grow.

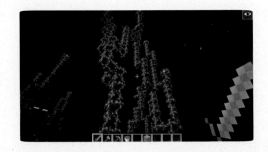

After you've gathered End Stone and Chorus Flowers, you can make your own farms of these plant formations without too much trouble. Manual harvest of them is easy via chopping down the bottom block of the tree, but more advanced farming methods work better. Water pools can be made to help drag the falling plants to the center of an area for easy harvesting. You can put a Hopper and Chest below or gather on your own.

Chorus Fruit restores four points of hunger when eaten and has a chance to teleport the user a short distance away.

Smelting Chorus Fruit turns it into Popped Chorus Fruit. Though now inedible, these items are used to create Purpur blocks and End Rods.

End Ships and Elytra

Some End Cities have a pier that spawns an End Ship beside it. These too have great loot, including a few things you aren't going to see often on their own. End Ships have more Shulkers to contend with, but they're also filled with Potions, a Brewing Stand, an Item Frame of Elytra, and a Dragon Head. This is must-have material, so hunt aggressively each time you encounter an End City.

Elytra are Chest items that grant gliding powers to your character. When you're falling, tap the Jump button to start a glide. Your Elytra lose durability when in use, but these items can be repaired by merging two together or using Leather and an Anvil to reforge them (this being a much less-costly method in the long run).

Gliding is really, really fun. There's something magical about leaping off of mountains and towers and soaring over the land. Keep your view slightly above the horizon to glide for as long as possible, or dive down to gain speed (but at the cost of your total glide time and distance covered).

If you try to raise your angle of flight too high, you can effectively stall out. This is dangerous, because you can take falling damage while using the Elytra if you hit the ground while going too fast. Be careful!

Start off with gentle flights to test the mechanics of the wings, and then get bolder as you become comfortable with the way everything works.

Fighting Ender Dragons

Once you're comfortable going to the End and getting your bearings, start arming yourself for the final engagement. You want a Bow with the best Power enchantment you can get. A few stacks of Arrows won't hurt, though you likely won't need all of them unless things go very badly.

A good Sword helps, too. The Ender Dragon is too mobile to kill with a Sword, but Endermen also inhabit the End, and they're an additional threat. Swords should have either Fire Aspect or the highest possible damage output.

Diamond armor with Protection IV is your smartest bet for safety. Your helm can be either a Pumpkin or a Diamond Helm. The latter is better for survival. Pumpkins are better for avoiding extra fights with Endermen, because they don't attack when you look at them. This is a matter of personal preference.

Potions of Healing and Regeneration are both useful during the battle. Golden Apples or Enchanted Golden Apples are great, too.

Ender Pearls are helpful as well. They let you teleport from smaller islands over to the main island, possibly saving you if you're knocked over the edge during the boss fight.

Keep a Bucket of Water handy so that you can cushion your fall if you're knocked high into the air. Deploy the water directly under your character right before you land. This saves you from massive damage when things go badly!

Slaying the Dragon

A series of Ender Crystals keeps the Ender Dragon alive and healthy. Each crystal is placed on top of an Obsidian pillar, like the ones on which you arrive. Destroying these is a critical part of the boss fight. If you don't break the crystals, the Ender Dragon can stay at or near full health indefinitely, despite your best efforts.

Watch for the healing beams that emanate from the Ender Crystals. Their energy flows toward the Dragon. Trace it back to figure out where the crystals are, and use your Bow to shoot at them until they explode.

A couple of the crystals are usually protected by Iron Bars. They can't be shot as easily as the others. You have to either pull the Dragon away from them so that it doesn't get much healing, or you have to quickly build your way up to the protected crystals so that they can be destroyed directly. It's challenging, but may need to be done if the crystals are well-placed and providing substantial healing.

When you're done destroying as many crystals as you can, turn the Bow on him! Head shots are the way to go if you want to win this fight anytime soon; they inflict quadruple damage. The best way to achieve these hits is to wait for the Ender Dragon to come after your character. Nail it in the head with a fully charged attack. Get another shot in immediately afterward, and then watch the Dragon fly away. Chase it and wait for the boss to turn and come after you again. Repeat your attacks and wait for the kill!

A risky trick is to dig a small hole, place a Bed into it when the Dragon is ready to charge you, and set the Bed off just before the Dragon attacks. You need to have a safe spot to jump when this happens, so the technique requires practice, setup time, and precision. It isn't a technique for first-time Dragon killers, but it shaves tons of time off of the battle once you know how to do it reliably.

Another tactic is to craft Ender Crystals (with Glass, Eyes of Ender, and Ghast Tears). Place these is spots where the Dragon is likely to charge, and then detonate the crystals as the Dragon passes. They do very high damage.

The Aftermath

The Ender Dragon drops so much experience that even a character with no experience will gain dozens of levels almost immediately. It's better to bring a few friends to spread around the experience, or bring in materials for enchanting work so you can enchant multiple items and still max out your experience.

The Ender Dragon also drops a Dragon Egg. This doesn't have a use (yet). However, you can collect it. Clicking on the Dragon Egg causes it to teleport. Do this one time to get the Egg away from the End Portal, which appears to take you home. You don't want the Egg to fall into the End Portal and break.

After the Dragon Egg teleports, track it down. It sometimes appears below the ground. Tunnel until you find it, and then get two blocks beneath it. Destroy the End Stone there, place a Torch, and then destroy the block above to drop the Dragon Egg onto the Torch. This turns the Egg into a resource and allows you to collect it.

You've now completed the End. Come back here to farm Endermen or End Stone, and use your new End Portal to return home at any time.

If you craft Ender Crystals and place one on each side of the Exit Portal, you can respawn the Ender Dragon. This is done to practice killing it, to harvest Dragon's Breath (in Glass Bottles), or for pure fun.

Redstone

You can mine Redstone deep underground in the Overworld. Once you start mining down there, Redstone collects quickly. Each vein yields a fair number of pieces, and it's hard to miss these veins even when you're running through a cavern, because they're bright red. Always keep an Iron Pickaxe handy. Lesser materials fail to break Redstone properly. Iron tools are required for quite a few of the special metals and ores, so an Iron Pickaxe isn't a particular burden here.

You can craft blocks of Redstone to make pretty crimson decor around your house, but its real uses are much more impressive. Redstone is used to make Clocks, Compasses, Detector Rails, Dispensers, Droppers, Note blocks, Powered Rails, Redstone Lamps, Redstone Repeaters, and Redstone Torches. That's a pretty big list!

This amazing material is also used in brewing to make Potions last longer. If that's not enough for you, you can also place Redstone on the ground as a red trail of dust. Redstone Dust lets you channel power from one area to another, allowing for the construction of complex machines.

Transmission of Redstone Power

Trails of Redstone Dust send power up to 15 blocks from their source. Power is generated by a number of objects. Pressure Plates, Redstone Torches, Levers, and Buttons are just a few examples of items that trigger some type of power. Placing Redstone Dust on a block next to these items lets their power transmit to somewhere else.

Create a trail of dust that goes where you need it to go, and make sure you don't shift the height of your trail more than one block at a time. Redstone Dust stops sending power if its elevation changes more abruptly than that. It also fails if you shift the trail up or down one block and don't leave either air or Glass in between. Trying to send the trail up and under another heavy block doesn't work.

When power is continuous along a line of dust, the material turns bright red instead of dark red. This lets you see how well power is flowing along your lines. If the energy isn't going far enough, add additional sources of energy, such as a Redstone Torch.

Redstone Machinery

Now things get a bit more complex. You know that Redstone can carry energy around, but what does that actually do? A good question! The energy from these signals lets you operate a range of mechanisms in the game, providing automation for farms, traps, transportation, and more. It's hard to get a handle on all of this when you first start *Minecraft*. In fact, this presents a steeper skill/learning curve than almost anything else in the game. Don't try to master this right away. Take your time, dabble in Redstone, and figure it out as you go.

When you're starting out, don't be afraid to look at other people's machines for inspiration. See how they did what they did. Most people need to see a few machines set up in the game before they start to understand Redstone's use and potential.

Having said that, let's move forward. We'll keep this as simple as possible. Let's start by breaking down the major parts of a potential machine.

Pieces of a Machine

- ◆ Power: some device needs to provide power for your machine
- ◆ Transmission: the power needs to be sent from its source to somewhere else of your choosing
- ◆ Mechanism: this device needs to receive power and use it to accomplish your goal

Items that Produce Power

Power is produced by a wide range of items.

ITEM	HOW TO ACTIVATE IT	POWER PRODUCED
Button	Interact with it or use a Bow to shoot it.	Activate nearby dust/components for 1.5 seconds when touched, or one minute if shot by a Bow.
Daylight Sensor	Turns on during the day and off at night; the opposite is true if used belowground.	Adds more power as the day/night progresses.
Detector Rail	Adds power when a Minecart is detected nearby.	Powers itself and adjacent blocks.
Lever	Produces power when turned on.	Power remains on as long as the Lever is not turned off.
Pressure Plate	Provides power when touched; Wood Pressure Plates can be shot with Arrows to produce power.	Powers the block underneath it; any trails/components next to either the plate or the block below are activated.
Redstone Block	Always on.	Strong power for all nearby components.
Redstone Torch	Provides continuous power unless it receives power from another source—this turns it off.	Powers adjacent blocks but not the block to which it is attached.
Trapped Chest	Provides power when someone opens the Chest.	The Trapped Chest and the block underneath it power adjacent dust/mechanisms.
Tripwire Hook	Turns on if the wires are damaged or crossed.	The hook and the block it's placed on produce power.
Weighted Pressure Plate	Adds increasing power based on how many objects are on top of it.	The plate and the block it's placed on produce power.

How to Transmit Power

Power sources add energy to adjacent blocks, which is sometimes all you need. Add a mechanism next to a power source, and you're good to go. However, power transmission is wonderful if you need to make something happen several blocks (or more) away from the power source. The following three items let you send power this way.

Redstone Dust

This is the most basic way to send a Redstone signal along a short length of blocks. The power goes as far as the strength of the original signal. This means that a strong power source can send power 15 blocks away; a source with less power can transmit power only a portion of that distance. For example, a Daylight Sensor will send its signal farther as the day goes on and the sun rises higher in the sky.

Create a simple test to observe this. Make a Daylight Sensor with a trail of Redstone Dust that leads 15 blocks away from it. Watch the line of dust turn bright red across a greater distance as the day progresses—pretty neat!

Redstone Repeater

Sometimes, you may want to send a signal along a greater distance than 15 blocks. Redstone Repeaters let you strengthen a signal in a single direction. Place your line of Redstone Dust so that it leads up to the rear of the Redstone Repeater and then continues out its front side.

This strengthens your signal and allows it to reach greater distances. If you want, add more Repeaters so the signal continues toward any destination. There's a short delay in this process, but that's good too. Redstone Repeaters are often used as a way to slow down a signal so that it doesn't get to its final mechanism too quickly.

Redstone Comparator

Comparators are the most complex way of transmitting power. Like Repeaters, they have a front and a back, but they don't reinforce the signal. Instead, they have two modes: Comparison Mode and Subtraction Mode.

Comparators send their signals from back to front, and they output a signal that's equal in strength to the signal they receive. Thus, a trail of activated Redstone Dust that would normally travel five more blocks can enter the back of this device and exit the front to power five more blocks of dust. You might be thinking, "That doesn't seem to do anything important at all." Well, not yet.

The Comparator comes into play when there are signals coming into the back and the side of the device. This changes its output. In Comparison Mode, the signal is shut down if the value of the side signal is stronger than the one entering the rear. Thus, Comparison Mode gives you a way to shut down machines based on a separate circuit.

Subtraction Mode reduces the signal strength of the main line by the strength of the signal entering the side of the comparator.

Mechanisms

At the end of your signal, place a mechanism of some sort to use the power you're sending. Mechanisms can accomplish a wide range of tasks.

MECHANISM	EFFECT
Activator Rail	Triggers Minecarts that pass over it, detonating TNT, executing Command blocks, or silencing Hoppers.
Command Block	Power causes the block to execute its command a single time.
Dispenser	Shoots one item from a random slot.
Door	Toggles between open and closed.
Dropper	Drops one item from a random slot in its inventory.
Fence Gate	Toggles between open and closed.
Hopper	Power stops Hoppers from pulling items into themselves.
Note Block	Creates sound.
Piston	Pushes the block in front of the Piston (and up to 12 total blocks beyond that).
Powered Rail	Speeds Minecarts.
Rail	Toggles Junctions.
Redstone Lamp	Creates powerful light.
TNT	Begins the detonation sequence for the block of TNT.
Trapdoor	Toggles the position of the Trapdoor.

What to Make

Even though we just explained Redstone functionality, this barely scratches the surface. None of this information really means anything until you start to build your own devices.

Following are some simple ideas to get you started with Redstone.

Heavy Doors

Iron Doors keep out monsters on any difficulty, no matter how many of them there are. They don't even try to pound their way through. Use six Iron Ingots to craft a Door, and use power to open and close it. On the inside of your house, a Pressure Plate in front of the Door works perfectly for easy escape. On the outside, you don't want that because monsters might walk right in.

Instead, use a Button outside your Door. Neither of these items leaves the power on continuously, so your Door closes as soon as you move away or wait too long.

Fast Minecarts

Place Powered Rails over long stretches so your Minecarts can travel across great distances. You can climb large inclines as well, making it easier to travel up and down from your mines without wasting time.

Easy Pits

Dig a pit near the front of your house and place a Trapdoor over it. On the inside of the house, place a Lever on a block that's adjacent to the Trapdoor. When you use the Lever as a power source, the block it's attached to gains power. This, in turn, transmits to the Trapdoor and activates it. You can now drop creatures into a pit from the safety of your home. If anyone you don't like comes up to your house, drop them into the pit. A deadly fall should do the trick nicely, but Lava and other fun toys work just as well.

Night-Lights

Redstone Lamps, Redstone Torches, and Daylight Sensors let you craft lighting that turns on only when the light level falls to a certain point. Put the Redstone Lamps and the Redstone Torches next to each other, so they're turned on by default. Then place a line of Redstone Dust that leads to the blocks underneath the Redstone Torches. Connect this to your Daylight Sensors. When there's enough light during the day, they'll provide power to the dust and turn off the Redstone Torches. As night falls, they'll lose power and the Redstone Torches will begin powering the Redstone Lamps again. This is an example of an inverter (i.e., using Redstone Torches to turn off a signal rather than turn it on).

The same technique lets you close Doors and Fence Gates in the evening, to prevent monsters from coming into your areas.

General Tips

The biggest tip that can be given is, if you have the right equipment to do so, plug in mouse and keyboard, or a controller. Performing the simplest actions, such as looking around and walking, can be irritating with mobile controls.

If you aren't worried about Achievements or cheating in general, you can change the difficulty or mode at any time in the settings. If you're not relatively close to a Water source at your home, it's a good idea to make is an unlimited Water source nearby. This can be done by digging a 2x2 (only need to be one block deep) hole and placing a Water Bucket in one corner of the hole, then dumping another into the block diagonal to the one you filled. When you do this, you can get Water from it without having to refill it forever.

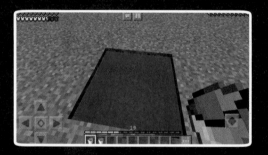

Your Home

KEEP YOUR HOME LIT UP. You don't want your home to be dark at night. The moment you walk outside, a Creeper could blow the front out. Place Torches around the house walls (INSIDE AND OUT) and grounds. To make it look a little prettier, make some Fences and stack them up like streetlights, and hang some Glowstone.

Livestock

Make a large area and surround it in Fences to keep livestock in. Once you have a large amount of each type of animal you can breed, start killing them, and keep the process going for a good supply of meat.

Farming

Make your own farm behind your home. Instead of finding a river, pond, or ocean to plant around, make the farm near your house. Keep a Fence around it so mobs don't stomp around it. To prevent unwanted animals from jumping in, build about three blocks away from any higher blocks.

A little fashion tip for farmland and to make sure you have fewer accidents in un-plowing the land, place a Wooden Slab (color of your choice, but Birch looks great) over the stretch of Water so you can walk around without having to swim in the Water or accidentally destroying crops.

Secret Room!

If you play on multiplayer servers and want to hide secret rooms, here are a few tips for you. You can place a picture over a doorway, and if it's big enough, it can hide that entrance. Ladders and Signs can stop the flow of Water. With that in mind, consider having a secret room under a pond—dig out a room, then place Ladders or Signs to block the flow. Furnaces

If you have need to cook or smelt a large load of materials, a Lava Bucket or Blaze Rod is much more efficient than using all your Coal.

◆ A piece of Coal can keep a Furnace going for 80 seconds.

◆ A Blaze Rod can keep a Furnace going for 120 seconds.

◆ A Lava Bucket can keep a Furnace going for 1000 seconds.

It's a good idea to have a load of Furnaces ready so you don't have to cook one stack of items at a time. You could even build your own Furnace room.

Mining/Digging

If strip-mining is your thing, the best place to mine is at Layer 16 and below, although many believe it's best to do it between Layers 12 and 16. Layer 16 is the layer where Diamond Ore starts to spawn.

One irritant when digging up or around is when you hit Sand or Gravel. A fast way to get rid of a column of falling Sand/Gravel is to put a Torch under the block. The Torch makes the blocks break automatically.

When mining, keep a Water Bucket with you. If you come across a Lava pool, dump the Water above it to make a walking path.

If you don't have a Water Bucket—or in general, when mining around a Lava pool, or high in the air—crouch while mining so you don't fall.

MODERN COMBAT 4: ZERO HOUR

Developer	Gameloft Montreal
Publisher	Gameloft
Year Released	2012
Platforms	iOS, Android, Windows Phone 8, BlackBerry 10, and PlayBook
Type	First-person shooter
Suggested Age	13+
Cost	Free to download

$ IN-GAME PURCHASES
In-game currency, Character upgrades

Game Overview

If you've ever been *called* upon to do your *duty*, you'll have more than a passing familiarity with *Modern Combat 4: Zero Hour*. This fast-paced first-person shooter is the fourth game in the franchise, and is set in the near future, pitting an undercover armed force (the SGS) against the Phantom Unit, with you having the opportunity to play as or against both sides.

What You Need to Know

You control your soldier using virtual on-screen buttons, with included (and optional) gyroscopic controls. You can use grenades, crouch, reload, change weapons, employ melee attacks, mantle across obstacles, as well as aim using iron sights. There's a single-player Campaign (comprising 12 missions), and a robust Multiplayer mode (with 11 maps and 10 modes).

From Zero Hour to Hero Hour

It's important to note that there are a number of instances throughout the game where you can upgrade your soldier's statistics. These, along with your soldier's Specializations, which allow you to add more Perks to your repertoire as you gain Ranks, are the keys to improving your game. That, and accruing copious Blue and Gold Credits to unlock better equipment, of course!

RFO SUMMIT
MISSION 1

LOADING...

Preparation

If you're playing for the first time, there are some initial tips to try before facing foes in either Campaign or Multiplayer:

How Sensitive Are You?

Don't overlook the Sensitivity slider in the Controls menu; it allows you to increase or decrease how rapidly your movements are conveyed from screen to in-game. If you're having trouble making accurate movements to aim at a foe's head, think about tweaking the sensitivity. If your controls are sluggish and you aren't aiming at an enemy fast enough, increase the sensitivity. If you're overcompensating or exhibiting an aim that's too "twitchy," try decreasing the sensitivity. Don't just ramp the sensitivity up to maximum thinking that's how the pros do it!

The Aim Game: Turn It Off!

Aim Assist can be found in the Settings menu, and there are reasons to play this game with and without this feature. The biggest reason to switch this off is that it helps you train for Multiplayer matches, where (unless you're playing a Custom match) all your enemies use manual aiming anyway. Don't rely on this crutch, as you'll be outclassed by human foes once you finish the Campaign mode. With the practice of manually aiming at foes in Campaign, transferring this skill to Multiplayer becomes much easier. Practice makes perfect!

The Aim Game: Turn It On!

Or, if you want to accrue more points at a quicker rate throughout Campaign mode, keep Aim Assist on. Aim Assist automatically tracks the enemy nearest to your location and allows for quicker takedowns, easier headshots, and faster gameplay, and keeps you alive longer. To gather bonuses (including Credits) at a more rapid rate, it's more straightforward if to just do the firing, rather than worry about the aiming too. But don't be surprised if you're outclassed when facing foes in Multiplayer!

Gunning with the Gyroscope

It's also worth fiddling with the Gyroscope in the Controls menu, turning it on and adjusting the sensitivity to your satisfaction, as it makes pistol and shotgun attacks a little easier to land. It also helps when you're aiming down your weapon sights.

Change the Grenade Button

The default location of the Grenade button can cause you to inadvertently press it during particularly vicious combat. Minimize accidental carnage by changing the button to a spot where you don't keep accidentally pressing it.

A Sound Strategy

Check the Sounds menu, and turn off the Music while turning up the Sound FX. This way, you can more easily hear enemy movements, distant firing or footsteps, and other effects to pinpoint where they are and act accordingly. The sooner you hear a foe (sometimes before visual contact is made), the quicker you can take them down.

TIPS

Movement

Wandering around aimlessly is going to get you killed. Instead, ensure you're a lithe and nimble killing machine by employing these movement-based tactics:

Be Like a Shark

Never stop moving. If you're stationary, or even remaining in a specific area for a long amount of time, you're easy prey. Employ crouching and cover where appropriate, but only when under attack. Never appear in the same place twice, and your foe should never be able to learn your routes.

Control, Not Camping

If you find yourself in an area with cover (especially in Zone Control maps), it's worth learning where enemies are going to appear from, and train your (long-range) weapons at this spot. But don't simply camp there; constantly move so you can more easily react to a foe appearing in an area you didn't expect, as well as to remain mobile so you aren't hit yourself.

Hip-Firing Strafe

As you should be constantly moving while in combat (unless you want to die quickly), you need to learn how to effectively fire and move simultaneously. This is achieved (without the slowing penalty of sight-aiming) by attempting a circle-strafe—sidestepping in one direction while turning your weapon's aim in the opposite direction. Why? So you can more accurately utilize the inertia of your movement while manually aiming.

Getting High

If a particular area or map has multiple vertical levels, attempt to reach and lurk around the top floor, if there are good and open views of areas below you. It's always easier to aim at, and fire, on foes below you, especially as you can retreat and use the edge of the floor as cover, or drop down and finish the job.

Combat and Weapon Use

There are almost limitless playstyles and weapon combinations to try. But it's well worth figuring out some overall tactics before you start spraying foes with bullets:

Locked and Loadout

Before you adjust your gameplay style to weapons you prefer or unlock yourself, maximize your chances of success by equipping a lightweight pistol (to use when fleeing an enemy or running), along with a rapid-firing rifle (to employ when you take an offensive posture).

Getting Attached to Your Weapon

You may be thinking that adding all manner of attachments to your weapon could help you in combat, and to a certain extent (and for less-experienced gamers) this is true. However, if you can easily take down foes without extra attachments, opt to remove the heavier ones from your weapons so you can move faster and fire more quickly. For example, it's better to keep all your attachments light, even if that means sacrificing a bigger magazine. Why? Because you gain a constant advantage by moving slightly faster, compared to being able to fire for longer between reloads; you usually never use up a full magazine between reloads anyway.

A Marked Man

Some attachments you should definitely consider using, such as the Combat Telescopic Sight (CTS) at longer ranges, and the Tactical Holo at mid-range, both of which have a helpful marking laser that allows you to track enemies on your radar after you spot them. This obviously allows you to watch foes, even if they break away from combat with you.

Campaign Promises

Blue Credits are awarded during the single-player Campaign mode. In order to complete the 12 missions with a good degree of competence, it's worth spending some of these credits on upgrades. Apply faster reloading and a laser-sight attachment to your weapons. Choose the automatic turrets and body armor to help you succeed, and then think about other upgrades afterwards.

Check Yourself and Mop Up. Don't be above spawn-killing enemies. If you find a foe who's just appeared, they're likely to be a little disorientated, so focus and attempt to slay them before they can react in time. Is combat occurring up ahead of you, or in the distance, or in an adjacent chamber? That's usually great news, as you can step into the chamber and ideally defeat all the enemies in there (who are likely to be wounded and about to finish each other).

Weapons Detail

So you've won a few matches, but you want to learn a bit more about the arsenal you can choose from. While everyone has their own favorite attachments and loadouts, it's worth learning what the different weapon types are, along with Multiplayer-centric advice.

Recommended Weapons

For the following descriptions, we've flagged our favorite weapons in every type with an asterisk.

Assault Rifles

Primary Weapon: Well-rounded with copious customization options. Useful during medium-to-long-range combat.

Charbtek-28*

One of the most versatile weapons, especially if you're seeking the highest damage per second of any primary weapon, impressive rate of fire, and with a long range and the largest magazine size (45). It suffers from hip-fire inaccuracy and is tricky to aim at long range, with poor handling. However, attachments can compensate for this.

Compakt-665*

If you're more concerned with firepower, mobility, an exceptional rate of fire, and excellent damage potential, while less concerned with the weapon's visual recoil, expense, and lack of long-range capabilities, this should be your primary weapon.

KR-200

If your playstyle includes accurate, well-taken shots, consider this versatile weapon, with great long-range and burst rate-of-fire capabilities. This is accurate (especially through iron sights), and with its burst fire, it can drop a foe quickly, despite a delay in firing.

SOCAR-S A1*

Though this is the default weapon you use, many still utilize it, despite giving up damage at closer ranges and rate of fire to the Compakt and Charbtek rifles. Pair it with a recoil booster to increase damage, and learn to love the gun's range and accuracy.

UFIA PSD-2*

If you favor iron sights or hip-firing accuracy, good headshot (and headshot multiplier) potential, and great mobility, pick this. Be aware that its damage is light (so a recoil booster is recommended), and it has a slow rate of fire and poor range.

VECT9

Slot in an extended magazine (bringing the clip from 20 to 30 rounds) and be wary of the poor mobility, especially at closer ranges. Expect high recoil and a low rate of fire. However, it offers strong long-range and hip-firing killing potential, and has good damage.

TIPS

Shotguns

Primary Weapon: Massive damage and limited range mean shotguns are an excellent option for close-range firefights.

CTK-1410

Those favoring long-range blasts, reasonable damage potential, and a passable rate of fire should try this shotgun out for size. Only then might you try to ignore the high recoil, inaccuracy (especially at close range), laborious reload, and small capacity of this weapon.

R780*

If you can get over the long reload time, short range, and slow rate of fire, this shotgun is a blast—literally, as it's murderous at close ranges, is cheap to purchase, handles well, and has the flexibility to be used between melee and medium ranges.

Volkhov-12

Overcome this shotgun's problematic recoil and inaccuracy when firing at medium ranges, and you'll be wielding a weapon with large (12-shot) capacity, fast reload (for a shotgun), and excellent rate of fire and damage potential.

Sniper Rifles

Primary Weapon: Click on a scope, stand at a distance, and take down foes from afar, ideally without being spotted.

E24 SASR

You're likely to compare this to the X6. This has lower damage for each firing, but a quicker rate of fire. It may be unwieldy, offer limited potential when iron sights aren't utilized, and be slow to reload, but it can be fitted with extended magazines, and offers unmatched damage per second at long ranges—usually resulting in one-shot kills.

SFS CTK-12*

While the price is high, the damage is low, the mobility is poor, and the reload time is long, this rifle has excellent attachment possibilities, is faster at firing than the X6, and offers higher damage at closer ranges. Purchase attachments (like the Deep Impact rounds) to negate any shortfalls.

X6 .338

Being a bolt-action rifle, this suffers from poor rate of fire, and isn't accurate when hip-fired. But it's cheap, has a reasonably sized clip (10), has excellent iron-sight takedown potential at long ranges, and inflicts the most damage of all sniper rifles. Just make each shot count!

Handguns

Secondary Weapon: Both regular and machine pistols are useful backup weapons, especially at close and middle ranges.

Black Mamba

Highly powerful, with good range and lethal—single-shot kills at close range (as long as you're sight-aiming). Partner it with JHP rounds for even more potent damage. It has a slow rate of fire and small six-shot capacity (four if using Bird Bomb rounds for extra explosive damage).

Schoc 33

Low damage, and not automatic compared to the other handguns, but mobile and with a quick reload. However, its low damage, high recoil, and the availability of much more proficient secondary weapons (such as the OPS65) relegates this to those wanting a quick rate of fire, without the damage.

Viny Pro*

Though it features a visible recoil and a small magazine capacity (20), the high rate of fire, mobility, and excellent iron-sights visibility make this a choice backup weapon to utilize. Add JHP rounds and an extended magazine for even more potency. Did we mention it's almost as quick at firing as an SMG?

Submachine Guns

Secondary Weapon: If you want portability as well as rapid firepower, choose this for close or mid-range confrontations.

Jolt-7 MP

Granting you a high rate of fire, good mobility, a quick reload, and a large magazine, this inflicts good damage at both mid and close ranges, though it trails off at longer ranges. It's expensive; many prefer the OPS65, as it's more potent at closer distances, even with attachments.

OPS65*

As long as you combat this weapon's poor accuracy by attaching a grip, and you aren't worried about its short range (compared to other SMGs), this is an excellent choice. It's cheap to buy and features a quick reload, great mobility, and impressive rate of fire and damage.

Tygr X3

Looking for an SMG with insane reload speeds, a high rate of fire, low recoil, and excellent mobility? How about long-range and large magazine capabilities? Then choose this, if you can ignore the expense, the lack of close damage, and the fact it loses out to the OPS65 at long range, or if foes are using armor Perks.

Launchers

Secondary Weapon: Slow, projectile-firing behemoths. If you can time your attacks right, you can take out groups of foes or vehicles with these. Time your attacks wrong, and you can kill yourself just as easily.

40mm Thor GLP*

Expensive, with a pronounced arc to each shot making it inaccurate over range, plus it comes with a lengthy reload time, is expensive to purchase, and is less effective against drones and turrets compared to the other launchers. But wait! It's great for crowd control and those foes who like to camp, is better against players (rather than machines), and has high mobility.

CTK-88 Crumplor

Need medium-to-long-range projectiles launched? Pick this. It's excellent against recon aircraft, drones, and turrets; is reasonably priced; and can drop foes at range. It suffers from poor damage against multiple human opponents, with slow-moving projectiles, and unimpressive mobility and reload times. It's also massive, blocking some of your screen!

Kolbaszky S-40 GL

Don't use this at long range, as the arc of the projectile is tricky to aim. It has a long reload time too, though if you can connect with its projectiles, it delivers the highest damage, with the largest area of effect, and is great to fire at those dug in who aren't moving.

TIPS

Projectiles

Whether or not you've mastered the weapons with triggers, it's also pertinent to learn how to properly punt the nine different projectiles, as they all have different effects:

Rosarms Industries R67 Fragmentation Grenade

The R67 Frag Grenade is good for longer, ranged attacks, as it has a highly damaging and large blast radius, but is less effective (due to its lethal damage) at closer quarters if you're attempting to defend. It can be thrown a long distance, and is also "cookable"—keep it in your hand and lob it so it explodes as it lands, but without taking too long and killing yourself.

Charbtek CTK-84 Incapacitating Grenade

Though rarely encountered in Multiplayer, combine this with the Opportunism Stealth Perk so you can inflict more (gun-based) damage to those you've stunned when using this Flashbang or Stun Grenade. It has a large area of effect, blinds foes for around four seconds, and is excellent to use as crowd control. If you're on the receiving end of this attack, turn away or retreat to lessen the effects.

Rosarms "Bee Swarm" R70-CS Incapacitating Grenade (8,000 Gold Credits)

The Stun Grenade inflicts mass shrapnel damage over a radius of five meters, disorienting victims due to the CS gas also emitted from the explosion. This is a great defensive tactic to use against enemies at close range, and lobbing two of them can cause fatal damage if the foe is close enough. Just make sure you're backing up and out of the blast radius. Otherwise, employ this to lessen an enemy's counterattack.

Bernier-2 Titanium Steel "Tactical Poignard"

An instant kill if these connect with a foe? Sounds amazing! No automatic aim and a tendency to bounce a lot? Sounds less amazing. If you can get pass the inaccurate nature of this throwing knife, and the fact this is only useful against a single foe (there's no area of effect), then try this out. Usually reserved for pro-players, this has a longer range than any other projectile you can carry.

Kremlin Rifles KR-G3 White Phosphorus Smoke Bomb

This Tear Gas Smoke Bomb detonates into a five-meter cloud, dispersing after 10 seconds. During the time it's effective, it incapacitates one or more foes, helps you to block routes, slows or stuns enemies, and can be aimed through if you've equipped the Thermal LCD. This is the grenade to use to control multiple foes, stopping them from entering certain areas. Follow up with gunfire, as this grenade doesn't inflict damage.

Chralz Technik GMBH Anti-Tank ST174

This Sticky Bomb inflicts the most damage of all the grenades, is cookable (as long as you throw it before it explodes in your hand), and is one of the most popular ways to defeat enemies using a projectile. It can damage foes on the other sides of walls, can be thrown to "stick" onto walls so enemies arriving around three seconds later are caught in the explosion, and can even be stuck on foes. It has a large damage radius, and despite the lengthy detonation time-frame, it's usually the most effective grenade in the game. Pick Grenades Expert or Explosives Expert to increase its potency still further!

Thermate-TH3 Mark 7 Grenade

The Incendiary Grenade creates intense and deadly heat within a one-meter radius once it explodes—more than enough to defeat any foe in the vicinity. It's used in a similar fashion to the Smoke Bomb, though this kills foes. Throw into hallways and thoroughfares to prevent enemies from progressing. It detonates instantly, lasts around eight seconds, and quickly kills. The only drawback? It's easy to get caught and kill yourself, so don't use it in close quarters.

Kremlin Rifles KR-X Ultralight NNEMP Bomb

The EMP Grenade temporarily disables your HUD, turrets, jammers, and radar for 20 seconds, within a radius of 10 meters. If your foes are using a lot of these types of equipment, it's worth annoying them with this, then following up with gunfire attacks while they're disorientated.

CTK-160 LRHE Concussion Grenade

Compared to the similar Frag Grenade, this Concussion projectile explodes instantly upon impact, has a good throwing distance, and has a lethal central radius, with an outer radius that stuns foes (though it's not as potent as the Stun Grenade). Though the lethal area is small, and the grenade is harmful to both friend and foe, it's excellent to lob at the feet of an enemy, which pretty much guarantees a kill. If the foe staggers out of the area, back up the grenade with small-arms fire to finish the job.

Recommended Add-Ons

Need to survive a grenade blast? Invest in the Nanofiber Vest (Front Line Specialization).

Need to shrug off the effects of a Flashbang or Smoke Grenade? Invest in a Tactical Mask.

Need to carry three grenades instead of two? Invest in a Grenade Belt

Specializations

Modern Combat 4: Zero Hour gives you the opportunity to play in one of five styles, or Specializations. It's worth checking out the additional Perks you acquire for reaching the various Ranks, by consulting the following table. Then focus on obtaining the set of Perks that best suits your style of play, or the Perk you really want as part of your repertoire.

SPECIALIZATION	RANK 10 PERK 1	RANK 10 PERK 2	RANK 20 PERK 1	RANK 20 PERK 2	RANK 30 PERK 1	RANK 30 PERK 2	RANK 40 PERK 1	RANK 40 PERK 2
Intervention	Sharp Shooting: Enemies you hit are stunned slightly.	Team Player: Your kill assists count toward the kill streak required to call in military support.	Grenade Belt: Spawn with two grenades instead of one.	Personal Jammer: Jams the radar of enemies in your vicinity.	Integrated Radar: Enemies on radar are highlighted on the battlefield.	Helmet: Reduces damage taken from headshots.	Paragon Striker: Increases movement speed while in iron sights.	Athleticism: Increases movement speed while sprinting.
Stealth	Opportunism: Deal more damage against incapacitated targets.	Sneak: Move and sprint silently.	Grenade Belt: Spawn with two grenades instead of one.	Decoy: Deploys a device that creates a diversion on enemy radars.	Readied Shot: Crouched shots further increase accuracy.	Tactical Mask: Protects you from cripple, blindness, and stun effects.	Paragon Senses: Receive an alert when an enemy aims in your direction.	Camouflage: Sensors and recon aircraft cannot detect you.
Front Line	Privilege: Health and movement speed are increased and your killer is highlighted as you respawn.	Military Tactician: Reduces by one the requirements needed to call military support.	Grenade Belt: Spawn with two grenades instead of one.	C4 Explosives: Deploys a device that explodes once triggered, dealing large-radius damage. Can be destroyed.	Martial Arts: Automatically perform a melee attack when an enemy is in range.	Gun Expert: Increases reload speed.	Paragon Juggernaut: Increases maximum health significantly.	Nanofiber Vest: Absorbs an amount of damage from each bullet received, except from AP rounds.
Support	Duty Calls: Increases zone-capture speed as well as movement while carrying flags.	Improved Strikes: Airstrikes and Bombers perform radar scans when you call them.	Grenade Belt: Spawn with two grenades instead of one.	Grenades Expert: Increases the area of effect of all grenades.	Sentry: Deploys a device that stuns and affects with EMP enemies who walk nearby.	Sensor: Deploys a sensor that identifies enemies with a red dot on the radar. Can be destroyed.	Paragon Saboteur: Shows enemy devices on radar and jams those near you.	One Last Thing: Drop a lesser Frag Grenade upon death.
Demolition	Resistance: Reduces damage taken from explosions and area damage.	Dedication: Deaths from explosions don't stop your kill streak for the purpose of calling support.	Grenade Belt: Spawn with two grenades instead of one.	Ammo Pack: Increases the quantity of ammo carried by 50% for all launchers.	Proximity Mine: Deploys an armed mine that explodes when a foe walks near. Can be destroyed.	Incendiary Device: Deploys a device that ignites a fire when triggered, causing damage over time. Can be destroyed.	Paragon Destroyer: Makes all attacks deal additional damage against objects and makes them explode.	Explosives Expert: Increases damage and range of explosions.

MONSTER LEGENDS

Developer	Social Point
Publisher	Social Point
Year Released	2013
Platforms	iOS, Android, Facebook
Type	RPG/collecting
Suggested Age	12+
Cost	Free to download

IN-GAME PURCHASES
Gems, chests, special event items

Game Overview

Monster Legends combines elements of monster collection and base construction, then adds an assortment of dungeons, special events, and mini-adventures to create a sprawling gaming experience.

There's a great deal to learn, but *Monster Legends* introduces elements gradually. It uses tutorials and videos to help explain each new element as you encounter it.

What You Need to Know

The game requires a considerable time investment in the long term but not a great deal of time on a daily basis. Your workers are limited in number (only two at first), and some projects require many hours—and sometimes days—to be completed.

There are other activities that don't require workers, such as breeding monsters, running dungeons, and fighting PvP battles, that you can do while waiting for work to get done, but they also have downtime built into them.

Becoming a Legend

Pandalf walks you through the basics of setting up your base and populating it with monsters. You learn about hatching eggs, feeding monsters to boost their levels, and building a farm to grow your own food.

While completing Pandalf's tasks, your overall **level** increases. Your level appears in the top right corner of the screen. Tap on it to see your progress and what will be unlocked at the next level.

Follow the Goals

Completing goals (the scroll icon under your level) sometimes awards points. The goals also provide guidance for steps to follow while you're learning the game.

Player Level

You earn **experience points** (in the form of big yellow **stars**) from multiple activities, such as clearing debris from your islands, growing food, fighting in dungeons or on islands, or engaging in PvP battles.

Gaining levels allows you to add more buildings and upgrade existing buildings. You also unlock new activities and pre-existing buildings floating around your base. They'll need repairs before you can use them, so be prepared to spend some gold and lose a worker for long stretches of time. To learn more about these new buildings and aspects of the game, watch the tutorial videos when they pop up.

Building a Better Base

Your base must grow to meet the needs of your monster collection; however, you must balance expansion with your player level, available space, and the resources needed for growth. To maximize the value of your farms, habitats, and other buildings, you must upgrade them periodically. You spend gold, food, and sometimes gems to upgrade buildings and habitats.

The **hatchery** and **breeding mountain** are available from the start. When you're able, upgrade the hatchery and build the **breeding tree.** These actions increase the rate at which your monster collection can grow.

Your monster collection is limited by **habitats.** Each habitat holds two monsters initially but can be upgraded to make room for more. Until you build a **temple** of the same element, monsters are limited to level 10. Upgrading temples allows monsters to achieve higher levels. Check your habitats regularly to claim the gold generated by the monsters residing on it.

Build **farms** to grow food, which is then given to your monsters to increase their levels. Upgrading farms opens up a greater variety of food. There are other buildings to add to your base, but habitats, temples, and farms are the start of everything.

Monster Basics

Monsters are the main attractions in *Monster Legends*. You buy them, breed them, level them up, attach runes and relics to them, and send them out to fight. There are hundreds of monsters, with more being added regularly. The game provides a great deal of information already, but understanding elements in combat is vital to your success.

Elements and Element-Based Attacks

Every monster is attuned to one or two **elements.** This is what allows them to live in certain habitats,and what makes them resistant or vulnerable to element-based attacks. The exception to this is **legendary** monsters. They treat all other elements the same.

Monsters are resistant to attacks that are of the same element as they are ("weak" will appear during an attack). For example, Rockillas take half damage from Earth-based attacks. Monsters of two elements are resistant to attacks based on either of their element types.

Monsters are vulnerable to another type of attack if they're a single-element type. That same Rockilla will take critical damage from Dark-based attacks ("strong" will appear during an attack). Monsters of two elements are vulnerable to two types of attacks, unless it is the same as one of their elements. That means an Earth/Dark monster would take half damage from Dark-based attacks, not 150 percent damage.

When you're selecting your team for battle, remember the following:

- Fire does critical damage to Nature.
- Nature does critical damage to Magic.
- Magic does critical damage to Metal.
- Metal does critical damage to Light.
- Light does critical damage to Dark.
- Dark does critical damage to Earth.
- Earth does critical damage to Thunder.
- Thunder does critical damage to Water.
- Water does critical damage to Fire.

In-App Purchases

The primary in-app purchase is gems. You can exchange gems for items, buildings, and resources. Other in-app purchases include treasure chests and items that are used during special events.

Join a Team

Being part of a team opens up Team Wars, which is another way to obtain monsters and runes. In addition, you can learn from experienced players, which are always the best resource in any game.

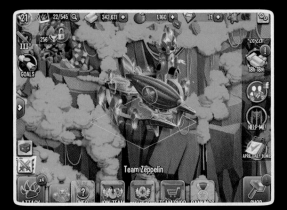

Don't Spend Ahead of Need

Gold is a valuable resource, so don't spend it until something is necessary. You don't need habitats for monsters you don't have yet. Hold off on building or upgrading temples until your monsters hit max level.

No Idle Time

Always keep your workers busy with building, upgrading, or cleaning up your base. In addition, it's possible to clean up secondary islands even before you buy them.

Don't let your hatchery sit empty; keep it working on eggs. When you upgrade to hatching two eggs at the same time, keep one side available for quick-hatching eggs.

There are limits on the number of **attack points** (for multiplayer) and the amount of **stamina** (for dungeons and islands) you can store. Once you hit that maximum number, get out there and fight.

Earning Gold

While you'll earn gold from activities like clearing debris and selling excess items, monsters, and eggs, most of your gold comes from leveled up monsters on upgraded habitats. Every monster and habitat contributes, but Nature habitats have the best gold storage, and **Pandaken,** which are available early on, have notable revenue stats. Add in **boost** buildings and watch your gold production skyrocket.

Earning Gems

Gems are the most versatile resource in Monster Legends, which makes them the most valuable. They're used to buy everything, including treasure chests, eggs, legendary monsters, and much more. In fact, you can even trade gems for time. Every project, whether it's building, breeding, or hatching, includes an Instant option and the number of gems required for the Instant option.

Unless your wallet is wide open, gems are difficult to obtain in the numbers required to keep everything moving along. You will get a few while clearing debris from your base, but most gems require work. The following are a few rules to follow to get the most of your gems.

No Waste!

The first rule of gem use in Monster Legends is this: Don't spend them to save time. Keep gems for the things that can't be obtained any other way, such as upgrading the hatchery and purchasing the breeding tree. Buy only **legendary** and (some!) **epic** monsters, since everything else is available through breeding or as rewards during special events. If possible, buy monsters and buildings when they're available through a special sale.

Make Friends

Click on the Social button in the lower left corner of the screen. Making friends can be its own reward, but it's also a great way to get gems. Don't forget to check the achievements related to friends!

Check Achievements

Achievements appear under Goals. Achievements award both stars and gems. Scroll through the list from time to time to see how close you are to completing an achievement, then work to get that achievement done.

Participate in Competitions and Special Events

Competitions and special events start and end often. Always check rules to see how you to earn the rewards. These competitions and special dungeons don't stick around for long, so watch the countdown timer so you don't miss out!

Get Out and Fight

After some battles, you get to spin a **roulette wheel**. Gems are typically among the items you can win with a spin. Gems may also be rewards for completing some dungeons, which change regularly.

MONUMENT VALLEY

Developer	**Ustwo Games**
Publisher	**Ustwo Games**
Year Released	**2014**
Platforms	**iOS, Android**
Type	**Puzzle**
ESRB Rating	**E**
Cost	**$3.99**

$

IN-GAME PURCHASES
Expansion (eight more levels)

Game Overview

Monument Valley is known as much for its visuals (it won an Apple Design Award the year it was released) as for its gameplay. You play as a princess named Ida, who is in search of forgiveness for something she doesn't remember clearly.

What You Need to Know

You guide Ida through 10 levels by moving the environment and changing perspectives to reveal new pathways. Geometry (impossible geometry, really) similar to the artwork of M.C. Escher is the main mechanic at work in Monument Valley.

If you want to replay a level after you complete it, spin the building with roman numerals left or right. There aren't any secrets that require return trips, but many players find the sights and sounds of the game soothing and enjoy return trips to familiar areas.

Impossible Only Until It Isn't

The goal on every level is to reach an **endpoint**, which is most often a square set in a starburst. To reach that endpoint, you must change the configuration of each level with buttons and gears while avoiding blackbirds.

As you work through each level in the game, you will need to suppress the parts of your brain that tell you that it's impossible for Ida to reach certain locations. To enter a doorway on the ceiling, for example, you must turn a crank to spin the entire level. Spinning the level may change a support column into a walking path, or after you change the way you view the level a wide gap becomes a solid path.

Doorways

Treat any darkened doorway as an objective, but not the final objective, on a map. Anytime you see one, assume you need to get Ida through it at some point. Doorways transport Ida to a new location, sometimes on the same map and sometimes to a new map on the same level.

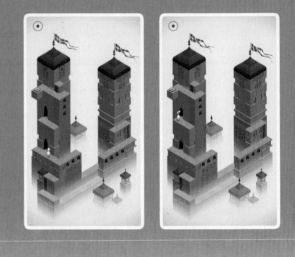

Characters

Ida

Ida is the main character you control during the adventure, and it is her story you are uncovering. Touch any point on the path to command Ida to move to it. If she doesn't move, then she has no path to that point.

Totem

Totem is introduced in Chapter VI: The Labyrinth as an ally that helps Ida complete her journey. You have limited control over the yellow totem. It can slide freely along clear paths and rest on buttons, but it can't use stairs.

Blackbirds

Blackbirds are more nuisance than threat. They don't appear on every level, and only the ones in motion will block your path. Blackbirds follow set patterns that you can alter if you move the path from their feet. A few blackbirds become unwitting accomplices when Ida needs help with buttons.

Interactive Environment

Buttons

To help them stand out, multicolored buttons are raised higher than the path around them. There are two types of buttons: those that are pressed once, and those that will spring up if weight isn't kept on them. For the second type of button, any weight left on it will do the trick—it could be Ida, Totem, or a blackbird.

Gears & Pulls

Gears are the most obvious way for you to manipulate the environment. Touch them with your finger and spin them. If turning a gear in one direction doesn't help, turn it the opposite way. Gears become unusable while Ida stands on the path they manipulate. Pulls are simple to use. When you see one, put your finger on it and slide it in or out to grow or shrink the path.

Raised Circles

Raised circles indicate pieces of the environment you can manipulate directly. Touch the circles and slide your finger in different directions to see what changes are made. In some cases, what you change is the side of the level you're viewing. Just as with gears, make the changes slowly and move the circles in multiple directions.

In-App Purchases

You can buy an expansion called Forgotten Shores, *which includes an additional eight levels, for $1.99.*

Change the Environment Slowly

Anytime you're changing the environment, do it slowly. Some alterations are so deceptively simple that you'll miss them if you change things too quickly. For example, two broken paths come together briefly to make a whole one, or a doorway is visible (barely) only while a column rises or sinks.

Changing Floors

Ida doesn't jump, fly, or climb, meaning she can't change floors on her own. She needs steps, a ladder, or columns that carry her up and down. If you don't see any of those, then use any visible gears, pulls, or raised circles to change the lay of the land.

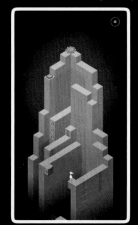
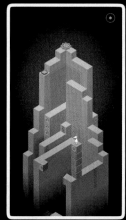

If She Won't Go

If Ida refuses to go to a spot you touched, she has no way to reach it. You must change the environment around her to create a clear path.

Sticky Shoes

Ida always remains attached to the ground, even when that ground is spun under her feet or she's walking upside down. She even sticks to the ground when she walks up a curved path that changes her orientation to the ground.

Work Backward if You're Stuck

If you're not sure what to do next, start with your objective and work backward from it to see where Ida needs to go next. If, for example, there's a gap in the path but no button or raised circles that could be used to fill it in, then you know that you need to change the view of the level until the gap vanishes.

NEKO ATSUME: KITTY COLLECTOR

Developer	Hit-Point
Publisher	Hit-Point
Year Released	2014
Platforms	Android, iOS
Type	Idle / Cat Collecting
Suggested Age	6+
Cost	Free to download

$ IN-GAME PURCHASES
Fish and Gold Fish
(in-game currency)

Game Overview

If you've ever dreamed about your home being the hot spot for neighborhood cats, *Neko Atsume* is the perfect game for you. Transform your backyard into a haven for cats with food, toys, beds, and random objects that shouldn't appeal to cats at all but, for inexplicable cat reasons, draw them in droves.

Neko Atsume is a relaxed gaming experience and one that doesn't demand constant attention (in fact, the cats won't appear until you shut down or minimize the game). Cats come and go on their own, and the gifts they leave behind will wait for you to return to the game. Every cat and goody is available immediately, but you need patience and persistence to uncover everything the game has to offer.

What You Need to Know

After you complete the tutorial, the gameplay follows a simple cycle: Buy goodies from the shop, place goodies in your yard, wait for cats to visit, then collect the fishy gifts (in-game currency) left behind by the cats after they depart your domicile. Over 60 cats may grace you with their presence. The majority are lured by just food in the dish and a goody in the yard. Others are more finicky and demand either premium food or specific goodies.

Kitty Activity

The menu (paw print in the top left) is where you do most of your work. Tap the button to bring up the following options: Cats, Shop, Goodies, Camera, Yard, Gifts, Settings, News, Other.

Cats

The Cats button brings up three options: Catbook, Album, Mementos.

Catbook

The Catbook tracks the cats of Neko Atsume. Question marks mean the cat hasn't visited your yard. A cat's name on display with a face on a solid background means the cat has visited your yard but does not have a Best Shot selected in its album. You can change a cat's name in its Catbook entry. Touch the nameplate at the top of the entry, then enter a new name.

Touch on a cat's entry to learn its personality and power level (neither impacts gameplay), as well as the number of visits to your yard and the top three goodies used during its visits. Take note of the goodies if you'd like to encourage a specific cat to visit again.

Album

Your Album is the collection of pictures taken with the Camera. You begin with an empty album (with 72 free slots) that can be used to store any photo you take. New albums (with 18 free slots) appear each time you photograph a new cat. To set a cat's BEST SHOT, tap twice on a photograph in that cat's album. If you fill an album, you can add additional pages for a price.

Mementos

Mementos are gifts from the cats that visit. Each cat offers a unique memento, but there's no set way to earn them. Just keep enticing cats to visit your yard and they'll leave it for you. Eventually

Shop

The cats that visit your yard leave behind fishy gifts that are spent in the game's shop. Select Shop in the menu to exchange fish and gold fish, as well as to purchase food, goodies, and even a yard expansion. To access the items purchased in the shop, open up the menu again and touch Goodies.

With the exception of food, goodies only need to be purchased once. After they're purchased, you're free to swap goodies in and out of your yard.

Goodies with an S in a blue box are small and take up a single space in your yard. An L in a red box means the goody is large and takes up two spaces, which limits where the goody can be placed.

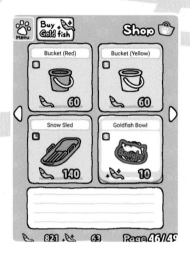

Camera

The camera has two options, located at the top of the screen. The default option is to take a picture of an area of the screen and save it to an album. The second option allows you to save a snapshot of the game to your device (these shots won't appear in an album).

You aren't required to use the camera at any point, but it's the only way to get custom pictures of the cats as they visit your yard.

Goodies

The Goodies option brings up a list of the items you've already purchased. Categories of goodies include food, balls, boxes, beds (an aluminum bowl appears in the bed category because…cats), furniture, tunnels, and toys. Use this option to place them in your yard. Your yard has five distinct locations, but only one can accommodate a large goody.

Yard

This button returns you to the yard view. There are five goody spots total, but remember that large goodies take up two spots.

In the yard view, touching a cat takes you directly to its Catbook entry. Touch a food bowl to bring up a refill screen. The status bar under the food shows how much food remains in the bowl.

Food

Food appears under the Goodies menu but has a dedicated spot in your yard. Food is the only item that has a shelf life in your yard (it lasts indefinitely before you place it). Thrifty Bitz (the free food) remains in the bowl for eight hours. Frisky Bitz (the only food purchased with Fish) lasts six hours. The four types of food bought with gold fish all last three hours. You can save on food by buying in bulk.

Daily Password

Every day that you enter the daily password, you are rewarded with fish or gold fish and earn a stamp on a card. Five stamps fill a card, and you get a can of Ritzy Bitz. Don't worry if you forget about the password. There's no penalty if you don't get a stamp every day.

Gifts

To claim the fish left behind by visitors, you can either select Gifts in the menu window or touch the Gifts Await prompt when it appears near the bottom of he screen.

News

There are web links under News, but the main attraction is the daily password, which is entered under the Other menu. A new password appears at the same time each day.

Other

The two initial options under Other are Help (an in-game manual) and Connect. Select Connect to input the daily password, submit feedback, and view the official game FAQs (they open in a browser). The Remodel option appears after you purchase the yard expansion.

Expand Your Yard

Since more space means more cats can visit, save Gold Fish until you have enough to buy the Yard Expansion in the Shop. Not only do you double your available space, but you also unlock the Remodel feature, which changes the look of your Yard. Remodels don't come cheap, meaning they're a purchase you can put off for a while.

More Cats in Less Space

Another way to expand cat population is to buy Goodies that allow more than one cat to use it at the same time. A few Small goodies (such as cubes), have room for two cats. Large goodies all fit multiple cats. The Cat Metropolis leads the pack with room for six cats.

When Tubbs Appears, Let Him Be

Tubbs appears only next to a freshly emptied food bowl, looking extremely pleased with himself. Don't do anything with the food bowl until he leaves on his own. The longer he sticks around, the more Fish he leaves for you.

Keep Updating Goodies and Food

If you continue to see the same cats in your yard, change the goodies and food. Remember that the expensive food expires in three hours, so fill the bowl with Thrifty or Frisky Bitz when you'll be unable to check the game for longer periods of time.

Rare Cats

Rare cats appear only when specific goodies are placed in your yard, and higher quality food is available. Use the following table to get a visit from everyone.

CAT	GOODIES
Bengal Jack	Luxury Treasure-Box
Billy the Kitten	Cowboy Hat
Bob the Cat	Cat Metropolis
Chairman Meow	Sunken Fireplace, Earthenware Pot
Conductor Whiskers	Twisty Rail, Cardboard Choo-Choo
Frosty	Any pillow (Snowy works best), Cooling Pads (Aluminum, Large, Marble, Thick)
Guy Furry	Heating Stove, Glass Vase
Hermeowne	Egg Bed (Nightview)
Jeeves	Fairy-Tale Parasol, Tower of Treats
Joe DiMeowgio	Baseball
Kathmandu	Temari Ball, Lacquered Bowl
Lady Meow-Meow	Luxurious Hammock
Mr. Meowgi	Scratching Log, Sakura Pillow
Ms. Fortune	Cardboard House
Ramses the Great	Tent (Pyramid)
Saint Purrtrick	Silk Crepe Pillow, Kotatsu
Sapphire	Fairy-Tale Parasol, Tower of Treats
Sassy Fran	Cardboard Cafe
Senor Don Gato	Mister Mouse
Tubbs	Food bowl with anything that isn't Thrifty Bitz
Whiteshadow	Remodel your yard
Xerxes IX	Royal Bed, Zanzibar Cushion

Wallpapers

As you meet certain conditions (typically obtaining a memento, or cats visiting your yard a number of times), Wallpapers become available in the Shop. These Wallpapers are saved to your mobile device but do not affect Neko Atsume's gameplay.

Obtaining the following mementos unlocks wallpapers: Bengal Jack, Frosty, Ms. Fortune, Sassy Fran, Socks (also requires 40 visits from Ginger, Marshmallow, Spooky, and Spud), Snowball, and Speckles.

After you purchase all the goodies on 21 pages of the shop, the 15th visit by each of the following cats unlocks wallpapers (three total wallpapers): Ginger, Patches, Peaches.

Repeat visits from the same cats unlock wallpapers:

◆ 10 each from Lexy, Pepper, Pickles, Misty, Bolt, Sunny, Peaches, Bandit, Smokey, Princess, Pumpkin, Tabitha, Rascal, Shadow, Ginger, Socks, Spots, and Mack (and purchase all buckets, pots, and the Planter)

◆ 25 from Ms. Fortune (Gozer and Patches must be in your Catbook)

◆ 25 from Sassy Fran (Mack and Shadow must be in your Catbook)

◆ 40 each from Snowball, Gabriel, Sunny, Pickles, Fred, and Ginger

◆ 50 each from Socks, Pepper, Gabriel, and Smokey

◆ 50 each from Fred, Lexy, Marshmallow, Smokey, and Sunny

◆ 100 each from Callie and Sunny (and purchase Goldfish Bowl)

◆ 100 from Snowball (Pumpkin must be in your Catbook)

NEO SCAVENGER

Developer	Blue Bottle Games
Publisher	Blue Bottle Games
Year Released	2014
Platforms	iOS, Android, Steam, Windows, Linux
Type	Survival
ESRB Rating	M
Cost	Free to download (demo)

IN-GAME PURCHASES
Full version ($9.99 mobile, $14.99 Steam)

Game Overview

In a not-too-distant future, warfare and supernatural forces have nearly destroyed humankind. Small settlements struggle to establish themselves while large cities survive by militarizing. And yet, the areas with no living humans might be the most dangerous of all. It's safe to say that if NEO Scavenger included unlimited hair spray, it would be eerily similar to every post-apocalyptic movie filmed in the 1980s.

What You Need to Know

NEO Scavenger is not a forgiving game. You begin with almost nothing and your first action is surviving an encounter against a dangerous creature. The full version of the game allows you to save your progress, but an in-game death deletes the save. Once you learn how to survive the first few nights, your reward is a challenging sandbox-style game with elements of mystery, survival horror, and text-based nostalgia.

At Least It Comes with a Manual

While there will be a great deal of trial and error (and death) while you learn how to survive the world of *NEO Scavenger*, the game doesn't leave you totally in the dark. The **Help screen** includes a PDF manual that covers the commands available to you. If you're playing on mobile, ignore the Controls section in the manual and use what's on the Help screen.

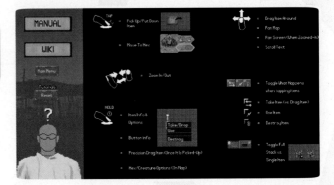

Abilities and Flaws

The first action you take in each game of *NEO Scavenger* is to select abilities and flaws. **Abilities** increase the number of options you have when interacting with the world and its inhabitants. **Flaws** increase the difficulty of the game. Touch and hold any ability or flaw for a brief description.

The dots in the upper right indicate the value of the ability or flaw. You start off with 15 points you can spend on abilities, but choosing flaws adds points to your abilities pool. Some flaws and abilities are incompatible (e.g., Eagle Eye and Myopia), meaning you can't choose both.

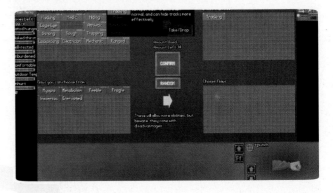

Increased Difficulty

You aren't required to select any abilities. If you want an even more challenging NEO Scavenger experience, start the game with no abilities.

Navigating the World

NEO Scavenger is essentially a text adventure with still images. To get around the world, you need to be familiar with the various screens used by the game.

The left edge remains the same on every screen. The **main menu button** appears at the top, directly above the number of actions you can take, your current status, and the outdoor temperature. Yes, even the temperature is out to kill you, so you must find clothing before the onset of hypothermia.

Time of Day

Each day is divided into six segments: dawn, morning, day, evening, dusk, and night. At a time of day with less light, the number of hexagons you can see on the map decreases. If you lack a source of light at night, you're limited to a single action point.

Map Screens

The world is a series of connected hexagons. The icons on a hexagon tell you what you might find there. A few examples are a **wooden chest** (items on the ground), a **magnifying glass** (locations you can scavenge), and **red footprints** (someone or something passed through the area).

Moving between hexagons typically consumes one of your action points. However, if you're suffering from penalties, or if the terrain is rugged or forested, moving may consume more than one point.

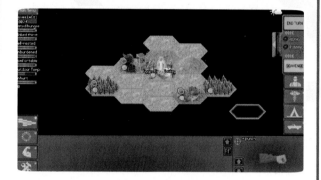

Encounters Screen

The Encounters screen comes up when you meet another person or creature. Tap your choice from the **Options for This Encounter** box to make it appear in the **Put Chosen Option Here** box. Check the summary text above the confirm button before confirming your action. The text box on the bottom of the screen updates you on the action and any changes to your status. You must resolve or escape the encounter to return to another menu screen.

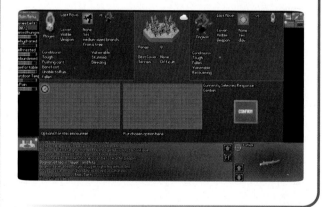

Items and Vehicle Screens

When you find items on the ground, use the **Items screen** to pick them up. You can carry items in your hands and in any pouches or pockets you have. Finding a **vehicle** allows you to store extra items. Vehicles are great until you get caught in a fight. Some cause you to lose the ability to run, and they also remove a few combat options.

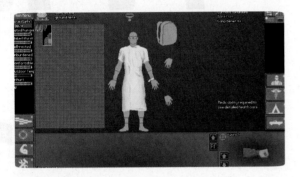

Player Conditions Screen

The Player Conditions screen shows **damage taken**. If you have medical items in your inventory, you can use them here. The **Medic** ability allows you to see three additional status bars on this screen: Blood Supply, Immune System, and Pain Tolerance.

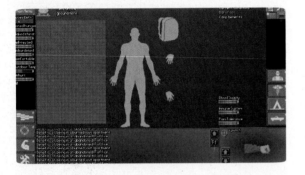

Camp Screen

Use the Camp screen to find a good place to **rest** in your current location. Not all campsites are equal, so compare the stats of each available site before you settle on one of them.

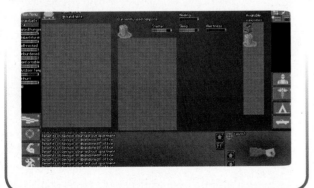

Crafting Screen

You start out with a few recipes already known, including ways to make fire. Check scraps of paper you pick up for new recipes. You can also learn from experimenting on your own. Your choice of abilities also affects what you can craft.

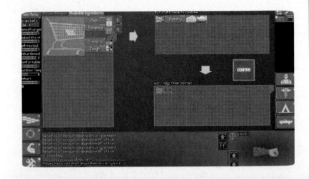

In-App Purchases

If you started with the free demo, you can purchase the full version of the game. The full version ($9.99 mobile, $14.99 Steam) unlocks all content, expands the game's map, and allows you to save your progress.

Basic Needs First

The necessities in *NEO Scavenger* are food, drink, and warmth. When you're first starting out, you can't be picky about what you wear. If it's clothing that covers a part of your body, put it on. For food and drink, you can be more selective. You begin sated, and not all food and drinks are safe. Carry whatever you find but wait until you can boil the water to consume it, unless you have no other choice.

Abilities & Flaws

All abilities have benefits, but for your early games, consider the following choices: Trapping, Botany, Strong, Melee or Ranged, Hiding, Athletic. Trapping is great because allows you to make fire without a lighter, as well as to trap and skin animals for meat. Botany provides additional food from scavenging and ensures the food is safe. Pair Strong with Melee or Ranged (or both), since combat will happen eventually. If you're not the confrontational type, choose Hiding or Athletic, since both expand your options to avoid conflict.

If you want to choose flaws so you can add abilities, go with Insomniac, Metabolism, and Myopia. Each of these flaws can be managed provided you pay close attention to your status indicators.

Live First, Fight Later

You win survival games by surviving. That means avoiding fights when possible, unless you know there's no other choice or that you will benefit greatly from winning a fight. If you must fight, don't be a good sport about it. Take down your enemy quickly to minimize the chance of injury to you. If you can spring an ambush, that's even better.

If you do get into a fight, avoiding hits is your number one concern. Don't attack until your opponent is vulnerable. Your chances of scoring a hit aren't good, so you need all the advantages you can get. Don't forget that you can change weapons—but only before the actual fighting begins.

Scavenging

Scavenging can be a life-saver, but it can also be a life-ender if you're not careful. Since scavenging can draw unwanted attention, never use your final action before the end of a turn to scavenge. You may need the points for an escape attempt.

When you are given the option to scavenge a structure, carefully check its description. You don't want to be caught inside a building that's about to collapse. Whatever might have been inside it isn't worth the injuries you may suffer.

When you're starting out and have limited space for carrying your goods, put plastic bags into your hands. Since they're compact when not in use and fall apart quickly, keep all the bags that you find until you obtain a proper backpack.

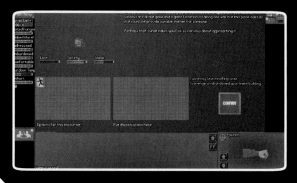

Don't Craft with Bad Material

Before you start crafting an item, go through the materials it requires and choose the **highest quality ingredients** available. You must split the stacks to view individual items, but you don't want waste your time making something that starts out almost broken due to one bad ingredient.

Crafting works in reverse as well. A number of items can be **deconstructed**, allowing you to reclaim the ingredients that make up the item. Expect some degradation of quality if the item had been used before being deconstructed.

N.O.V.A. LEGACY

Developer	**Gameloft**
Publisher	**Gameloft**
Year Released	**2017**
Platforms	**Android, iOS**
Type	**First-person shooter**
ESRB Rating	**T**
Cost	**Free to download**

 IN-GAME PURCHASES
Coins and trilithium

Game Overview

N.O.V.A. Legacy is a sci-fi, first-person shooter that offers a multiplayer and solo experience. Upgrade your weapon arsenal and defense to help you defeat your enemies in various game modes, or enjoy a player versus player matchup in multiplayer arenas to rise in the leaderboards.

In-App Purchases

You can upgrade and get more items faster if you buy coins or trilithium.

What You Need to Know

You must collect cards from packs to upgrade your items' effectiveness. Packs can be bought with trilithium, earned by watching ads, or earned through normal gameplay. You can use coins to buy the upgrade once you have enough cards of the same item.

Single Player and Multiplayer

Melee

In no circumstance should you ever engage in a melee, whether single player or multiplayer. In the time that it takes for you to recover from the melee, your enemy has time to shoot you. Hand-to-hand combat does little damage and you shouldn't have to do it; your pistol has unlimited ammo.

Health Regeneration

You do not regenerate health unless you are out of combat.

Headshots

As in most games, headshots do more damage. If you're comfortable dragging away from the aim assist on your phone, go for it. However, in the heat of a firefight in multiplayer, while getting more damage in faster is always good; if you take too much time breaking out of the aim assist, it may cost you.

Movement Speed

You can move in all directions, but you move significantly faster when facing forward.

Ammo Boxes

Keep an eye out for ammo boxes. They're the little boxes with a blue-green aura. The ammo boxes refill ammo. In multiplayer, these boxes are on a timer and can be picked up by all players, so be on the lookout to get to them first. Single player is more generous when it comes to the number of ammo boxes that appear.

Single Player

Challenges
Be sure to complete challenges for extra coins.

Assault Rifles
In single player, the assault rifle is a fine choice of weapon. With assault rifles you don't need to get so close to the enemy and you can just hold down the trigger and let the game's aim assist do the rest.

Shotguns
The shotgun is also a great weapon choice. There are very few situations where a shotgun isn't a good choice in this game.

Direction Assist
If you are lost, don't forget about the arrow below your health bar. The game is linear, but if you are outside the ship and can't find the next door to pass through to regain oxygen, the directional arrow is the ticket to your survival.

Invader Evasion
Invader enemies have a green laser attack. The lasers spread out quickly, but the space between the lasers is narrow. When facing this attack, take cover behind something or be quick to maneuver between two lasers.

Smashers
Smashers are enemies that use only melee attacks. The only exception is that they can throw their melee weapon (only once). Attack from long range and don't melee with them. Strafe to avoid the thrown weapon. The smasher in the picture is from a shadow mission.

Shadow Missions
Upon completion, shadow missions provide you with an enhanced pack. Play shadow missions as soon as they become available, because a timer counts down, and if it runs out you miss the opportunity to play the mission.

Green Toxic Waste Warning
Do not stand in the green toxic waste—it'll damage you over time.

Multiplayer

Shotguns
The shotgun is one of the better weapons to use in multiplayer. To get the most out of it, you need to barrel stuff enemies or you won't do a whole lot of damage per shot. If you're just inches from the enemy, one shot does a lot of damage.

Yellow Lifts
Yellow lifts are a great way of transportation, whether you are chasing an enemy or running away so you can heal.

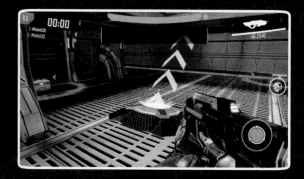

Loadout
A good loadout would be a sniper rifle, a fast-firing shotgun like the ECHO, and a heavy-hitting sidearm. Snipers are for long range, the sidearm is for close to medium, and the shotgun is for massive damage at close range. Your sidearm choice can be interchangeable, and of course you are free to use whatever you please, but this combination is an effective choice.

PLAGUE, INC.

Developer	Ndemic Creations
Publisher	Ndemic Creations/Miniclip
Year Released	2012
Platforms	iOS, Android
Type	Strategy/Simulation
ESRB Rating	E 10+
Cost	Free to download (with ads)

$ IN-GAME PURCHASES

Remove ads, buy scenarios, and unlock genes, bonuses, and new plague types

Game Overview

Humanity faces an epidemic of historic proportions. Countries are closing airports and seaports while working together on a cure. Your role is to ensure that doesn't happen, because the plague killing all humankind is your creation.

What You Need to Know

You begin the game with a modest goal: the elimination of every human alive on the planet. For each attempt, your primary tool is a plague that begins as a simple **bacteria, virus, fungus, parasite, prion, nano-virus,** or **bio-weapon.** As your plague infects more of the world's population, you gain DNA points that are spent to make your plague more virulent.

The world's population doesn't wait to die. As soon as your plague is considered a threat, researchers around the globe begin work on a cure. The game becomes a race between human research and evolving your plague to prevent the discovery and implementation of a cure.

Building a Better Superbug

Your first action is to select a type of plague. Without any in-app purchases, **bacteria** is your only option until you win a game. After selecting a difficulty level, name your plague and choose a modification for its genetic code.

Genetic Codes

You won't see the option to Modify Genetic Code until you either win a game or make an in-app purchase. There are five categories of genes, but only one category can be active per game. The special plagues (necroa, simian flu, and shadow plague) use genes specific to each.

With the preliminaries out of the way, the game shifts to a world map and you're prompted to choose a country. Countries can be rural or suburban, rich or poor; are arid or humid; and have a hot, cold, or mild climate. Note whether the country has seaport or airport icons, or both. Keep all these factors in mind when choosing where to start. They all have an impact on the choices you make while evolving your plague.

With all that settled, you're stuck waiting for your first DNA points before you can do more than read the Global News headlines. Pop the orange and red bubbles that appear to add to your DNA point total. DNA points are the currency you spend to evolve your plague. Pop any blue research bubbles that appear as well. They won't appear until the world starts to work on a cure. Once it does, watch for a blue jet flying between countries to see where the next bubble will appear.

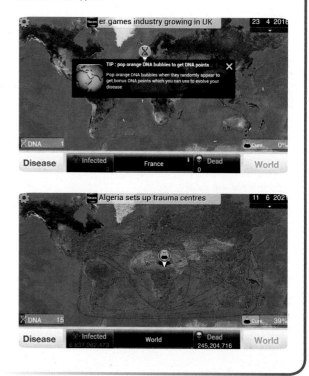

World Menu

Touch World in the lower right corner of the screen to learn more about the countries of the world, the progress on a cure, and data presented in charts and graphs. When something pops up on the Global News headlines, you can often find more information on these screens. Some headlines are purely for entertainment.

The **Infection Spread Summary** page is a good one to reference often. If you're struggling to spread your plague, review the **Healthy Countries** column. If the countries share a common trait, adjust your transmission traits (in the Disease menu) accordingly.

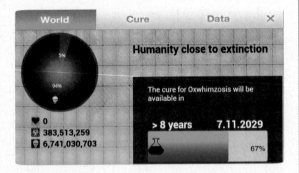

Disease Menu

Most of your work takes place in the Disease menu. The DNA points accumulated from the spread of your plague are spent here. Select the **Transmission** menu to expand the number of ways to spread your plague and how likely it is to mutate on its own.

The **Symptoms** menu choices start out cheap, which is fortunate considering how many there are. The pricier symptoms do double duty by being lethal to the afflicted and spreading the disease in often disgusting ways.

The **Abilities** menu is where you customize your plague's strengths. Generally, you spend a few early DNA points here to help your plague spread, then return to spend more points to slow the discovery of a cure.

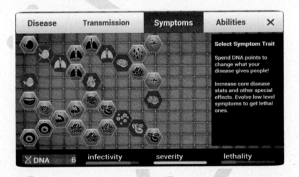

In-App Purchases

Upgrading to the full version of Plague, Inc. adds the ability to set the time to fast forward, unlocks more genes through gameplay, and removes ads. You can also purchase scenarios, genes, mutations, and bonuses, some of which can also be unlocked through gameplay.

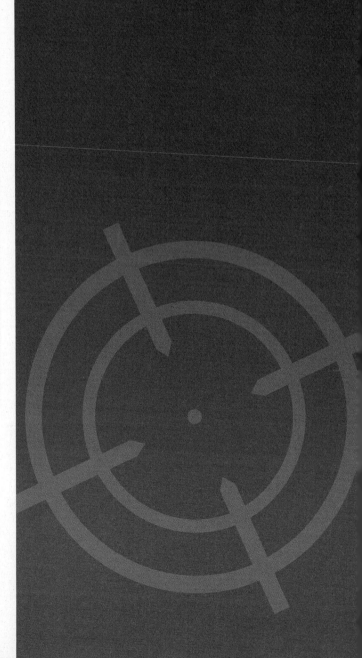

Disperse First, Lethal Later

In the early stages of each game, focus on spreading your plague before it becomes deadly. Select cold/heat resistance abilities and early transmission options based on your starting country. Infect as many people as possible before the first fatality, since that event often kick-starts the search for the cure. If necessary, devolve random mutations that may lead to a premature death.

Watch the News

In addition to puff pieces, the Global News headlines provide hints at future events and cues for you to check the World and Disease menus. Weather forecasts and predictions of animal behavior should be factors in your transmission selections.

When your plague is starting to gain traction, the News reports on proposed countermeasures and where society is starting to break down. Choose abilities that keep your plague virulent and incurable.

Island Countries

Island countries (e.g., Greenland, Madagascar) with limited contact with other countries are often the cause of lost games. If any island continually refuses to become infected, check for countries that have contact with it and start your plague there.

The Plagues

Bacteria

Bacteria is the plague type least likely to spontaneously evolve, meaning it's easier to keep control of it as it spreads around the world. Bacteria's unique ability, bacterial resistance, provides general environmental protection, but it's not as effective against hot and cold as heat resistance and cold resistance. If you're struggling in an extreme environment and have already maxed out resistance to either heat or cold, that's when you put points into bacterial resistance.

Virus

Virus stands apart from other plague types because of how it mutates rapidly and costs DNA points to devolve. Investigate every pop-up window about spontaneous changes in your virus, especially in the earliest stages of games. Viral instability enhances the number of mutations, so avoid putting points here until work begins on a cure. If you're looking to set speed records for victory, start with a virus.

Fungus

A fungus is the most difficult plague to spread, which makes investing in its unique abilities (spore burst, spore eruption, and spore hardening) an integral part of every fungus game. The evolution gene option patho-stasis seems tailor-made for fungus, but you must be on top of devolving potentially lethal symptoms if you choose it.

Parasite

A parasite plague likewise leans on its unique ability, symbiosis. Symbiosis negatively affects your severity score, allowing the safe addition of infective symptoms in the early stages of your game. A parasite won't evolve on its own often, but devolve anything that's potentially lethal until you're set up to start with the killing.

Prion

Prion's unique ability, neural atrophy, impairs neural activity in humans and increases the time before research into a cure will begin. Early DNA points should go entirely to ways to increase transmission, which includes transmission options and mild symptoms like coughing and sweating. Devolve spontaneous mutations until your prion reaches every country. At that point, dump your built-up DNA points into fatal symptoms.

Nano-Virus

A nano-virus plague starts with a big disadvantage: The cure (actually a computer code to deactivate it) is being worked on as soon as you select patient zero. You should have a number of genetic code options at this point. Two good choices are genetic mimic to slow the cure and metabolic jump to get more DNA from popped bubbles. Spend early DNA points on anything that slows discovery of the cure and boosts transmission of the plague. Nano-virus has two special ability trees, which are both focused on slowing the development and implementation of the shutdown code. Invest in both early. Build up DNA points while the nano-virus spreads, then spend heavily in a rush to make it lethal.

Bio-Weapon

A bio-weapon gradually increases its lethality without external input, which explains why its unique abilities are all related to lowering its lethality. Nucleic acid neutralization resets lethality to zero, so save sufficient DNA points in case of emergency. Check the lethality level in the Disease menu often; you won't be prompted by the game! Keep your bio-weapon in check and spend just enough DNA points to get it spread around the world. Once the world is infected, get the unlock annihilate gene. It's vital that the plague is everywhere before you make this purchase. It's so effective, it may kill the infected before they can reach a country that's still healthy.

PLANESCAPE: TORMENT

Developer	Beamdog
Publisher	Beamdog
Year Released	2017
Platforms	iOS, Android, Steam, Windows, Linux
Type	RPG
Suggested Age	T
Cost	$9.99 mobile, $19.99 Steam

IN-GAME PURCHASES
None

Game Overview

Set in the Planescape fantasy setting from Dungeons & Dragons, *Planescape: Torment* follows the story of **The Nameless One**, who has awoken in a mortuary in the city of Sigil with no memories of his past life. The Nameless One sets out from Sigil, determined to uncover his past. Along the way, he gains abilities and companions that help him journey through the planes of existence.

What You Need to Know

When *Planescape: Torment* was released in 1999, it wasn't a huge commercial success; however, its dedicated fans, along with many contemporary critics, hailed it as the best computer RPG of the year. The **enhanced edition** left the original game intact and added modern improvements, such as a 4K interface, tab highlighting, and area zooming.

Guiding a Nameless Search

Your first action in the game is generating your character. Each stat (Strength, Wisdom, Constitution, Charisma, Dexterity, and Intelligence) begins with a value of 9. You are given 21 additional character points to boost those stats. Attributes are capped at 18 at creation but can exceed that number during the adventure.

The Nameless One begins as a **fighter** (values Strength) but can switch between fighter, **mage** (values Intellect), and **thief** (values Dexterity) during the adventure by speaking to an appropriate NPC. Some of your initial stat allocation should be made with your desired class in mind.

Alignment

The Nameless One's alignment is fluid. He begins as true neutral, but the choices you make will push him toward lawful or chaotic, good or evil. The game tracks his alignment on the Statistics screen.

An Overview of Stats

Because of its overall value, Wisdom stands alone at the top of the stat heap. Strength, Dexterity, and Intellect are tied to class bonuses and are considered primary stats. Constitution and Charisma are secondary stats, not because they're less important but because they don't offer class bonuses.

Wisdom

Maximizing your Wisdom score from the start of the game pays for itself. You see better dialogue options, have different ways to solve problems, and earn additional experience points.

Strength

Strength determines your ability to hit targets in combat and the amount of damage you inflict on a successful hit. High Strength opens up threatening dialogue choices, allows you to carry more in your inventory, and gives you a chance to break open locked objects.

Dexterity

Dexterity is a combination of speed, nimbleness, and hand-eye coordination. It determines your ability to avoid enemy attacks, pick locks, pick pockets, and catch thieves trying to steal from you.

Intelligence

A high Intelligence stat influences potential dialogue with NPCs and boosts your Lore rating, which allows you to learn the properties of unidentified items.

Constitution

If you're looking for a stat to skimp on so you can boost Wisdom, look elsewhere. Constitution is your health. A high Constitution boosts the HP earned with every new level. Constitution also influences the rate of health regeneration.

Charisma

More than simply a measure of good looks, Charisma also determines charm and persuasiveness. A good Charisma stat improves interactions with NPCs, who can't help being taken in by The Nameless One, despite his scarred and pale body.

Controls

The controls in *Planescape: Torment* are simple. Touch (if you're playing with a mouse, substitute "click" for each instance of "touch") a spot on the screen and the characters under your control move to it. Touch objects to inspect them—although not all objects can be inspected. Touch other characters to interact with them, which always begins with dialogue options. If it comes to a fight, keep in mind that combat is limited. Melee attacks are automated and spellcasting isn't much more complicated.

In-Game Assistance

If you're having trouble remembering the controls of the game or the location of a UI button, touch the question mark at the bottom of the screen. The How to Play screen that pops up has the information you need.

TIPS

More Talk, Less Fight

The critical acclaim for *Planescape: Torment* comes predominantly from the storyline and dialogue. Combat is rarely necessary and can be avoided almost every time. To get the most of the game, speak with every NPC you meet and explore the dialogue options thoroughly. You also get more experience from talking and completing quests than from killing.

Hit Point Insurance

The amount of HP you get from early levels is random. If you want to ensure that you get the max HP (or avoid getting the minimum HP), save before leveling up and be prepared to reload from that save.

Inked Up

When you find Fell's Tattoo Parlor in The Hive area of Sigil, memorize its location. This is the only location that provides the tattoos that boost stats. Available tattoos change often. Visit it after major events, such as adding new characters to the party, completing major quests, or joining a faction.

Character Upgrades

There are opportunities to earn stat upgrades throughout the planes. Some come from the use of magical items, while others come from completing tasks or simple conversations, which is why it's vital for you to speak with every NPC, including party members. Your first opportunity for an upgrade comes in the opening moments of the game. When you meet Ei-Vene in the mortuary, act like a zombie and your reward is +1 HP.

Building Your Party

The Nameless One won't be alone during his adventure. You can add five total NPCs to your party, from seven possible candidates. Morte is with The Nameless One from the start, and Annah joins automatically during the adventure. The others require some searching, some conversation, and some luck.

When you encounter Dak'kon, Fall-from-Grace, Nordom, and Vhailor, always save before speaking with them! They do not join automatically, so you must make the proper choices in conversation. After each character joins the party, and every time something of significance happens, talk to them until you exhaust all possible conversation choices.

CHARACTER	CLASS	HOW TO RECRUIT
Annah	Fighter/Thief	Joins automatically mid-game.
Dak'kon	Fighter/Mage	Speak with him at the Smoldering Corpse Bar.
Fall-from-Grace	Priest	Speak with her at her brothel in the Clerk Ward of Sigil. High Intellect and Charisma needed.
Ignus	Mage	Get the Decanter of Endless Water, then speak with Nemelle.
Morte	Fighter	Joins automatically when the game begins.
Nordom	Fighter	Buy the Metallic Cube from the Curiosity Shoppe. Learn how to use it as a portal into the Modron Maze.
Vhailor	Fighter	Speak with him in Curst Prison.

REIGNS

Developer	Nerial
Publisher	Devolver Digital
Year Released	2016
Platforms	iOS, Android, Steam
Type	Card game/King simulator
Suggested Age	12+
Cost	$2.99

$ IN-GAME PURCHASES
None

Game Overview

As monarch of a fictional medieval kingdom, you must respond to the events brought before you by your advisors. Each decision impacts the four pillars of your kingdom (the church, the people, the military, and the treasury) in different ways. As soon as one of the four pillars becomes too powerful or too neglected, your reign ends and a new reign begins.

Other Exits

There are ways to lose the throne (typically from death on a hunt or a duel) that have nothing to do with the four pillars. You can also choose to escape the throne during a long stretch of boring prosperity after signing a 10-year peace treaty.

What You Need to Know

Your goal is to reign for as many years as possible. Once your reign ends you continue to rule; however, it's as the heir of the previous king.

During these many reigns, your choices will complete **royal deeds** (which grant a title), as well as unlock new characters and decision cards. There are even multiple death cards to unlock. Touch on the **castle icon** in the upper left to check your progress. Each time you uncover something new, a star appears next to the castle icon at the top of the screen.

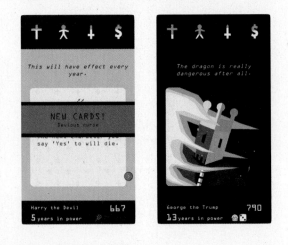

Swipe to Rule

As advisors and others come to you with their concerns, you generally have two choices for your response. For a preview of the responses, swipe just a bit in either direction. Most often, the responses are yes or no, or variations of them. Sometimes you're simply being fed information, so both left and right swipes bring up the same response.

Each response usually impacts one or more of the four pillars of the kingdom. The icon at the top (cross for church, stick figure for the people, sword for the military, and dollar sign for the treasury) flashes green when your stature grows with a group or red when your stature is diminished.

Some decisions result in an ongoing effect. There are four spots for icons at the bottom of the screen, just under the year. These icons track the current effects, since many last several years and continue even after a change in who occupies the throne. Regardless of how well you perform, every game of *Reigns* ends in 2001.

Close Enough...

Because of the way Reigns is designed, it's impossible to provide an exact description of how to complete certain tasks or earn titles. Use the following suggestions to complete some of the trickier tasks.

Royal Deeds

Royal deeds are titles you earn after meeting certain objectives. There's typically more than one path to follow to unlock each title.

TITLE	DESCRIPTION
The Alchemist	Find the frozen blood
The Ancient	Govern at least 40 years
The Bigot	Build 5 churches
The Blessed	Meet the clumsy prophet
The Boyfriend	Date a pigeon
The Coward	Look somewhere else
The Creepy	Lose yourself in the dungeon
The Crusader	Start a crusade
The Dazed	Try the blue one
The Devil	Meet the devil
The Devious	Invent modern politics
The Doomed	Unmask the senator
The Duelist	Win a duel
The Eternal	Govern at least 200 years
The Father	Have an heir
The Fossil	Govern at least a century
The Greedy	Build a personal fortune
The Grizzled	Govern at least 60 years
The Hat	Identify the terrorist cell
The Lover	Start a romance
The Mage	Talk to the vase
The Musician	Write a war song
The Old	Govern at least 20 years
The One-Handed	Lose a limb
The Patron	Recruit the minstrel
The Peacemaker	End a crusade
The Pious	Build a cathedral
The Pivot	Pass the first millennium
The Polyglot	Convince the barbarian to help
The Seer	See the future
The Senile	Govern at least 80 years
The Settler	Discover a new world
The Sorcerer	Meet the witch
The Survivor	Trick the devil
The Target	Hear about the conspiracy
The Tender	Arrange a bestial honeymoon
The Trump	Govern like a winner
The Wicked	Recruit the spy
The Wise	Recruit the doctor
The Writer	Discover printing
The Young	Govern at least 5 years

Status Effects

Some actions you take include status effects that may continue beyond your current reign. These aren't all the status effects, but they are ones you can actively select.

EFFECT	DESCRIPTION
Blue Mushroom	Eating the blue mushroom adds rabbit features to advisors.
Cathedral	The cathedral restores the church should its status hit 0.
Clarity	Eating an orange mushroom provides a clearer picture of your decisions' impacts.
Colonies	Increases both wealth and military.
Crusader	Reduces people, increases wealth.
High Walls	Fortifications restore your military should its status hit 0.
Lover	You can't say no to your lover, and the people are locked from changing their opinion of you.
Money Money	The central bank restores your wealth in case of a disaster.
Mount Care	The hospital allows you to recover your people status in case of a disaster.
Old Age	Your advisors seem to be speaking nonsensically, but this won't be an issue if you're familiar with most situations in the game.
Providence	The storage barn allows you to recover your people status in case of a disaster.
Silk Road	Increase your wealth.
Slaver	It's a terrible way to boost your wealth, but it will boost your wealth.
Theocracy	You can't say no to the church, but at least they'll handle your wealth.

Date a Pigeon

When the witch appears and asks if you want to learn white magic, say yes. Ask for something else until she offers a way to find love. When she asks about making a choice, respond with "What choice?"; choose "Like" when the pigeon appears as an option.

Excalibur

Excalibur becomes available once you speak with Loon the Seer and he offers questions to which you can answer "A king?" followed by "A sword?"

His response is the clue you need to find Excalibur on an upcoming trip to the **pungeon**. Wander the pungeon until the earth door is an option. Go through the earth door, then (in order) the fire door, water door, and acid door. The next room will have a door with a strange symbol over it (it's labeled the sword door). Enter the room, open the chest, and claim Excalibur.

Trick the Devil

Tricking the devil takes a great deal of set-up and an equal amount of luck. The devil appears every 666 years (666, 1332, 1998) and causes issues for the current king (and death for an unlucky advisor). Two people—a witch and an undercover senator, whom you need to unmask first—offer hints about how to trick the devil.

The senator suggests a course of action, while the witch provides numbers (1043, 683, 1214, 842, 1432, 1669) that match dates on the timeline that appears during the transition between reigns. You can scroll backward before starting a new reign to view them.

The timeline provides two clues. First, the symbols match those found above the doors in the pungeon. Second, the direction the king faces tells you which door to take when you see the symbol. On your next trip through the pungeon, look for gold doors until you get the torch. Avoid the arsenic door opposite the salt door, and you should be safe. Flee from the skeleton for now.

After lighting the hallway, look for the fire door. Go through it, then choose arsenic, acid, the broken wall opposite the gold door, the door opposite the pentagram, and then the pentagram door.

The symbols on the timeline at those dates match the symbols above the doors in the pungeon. Look for gold doors. Exploring is safe so long as you avoid the arsenic door across from the salt door and attack Kloc when he appears. After you get the torch and use it, cracks in the wall become visible. Go through doors in this order: fire, arsenic, acid, broken wall opposite gold, door opposite the pentagram. Finally, go through the pentagram door. Attack Kloc (the skeleton) but be ready for conversation. Always swipe right until you're allowed to leave.

You may have already met the homunculus in the vase (completing the Mage royal deed). If so, you should get a **red and cold ruby** at some point. If this takes place while the Crusader status effect is active, the homunculus can create a strawberry plant. Return to Kloc with the strawberry plant; he now offers assistance. Put him off until the devil makes a return visit. With the curse in place, say no to every advisor until Kloc pops up. Say yes to him, then yes to the dog to break the curse.

ROBLOX

Developer	Roblox Corporation
Publisher	Roblox Corporation
Year Released	2008
Platforms	Microsoft Windows, macOS, iOS, Android, Xbox One, Oculus Rift
Type	Adventure
ESRB Rating	E
Cost	Free to download

$ IN-GAME PURCHASES
Robux, items, Builders Club membership

Game Overview

Roblox is a massive multiplayer online game where users create their own games and experiences. It's a game where you go to create games and play games others have made. *Roblox* hosts over 15 million games created by users; the games are constructed of Lego-like virtual blocks.

What You Need to Know

Roblox Studio

Reached from the More option from the list of shortcuts at the bottom of the screen, Roblox Studio is the platform players use to create their own games. Players can create purchasable content through one-time purchases called Game Passes and micro-transactions through Developer Products. Developers exchange **robux** (earned from products in their games) for real money through Roblox's Developer Exchange System (DevEx). A percentage of the revenue is split between Roblox and the developer.

Robux

Robux is *Roblox*'s virtual money. It allows players to buy in-game perks, gear, and apparel. You can purchase robux with real money through menus that typically appear where purchases are made. If you don't have the robux needed to purchase something, a prompt takes you to your purchase options and bundles. You can also earn robux when another player purchases one of your items, or you can earn robux through a daily bonus that comes with membership.

Players

Roblox allows you to buy, sell, and create virtual items. Anyone can buy shirts and pants, but only those with a Builders Club membership can sell them. Only *Roblox* administrators can sell hats, gear, and packages on the platform. Limited items (like hats) are sold only through the *Roblox* catalog. They can also be traded with those who have Builders Club memberships.

Groups

Groups can be created only by Builders Club members. Groups allow players to join a group with other players. Group leaders can advertise their group, participate in group relations, interact with other group members, and manage the roles of members. The function of a group is to organize different types of communities and teams, ranging from game development to Roblox clans.

Groups can publish their own clothing and games, and the funds earned as a group from these endeavors enter a group fund. These funds can be used to market the group through advertisements or to run games under the group's name. Or, the funds can be distributed to the members of the group through the Group Payout system.

In-App Purchases

You can find in-app purchases anywhere in the game or in player-created games where items are sold. You purchase with robux, but if you don't have enough robux for the purchase there's always the option to purchase robux bundles for real money. From the home screen, you can click on the R$ in the circle at the top right corner. Here you have the option of purchasing 80 robux for 99 cents, 400 for $4.99, or 800 robux for $9.99. How much you need depends on the price of what you are buying in-game. Some games cost robux just to get in and play. Paying your way into the Builders Club is another way to spend money in this game.

Sign Up

When you first start *Roblox*, you are required to come up with a screen name, enter your birthdate, and state your gender. Then you're ready to dive in.

Finding Friends

Once signed in you land on the home page. Here you can search for your friends using their screen name and then land on their *Roblox* page. You can request to become friends in the game. On your friend's page, you can also see what games are their favorite and view their player badges.

Choosing Games to Play

The home page is full of recommended games to choose from, along with their ratings and a short description. You can filter what appears on the home page to help you zero in on what kind of game you want to play. You can sort all the games by: Recommended, Popular, Top Earning, Top Rated, Featured, Popular Near You, Top Paid, My Recent, My Favorite, or Friend Activity.

Look at Ratings

Pay attention to the star rating on the game so you don't waste your time with games that are not any fun to play. Follow developers who make good games so you can't go wrong with their creations.

Customizing Characters

You need robux to buy items to customize your character. You need real money to buy robux. You can see what people are wearing when you visit their profile pages, and you can choose to buy clothing items they are selling from there.

ROLLERCOASTER TYCOON TOUCH

Developer	Nvizzio Creations
Publisher	Atari
Year Released	2016
Platforms	iOS, Android
Type	Theme park simulator
ESRB Rating	E
Cost	Free to download

$ IN-GAME PURCHASES
Coins, tickets, cards, VIP perks

Game Overview

RollerCoaster Tycoon has been a popular series of games for nearly two decades, and *RollerCoaster Tycoon Touch* is the first game in the series designed specifically with touchscreens in mind.

What You Need to Know

You're in charge of attracting **peeps** by creating the best park possible. In order to attract peeps and encourage them to spend money on food and souvenirs, you must invest the coins they pay to visit the park into new and improved attractions.

The **stars** that you earn from completing tasks and upgrading cards act as experience points. Every time you reach a new level, additional attractions are unlocked for your park, but you must open decks of cards before you can build these new attractions.

Amusement Park Management

The game's tutorials walk you through the basics, chiming in each time a new element is introduced. Don't rush into anything until after the tutorial covers the topic. You often earn extra rewards or can buy items at reduced prices during a tutorial.

In addition to coins, you also earn **tickets**. Tickets are a premium reward that can be redeemed in the shop for additional coins, packs of cards, and special purchases. Tickets have additional uses, including auto-completion of missions and making purchases in buildings outside park boundaries.

No Tickets for Card Packs

Do not spend tickets to purchase card packs. Obtaining card packs is never an issue so long as you regularly complete missions, especially during bonus events.

In-App Purchases

Beyond purchasing coins, tickets, and cards, you can also buy a VIP perks pack that speeds up every facet of earning rewards, along with other exclusive features.

Don't Be in a Rush

Unless you're willing to spend real money, you need some patience. The cost of placing new attractions and upgrading existing ones far outpaces the income from the park. Keep your initial park design tight. You can always adjust things later as you earn more money and unlock new buildings. Plan your park by what can be covered by the service buildings.

Proper Coverage Is Essential

Information centers, restrooms, and janitor buildings must be spread throughout the park to maximize the overall coverage of each. Ride-maintenance buildings are necessary only around attractions. They keep attractions running smoothly, which ensures safe and enjoyable visits by peeps.

Decorations also affect a limited area. Just like ride maintenance, they work only for attractions. That means you should designate areas for attractions and decorations. Set up areas outside the reach of decorations and maintenance buildings for shops and possibly a food court.

Price Policy

Each time you add a new attraction, set the price of it at the high end of **good value.** Make it a habit to check prices on a schedule to see if they need adjusting to remain a good value.

Special Events

Special events happen regularly. Special events include holiday items, bonus reward weekends, and weekly ride challenges. These events offer special attractions or extra rewards for completing challenges and missions.

Upgrade by Demand

Upgrades become expensive quickly. Upgrade eligible cards only when necessary, not because you have enough coins and cards to do so. If you have more cards to upgrade than coins to pay for upgrades, choose upgrades based on what attractions draw the most peeps.

Earn Trophies Early

The requirements for many trophies are not hard to meet, and the rewards always include tickets. After you earn a trophy, check to see if it's a stand-alone award or part of a series of trophies you can earn.

Missions Have a Time Limit

If you're not interested in completing the current missions, leave the game and come back later. It may be hours before things change, but there are always three active missions.

Heat Map Help

When completing a mission requires that a percentage of attractions reach a certain satisfaction or decoration level, use the **heat map** to identify problem spots quickly. Place decorations where they're needed. Switch to the Information screen for the attractions to determine what steps are necessary to raise peep satisfaction.

Rebuild with Park Editor

Plan on a few total rebuilds of your park as you become more experienced with the game. Nothing placed inside your park is permanently anchored to the spot where it's built. Placing buildings costs coins, but moving them is free. Paths and fences must be erased, but they're always free to build. You don't need to use the Park Editor to modify your park, but it removes all the distracting peeps and makes it easier to see how much space each building requires.

Life Outside the Park

The buildings outside the boundaries of your park are unlocked as your park achieves higher levels. The **appreciation hearts** collected from happy thoughts are currency for these buildings, such as activating the Peep Train at the front of the park.

The Casino has a wheel-spin game where you can win prizes. The first spin each day costs appreciation hearts, but tickets are the price for subsequent spins. The Trading Fair acts as an exchange. Trade your surplus cards and appreciation hearts for cards of greater value. For example, common cards can be exchanged for a rare card. The Mall is a place to purchase cards with appreciation hearts, coins, and tickets. The Heliport is similar to the Mall, but there's a delay between ordering and the delivery of your order.

THE ROOM

Developer	Fireproof Games
Publisher	Fireproof Games
Year Released	2012
Platforms	iOS, Android, Microsoft Windows
Type	Puzzle
Suggested Age	11+
Cost	$0.99

 IN-GAME PURCHASES
None

Game Overview

The Room combines dark graphics, haunting sounds and music, and intuitive controls to create an immersive puzzle game experience. At first glance, the task in each chapter is simple: find out what's inside the box. The difficulty lies in finding the steps you must follow in order to open the boxes.

What You Need to Know

The Room has four chapters and an epilogue. Each chapter has the same objective: open a box. The game's controls are either touching the screen in different ways or tilting your mobile device.

You often find objects while trying to open the box. These objects range from an eyepiece to keys to old photographs. Some of these objects have a single use, while others stay with you the entire game.

Playing The Room

While there are instances of tilting your mobile device to influence the action on the screen, most of the controls require touch. **Swipe** with a single finger to move the camera view. **Pinch** with two fingers to zoom in or zoom out. **Double-tap** on points of interest to focus on them (you must pinch to zoom out again). **Tap** on items in your inventory to inspect them.

When you find objects of interest on the box, try different motions to interact with them. Their shapes typically provide a clue about what you must do to manipulate them. **Tap** on them to see if you can pick them up. **Slide** in different directions, or **swirl** your fingertip around to see if the object moves or turns.

Most objects that you find are used on the box to reveal a secret. Look for discolored or scratched surfaces on the box to see if there's a hidden panel or keyhole.

In the first chapter, you obtain an eyepiece that stays with you. The special properties of the eyepiece allow you to see otherwise hidden markings. If you're unsure of what step to take next, equip the eyepiece and carefully inspect the room for hints.

In-Game Assistance

The question mark in the top left corner of the screen provides hints if you've exhausted your other options.

The following are not step-by-step solutions, but they do cover the major steps to complete each puzzle.

Chapter 1

The opening of the tutorial is designed to show off the game's mechanics. When you read the note that says "Feed me and I shall survive, Give me a drink and I shall die," you're finally on your own.

Locate the **fire** symbol near the ground, then tap on it. Use the key you find there in a keyhole hidden behind a scratched panel. The key won't fit until you adjust it.

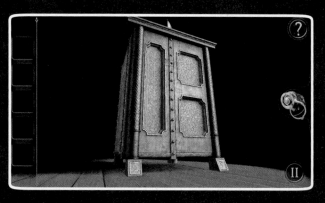

The engraved metal plate matches a **star-shaped screwhead** on the Talisman logo plate. Remove the screw to reveal a lens that attaches to your eyepiece.

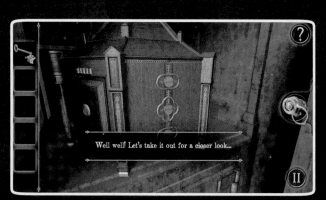

Swipe to the side of the box with a circle in the center. Slide the scratched panel to reveal another keyhole. Adjust the key to make it fit. The secret of the gold discs behind the panel is revealed with the eyepiece. Rotate the discs so there's an **ankh** on the top right and another on the top left.

Chapter 2

You must break three seals on this box before it opens. Start out by locating two **gold bands**. One is near the top of a leg. The other is also in a leg but near the floor. Spinning these gold bands reveals a telescope and a piece of cotton.

Focus on the square with number dials. Tap on the eyepiece and pan around to see **four numbers**. Enter the number 5 on the left, 2 on the top, 7 on the right, and 6 on the bottom. Flip the switch behind the panel to open a side of the box.

Place the **telescope** on the metal stands after you extend it to its full length. The piece of cotton goes into the lighter below the stands. Flick the igniter, then raise the lever to the right of the lighter.

Tap on a decorative leg to reveal a **book**. Rotate the discs so the clasp on the book can be opened. The **winding key** from inside the book turns gears near the stands where you placed the telescope.

Equip the eyepiece for both of the next steps. Look through the telescope, then turn the **rings** that were revealed to form a ram's skull. The **letter** you find goes into a blank spot next to four dials. Spell out T-R-I-A-L to open the first seal.

Open the top of the panel that just slid open. There are four **orbs** to light up inside by tilting your device. Note the symbol on top of the revealed panel. Equip the eyepiece and adjust the camera until that shape comes into view again.

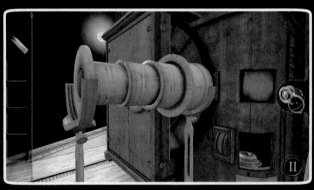

Focus on the **square plate** with four symbols on it. Spin each dial until the symbols match what is shown in this screenshot. The **cast-iron key** opens the keyhole you revealed earlier.

The **cabinet key** from the drawer fits the keyhole at the front of the panel. The **brass star** fits into a spot on the top of the box. Take the **metal ring** from the top and place it on the dial on the side of the panel. Turn the dial to slide the tumblers into the place. Left one tumbler, right until two tumblers move, left for one tumbler, and back right until two switches appear.

The key fits the large **keyhole** on the front of the panel but must be adjusted to fit. Use the **knob** on the round center of the plain door to open the second seal. Align the gears on the left side of the **clock panel** and turn the crank, which reveals the locks and the first key for those locks.

Turn the **dial** on the top of the leg halfway around and note that the top left lock moves at the same time. The **second dial** is at the feet of a knight on top of the box. The **third dial** is next to the gears. The **fourth dial** is on the opposite side of the panel, behind a white square.

Take the elastic band and cog to the gears. Add the **cog** to the gears to get a **screwdriver**. Remove four screws on the opposite side of the panel. Press the button to stop the gears at the right time to get a key. The key opens a drawer on top of the box once you adjust it.

Place your new cog in the center row and put it to use. Surprise! Another cog. Move both to the right-side row, then connect them with the **elastic band**. Press the button above the clock until a **steel tube** appears. The steel tube has two surprises inside.

The key opens a small panel that you must view with the eyepiece equipped to reveal a **shield**. The shield belongs to a figure on top of the box. Place the gemstone you receive on the clock's face. Equip the eyepiece and set the **clock** to 6:05.

Chapter 3

The switch behind the Talisman logo reveals a **box** and **letter**. Get the **key** from inside the box by moving the **gold ball** to the other side of the maze.

Use the eyepiece on the wood panel near the globe to reveal a square opening. Use the key on the nearby keyhole, then spin the **gold dial** left, right, left, and left to reposition all the tumblers. Place the **photo**, then collect and place the **square peg**.

Spell S-I-G-I-L on the dials. The **blue crystal** goes on the base opposite where you found it. Adjust the light beam to get a **flywheel**, which opens a double drawer near the base. Place the light reflector to change the path of the beam. Tapping the buttons drops panels in a timed sequence. The right button sequence rewards a **map piece**. The left side provides a **brass key**.

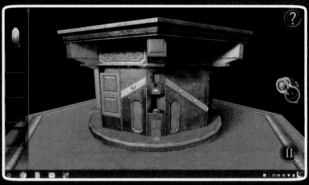

Use the key to get another **reflector**, which attaches to the first reflector. Equip the eyepiece and adjust the sliders around the edges to change the path of the light. Place the map fragments into the **globe**. Use the crank to open the circular panel. Equip the eyepiece and adjust the dial and your view to see a now-familiar shape.

Reshape the wooden box by spinning its base. Place it above the adjustable keyhole. Repeat the **star pattern** viewed through the telescope on the grid of stars built into the box for the final map piece.

Chapter 4

Focus on the **wires** on the top and tilt your device to light up both stars. The **handle** fits into another spot on top of the table, hidden under a flap. Equip the eyepiece and look at the wooden wall. Adjust your view and the dial to form the familiar shape.

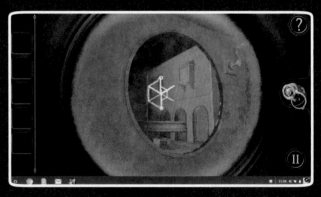

The **dagger** goes into the center of the table. Alternate between the square puzzle (hit the rectangle on the bottom to try your solutions) and pressing the button on the dial. When the wooden wall pops up again, adjust until you view the shape.

Place the **amulet** on the tabletop and solve the squares puzzle again. Get the energy source and stop the dial with a button press. Equip the eyepiece and view the wooden wall. Focus on the wooden walls and rotate the panels. Place the **null** element.

SKY FORCE RELOADED

Developer	Infinite Dreams Inc.
Publisher	Infinite Dreams Inc.
Year Released	2016
Platforms	Android, iOS
Type	Shooter
ESRB Rating	E 10+
Cost	Free to download

$ IN-GAME PURCHASES

Ads Removal, Planes Generator, SX2-Star Doubler, and Precious Cargo

Game Overview

Sky Force Reloaded is an action shoot 'em up game where you fly around in a straight path and shoot enemies in planes, helicopters, tanks, and other vehicles. The goal is to progress through levels to rack up points, with which you upgrade your ship, making it progressively stronger.

What You Need to Know

It costs **stars** to upgrade your ship. Obtain stars by playing the levels and collecting them from the enemies you destroy. The stats that can be upgraded on your ship are Health, Main Cannon, Wing Cannons, Magnet, Missiles, Laser, Energy Shield, and Mega Bomb.

In-App Purchases

In-app purchases become available once you reach the first boss fight. A shopping cart appears on the Ship Upgrade menu. Purchasing allows you to enhance your plane sooner than earning stars through gameplay. Here's what you can find in the Purchase menu:

◆ **Gift Shop:** Every three hours you can watch an ad to pick from three cargo crates. The chosen one gives you a certain number of stars to spend on upgrades.

◆ **Precious Cargo:** Gives you 5,000 stars instantly.

◆ **SX2-Star Doubler:** Doubles the number of stars earned.

◆ **Ads Removal:** Removes all ads from the game forever.

◆ **Planes Generator:** Dramatically speeds up plane production.

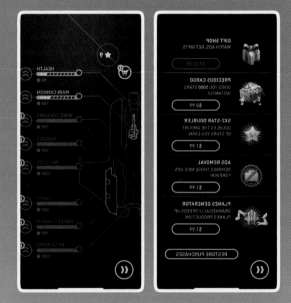

TIPS

Upgrade Health and Main Cannon First

Health and Main Cannon stats can be upgraded from the start of the game at a low star cost (the price rises after each stat upgrade), but the rest of the upgrade options are quite pricey at the start of the game. Instead of saving for those, upgrade Health and Main Cannon a fair amount to make your in-game experience easier. Making the Precious Cargo in-app purchase helps you put a large dent in acquiring the first two upgrades, allowing you to spend your time on the ones that are harder to get.

Upgrade the Magnet

After upgrading Main Cannon and Health, the next best thing to upgrade is the Magnet stat. The magnet attracts stars and weapon upgrade drops to your ship.

Farm Stars in Lower Levels

If you risk health to pick up drops, like stars, you may take some unwanted damage. You should instead consider moving back down to lower levels to farm stars after your ship has been greatly improved. Upgrades do come at a hefty price, and destroying enemy ships in lower levels becomes very easy and a great way to farm stars.

Try the Slow Motion Cheat

If you let go of the screen the game will put you into slow motion; you can use this mechanic to take a second to view your surroundings.

Use the Touch Anywhere Option

Enter Control Settings and choose the option that allows you to touch anywhere on the screen, instead of the option where you must hold the ship to move. The ship is fairly small, and you may not see some attacks coming if you are blocking the area with your thumb or finger.

Grab Weapon Upgrades

Make sure to pick up weapon upgrades while in combat to increase rate of fire. While in boss battles, you'll be constantly dodging attacks, so getting in as much damage as quickly as possible is key to defeating bosses. These weapon upgrade drops look like bullets with gold wings.

Overachiever Tactics

Completing all the challenges in a level unlocks a harder mode of the same level, complete with its own objectives. Completing each level's challenges is very difficult and sometimes nearly impossible to do all in one pass. Instead of trying to do multiple challenges in one pass, do each challenge individually. This is much more efficient, instead of trying to do them all at once and dying over and over. However, the two objectives that require you to destroy a certain percentage of enemy forces can be done in one go.

Underachiever Tactics

If you're not worried about challenges, maximizing stars, or your score, then there are plenty of things you can completely avoid doing. For starters, there's no need to rescue humans on the ground—they only give you a score and make you an easy target to hit. There's also no need to destroy certain parts of the map. For instance, in the first level there's a brick tower that gives you a few stars if you destroy it. Also, you don't have to focus on enemies with no chance of attacking you, like the dune buggy.

Humanitarian Aid

If you are in the vicinity and you want to rescue humans, you can collect more than one at a time; there's no need to waste time helping each one individually.

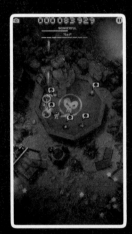

Final Boss Warning

Look out for a final boss's last attack wave. If you think you've killed the boss, think again. Don't go rushing in for the stars at what you think is the end. You may rush in for the star power-ups and be met by an outburst of explosives that can take you down, stopping you from actually passing the level. Make sure the boss is dead before collecting the spoils.

Mega Bombs vs the Laser

Mega bombs are a great tool for dispatching large groups of enemies or dealing a large amount of damage to a boss. The laser shoots out of the ship, unlike the bomb. The laser does a large amount of damage for a brief period. You should use this mostly on bosses.

Energy Shield

The energy shield only decreases the amount of damage you take; it doesn't eliminate all damage. So, don't rely on the energy shield or picking up health drops to get back to full health for achieving the Untouched challenge.

SMASH HIT

Developer	Mediocre AB
Publisher	Mediocre AB
Year Released	2014
Platforms	Android, iOS
Type	First-person action
Suggested Age	8+
Cost	Free to download

$ IN-GAME PURCHASES
Premium

Game Overview

Smash Hit is a first-person action game where you move in a straight line and throw metal balls at glass objects. You start with a few balls, but as you move along the path, glass pyramid and diamond targets can be hit to gain three or five balls, respectively. When moving down the path you must smash objects in your way or hit them and suffer losing 10 metal balls. If you run out of balls to throw, you lose and must restart form the very beginning.

In-Game Purchases

If you purchase Premium, you can replay from your last checkpoint when you lose, instead of starting at the very beginning. Premium also allows you to play more game modes.

What You Need to Know

When moving down the path, you encounter many different obstacles. These are mostly variously-sized glass panes, but there are some thicker, harder-to-break glass objects like the **swinging block**.

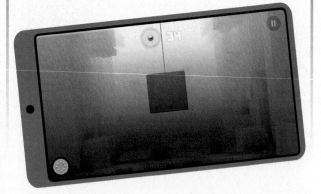

You'll also come by power-ups, such as **unlimited balls** (for a brief time), the **full-auto ball shooter** (with which you can tap and hold your screen to let loose a volley of metal balls), or the ability to **slow down time**.

- Using two **fingers** is way more convenient then using just one.

- If you pick up a power-up, don't instantly use it. Power-ups stack, so there's no need to use one to get the next.

- You do not need to break a whole obstacle to go through it. Instead, break it just enough to avoid hitting it with the middle of your screen.

- When moving toward the thick block, use a rapid-fire power-up or just tap shoot enough to make it swing backward before you hit the block.

- If you hit enough pyramids and diamonds without making any mistakes, a meter at the top of your screen fills. Each time it fills it adds one ball to each shot. If you shoot once, two balls will come out for the price of one. If the meter fills twice then you can shoot three balls at a time and so on.

SPLENDOR

Developer	Space Cowboys
Publisher	Asmodee Digital
Year Released	2015
Platforms	iOS, Android, Steam
Type	Turn Based Collecting
Suggested Age	8+
Cost	Paid download (price varies by platform)

IN-GAME PURCHASES
Game Expansion

Game Overview

Splendor is a Renaissance themed turn-based game where the goal is to acquire **prestige points**. At your disposal are **gems**, which are used to purchase development cards that depict sources of wealth, such as craftsmen, trade routes, and ships. Impressing nobles isn't a necessity, but earning the **tiles** bearing their likenesses can provide a boost to your score.

You can play *Splendor* with AI-controlled opponents, or humans through local pass-and-play, or find a game online. For pass-and-play, you can select a mix of AI and humans.

What You Need to Know

The goal in the main game of *Splendor* is to reach 15 prestige points by collecting gems (in the form of tokens), and then spending them to acquire different cards. Every card purchased includes a permanent gem that can be used for future purchases. Some purchased cards include prestige points, which count toward your goal.

In-App Purchases

The first expansion, titled The Cities, is available is an in-app purchase. The Cities changes the victory conditions of the game. Additional expansions are planned for the future.

Mercantile Moves

The main game begins with three decks of **development cards**, numbered 1, 2, and 3. Level 1 cards are the cheapest to purchase and only a few include prestige points. Cards from levels 2 and 3 are more expensive, but worth more prestige points. Four cards from each deck are placed face up, while the remaining cards go into individual draw piles. **Noble tiles** are also put in play. The number in the lower right of the tile represents their prestige point value.

Six stacks of **gem tokens** are placed next to the development cards. Five of the stacks represent different types of gems, and the number in use varies depending on the number of players. The sixth stack is always five **gold tokens,** which are wildcards. When making a purchase, gold tokens act as jokers, meaning they can be used in the place of any other gem.

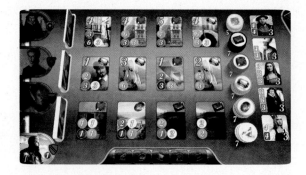

Actions on Your Turn

During each turn, you may take one of four actions: take three gem tokens of different colors, take two gem tokens of the same color, reserve a development card and draw a gold token, or purchase one development card.

The cost of a development card appears in the lower left corner. The colors of the circles match the gems needed for the purchase, while the numbers in the circles indicates how many of each gem is required. Tokens used to purchase development cards are returned to their respective stacks after you select a development card.

The gem in the top right corner of the development card becomes a permanent gem for future purchases, and for impressing nobles. The number in the upper left corner (does not appear on all development cards) indicates its prestige points value. When a development card is purchased or reserved, the top card from the draw pile is put in its place.

Only permanent gems impress nobles. You must earn enough gems to match the numbers on the left side of their tile to claim the tile and prestige points. You can claim only one tile per turn. Noble tiles are not restocked.

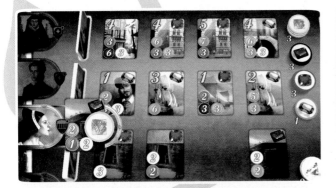

Ending the Game

When a player achieves 15 points, the game ends as soon as every player has taken an equal number of turns. If player 1 gets to 15 first, then the remaining players each get one more turn. If player 2 reaches the goal first, then everyone except player 1 gets another turn.

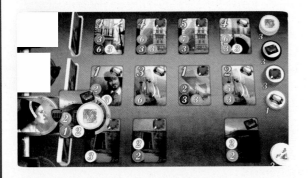

Stick With a Plan Until You Can't

With randomly drawn development cards and noble tiles in each game, there's no single way to win every time. That doesn't mean you can't build a consistent strategy to follow, but you must be flexible during games. AI (see next tip) is modeled after experienced players, so follow their leads to learn different ways to play the game, and how to counter their tactics.

AI Behavior

There are three personality types for the AI: Balanced, Opportunistic, and Specialized. If you choose Random AI, the AI's crest lets you know what style of player it is. If you choose Secret AI, the game doesn't provide any visual cues about the AI's playstyle.

The Balanced AI plays a conservative game, trying to build a stash of every color of gem token. They'll buy level 1 development cards before going after the level 2 and 3 cards, then try to sprint to the end of the game.

The Specialized AI focuses on the main two or three colors that appear on development cards and noble tiles. After building its stockpile of gems, it will go for high prestige point level 2 and 3 cards.

The Opportunistic AI likes to play spoiler. It is known for hoarding development cards (displaying a knack for taking one you're targeting just before your turn), and taking the last gem tokens in a stack.

Target Specific Development Cards

You can't get every development card, so focus on those with the greatest value for your strategy. What color appears most often on the visible Level 2 and Level 3 development cards? What color appears most often on noble tiles?

Don't be Afraid to Reserve Early

If there's a Level 2 or 3 development card on the board you must have, reserve it as soon as you can. Even if you are turns away from purchasing it, it's better to give up a turn to keep it away from the other players. The gold token that comes with a reserved card doesn't hurt.

Gold Tokens

Gold tokens can be spent on any development card, not just the ones you reserve. Despite being a precious metal instead of a gem, they count against your ten token allotment. The good news is that the game only spends gold tokens after depleting your supply of a gem. You can't accidentally spend one.

Challenges & Duels

Challenges use many of the same gameplay concepts as the main game, but instead of defeating opponents, you're solving puzzles. Tokens, development cards, and noble tiles all make appearances, but not in every challenge.

Duels, which are selected by touching the VS button on the Challenges page, are one-on-one matchups against historical European monarchs. Each duel uses unique rules.

Challenges

Understand the Goal

The first box under the historical text explains the goal of the challenge, but the explanation isn't always clear. When the text mentions the value of prestige points, it indicates the prestige point target value increases. That means the longer you take, the more prestige points you need to succeed.

Study the Restrictions

Read the rules carefully, taking note of limits on turns, gem tokens, reserving development cards, prestige point changes, and everything else the game may include as part of the challenge. The wording can be tough to decipher at times, so expect a few frustrating early attempts.

Plan Purchases

Planning ahead is especially important in challenges with limited gem tokens. Always spend gems so that you can select up to the maximum number of tokens during your turn. It will feel like a wasted turn when you're short gems for purchasing development cards, but there are only one or two tokens available, or all the tokens are the same color.

No Gold, No Problem

Working through a challenge that allows you to reserve development cards but lacks gold tokens? Reserve development cards that cost too much or won't help you reach the goal, to see if the next card is a better option.

Predetermined Challenge

When challenges use predetermined development card draws, there's generally a single solution to complete them. These challenges tend to be the trickiest ones to complete. Learn the order of the cards coming off the decks and plan your purchases to be ready for the best cards that are coming.

Duels

Charles V

The play style of Charles V is a mix of the Balanced and Opportunistic AI. Unless you slip up and leave him an opening to exploit, the real race here is against the turn limit.

You start with nine gem tokens (four are gold), so your first move should be purchasing or reserving a development card. For subsequent moves, follow your preferred strategy of obtaining prestige points. To get a better score, try to impress a noble tile on your winning turn to push your point total past 20.

Mary Stuart

You have zero margin for error in this duel. Used tokens are not returned to their piles. A chess-style timer counts down from one minute, so your choices must be quick and accurate. In addition, Mary Stuart is ruthless and starts out with two points.

If you're simply looking to win (improving your score can come later), monopolize the level 1 red development cards and go after noble tiles. When a red card is on the board, reserve it. Since the card order remains the same in every game, you can anticipate when one is about to appear.

While you're waiting on red cards, stockpile gem tokens before Mary Stuart grabs them all. Save the gold tokens obtained from reserving development cards for important purchases.

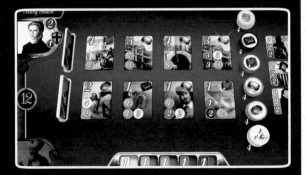

François the 1st

The only tokens in this duel are the five gold tokens that start out in your opponent's possession. They remain in the game no matter how many times they're spent. The result is early round actions must be spent building your purchasing power.

Focus on three colors. Use gold tokens to make up any deficiencies when buying level 3 cards, unless there's a development card with prestige points that will serve the same purpose. The value of the noble tiles makes them attractive targets, but they're not enough on their own to win the game.

Like Charles V, François generally won't win until the last round, so use that to your advantage when angling for high scores. Your highest scores come from reaching the 20 point target while impressing one of the nobles at the same time.

Isabella I of Castile

The duel with Isabella includes the highest prestige point target (25) and number of turns (33). The lack of level 2 cards and noble tiles results in games that start off slowly, but end in a rush for level 3 cards.

You're the first to act this time, but Isabella starts off with twice as many tokens. Isabella will try to control gem tokens, so refill your stacks after she makes a purchase. Expect lean times when she's holding a majority of gem tokens and purchasing level 1 development cards, likely out of spite. You won't see her tokens return to the board until she makes a level 3 purchase.

Reserve level 1 development cards worth 4 prestige points when they appear, unless you have the resources to buy them outright. They're as valuable as many level 3 development cards at a far lower cost. To close out the game, reserve and purchase whichever level 3 cards match the gems and level 1 cards you've been stockpiling.

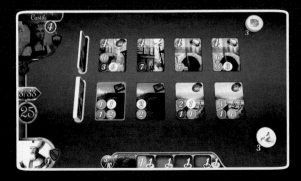

TEMPLE RUN 2

Developer	Imangi Studios
Publisher	Imangi Studios
Year Released	2013
Platforms	Android, iOS, Windows Phone 8, Tizen
Type	Platformer
Suggested Age	10+
Cost	Free to download

IN-GAME PURCHASES

In-game currency (gems and coins) and two characters (Bruce Lee and Usain Bolt)

Game Overview

Temple Run 2 is a single-player endless running platform game where you are being chased by **Cuchanck**—an enlarged monster monkey—until you run smack into a wall, you fall, or the monster finally catches up to you.

In-App Purchases

The in-game purchases are not required unless you want play as Bruce Lee or Usain Bolt. There are close to 30 characters you can unlock with gems earned through normal gameplay to keep gameplay fresh and keep you busy. However, buying coins or gems makes upgrading and buying maps and cosmetics much easier.

What You Need to Know

The Environment and Controls

While playing *Temple Run 2*, you don't just run in a straight line. You have to watch out for broken ledges, walls, river logs, etc. To dodge objects on the left or right of your path, **tilt** your device left or right. To dodge objects blocking the entire path, **swipe** either up or down to move out of the way. Swiping up makes you jump and swiping down makes you slide. Be careful when tilting your device to grab coins—the game often adds an obstacle at the end of a coin line.

Coins and Gems

Coins are used to buy characters and ability upgrades. **Gems** are used for buying clothing items for characters, maps, and power-up boosts.

Abilities

Abilities are stats, including Coin Value, Shield Duration, Coin Magnet, Boost Distance, Pickup Spawn, Power Meter, Save Me, Head Start, Score Multiplier, Wheel Bonus, and Bolt Distance (Bolt Distance requires the purchase of Usain Bolt). One particularly important upgrade is **Coin Value**—having a greater value for each coin makes getting other upgrades easier. Another great upgrade is **Power Meter**, which fills your meter a certain percentage faster.

- If you try to make a turn too early, you will hit a wall and the monkey monster will catch up to you, which also restarts your power-up bar (filled by collecting coins). Time your turns skillfully.

- You can only get away with one mistake while the monster is in your view; if you hit a wall or object a second time, you will lose.

- The small edges on the path can either be run around or jumped over; if you are near an edge while collecting coins, it's easier to jump over, but if no coins are around, it's your preference whether you jump over it or just go around the edge.

- While in river sections of maps, watch out for objects on your left and right. Keep in mind that tree logs block the river, so you have to dive under to avoid them. To get around a log, swipe down below it. You'll instantly lose if you hit it.

TICKET TO RIDE

Developer	Days of Wonder
Publisher	Days of Wonder/Asmodee
Year Released	2012
Platforms	iOS, Android, Steam
Type	Turn-based railway builder
ESRB Rating	E
Cost	Price varies by platform

IN-GAME PURCHASES
Expansions and map packs

Game Overview

Ticket to Ride has been an immensely popular board game for nearly 15 years and has spawned a number of expansions and sequels. The digital version of *Ticket to Ride* has been praised as a worthy adaptation of the popular game, with graphics and sound effects that enhance already excellent gameplay.

What You Need to Know

The original game pits up to five players against each other and allows you to select a mix of human opponents and four distinct AI personalities. Your goal is to score the most points by connecting cities by rail. Placing trains earns points, as does connecting the cities listed on destination tickets in your possession. Depending on which expansion you're playing, you may earn bonus points for creating the longest route or completing the most destination tickets.

Expansions to the game change a few rules, which we've covered in these pages. Expansions with smaller maps reduce the maximum number of possible players to three or four, instead of five.

Bonus Scoring, Asian Editions

Ticket to Ride's India expansion awards a unique bonus for connecting the same cities through two distinct paths. The Grand Tour bonus can add up to 40 points to your score.

Bonus points in Ticket to Ride Asia are given to players who connect the most cities in one continuous network of routes.

Building a Railroad Empire

Regardless of the number of players or the map selected, every game of *Ticket to Ride* begins the same way. Each player is dealt **destination tickets** and must keep some number of them. The game helpfully highlights the cities listed on the tickets when you select them. Each player also receives random **train cards,** which are used to claim routes between cities.

The remaining destination tickets are placed face down in a stack. From the remaining train cards, five are dealt face up and the rest are set up in a draw deck.

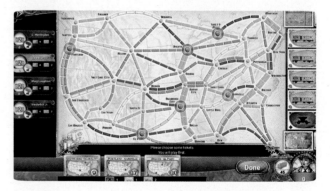

Actions on Your Turn

On your turn, you may take one of three actions: **draw train cards, claim a route,** or **draw destination tickets.**

Expansions' Additional Actions

Ticket to Ride Europe adds a fourth possible action: build a station. Placing a station on a city allows you to claim one route from that city. Unused stations count as four points at the end of the game.

Ticket to Ride United Kingdom adds purchasing technology cards as an optional action you can take before your turn. Purchasing a technology card does not end your turn. Technology cards expand your capabilities after they're purchased.

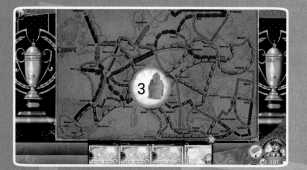

Draw Train Cards

There are eight colors of train cards (the colors are not related to the trains used by the players!), with each color depicting different rail cars and using a different symbol to assist color-blind players. The ninth type of train card is the locomotive, which acts as a wild card—unless you're playing the Switzerland or Nordic Countries expansion. In many versions of *Ticket to Ride*, if three of the five face-up cards are locomotives, then all five are discarded and replaced.

The restrictions for drawing cards are as follows:

- ◆ You may draw one face-up locomotive.

- ◆ You may draw one card blindly from the top of the draw deck. Regardless of what card you draw, you may then select one more card from the draw deck or any face-up card that is not a locomotive.

- ◆ You may draw one face-up card that isn't a locomotive, which is replaced immediately. You may then draw another face-up card that isn't a locomotive or select

Claim a Route

To claim a regular route between two cities, play the same number of cards of the same color, or locomotives, as are shown on the map. Gray silhouettes on the board indicate that any color of card can be used to claim the route, but all cards must be the same color or be locomotives.

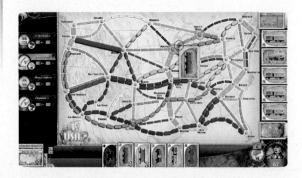

Draw Destination Tickets

Your final option, drawing destination tickets, is one that should be used sparingly. Depending on which version of *Ticket to Ride* you're playing, you draw a number of destination tickets and must retain at least one of them.

Ending the Game

The first player to end their turn with zero, one, or two trains begins the final round of play. Each player, including the player down to two or fewer trains, gets one more turn.

The game then calculates each player's score and any bonuses active in the game. Completed destination tickets are added to scores, while incomplete destination tickets reduce scores. The winner is the player with the highest score.

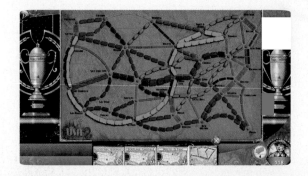

Tunnels, Ferries, and Mountain Routes

Tunnel routes, which appear in most expansions, are marked with notches around the car silhouettes on the map. Claiming these routes may cost you up to three train cards of the same color or locomotives.

Look for ferry routes over bodies of water with a locomotive symbol on some or all car silhouettes. To claim the route, you must play a locomotive for each symbol on the route. The United Kingdom and Nordic Countries expansions allow you to substitute a number of train cards of the same color for locomotives.

The mountain routes in Ticket to Ride Asia require an extra train car, but not train ticket, when you claim them. The car silhouettes for mountain routes are marked with a black or white X.

The points you earn from claiming a route are based on the number of trains used on the route. The scoring is not a simple progression. Claiming one-car routes awards a single point, while routes with six cars are worth 16 points.

Stock Certificates

Upon claiming certain routes in the Pennsylvania expansion, you earn one share of stock, sometimes with a choice of stocks. At the end of the game, you earn points based on how many shares of a stock you own relative to other players.

In-App Purchases

The expansions (USA 1910, Pennsylvania, Europe, Germany, Switzerland, United Kingdom, Nordic Countries, Asia, India) are available as in-app purchases.

TIPS

Stockpile Resources

If any of your destination tickets includes a city with limited route options, secure one of them early. Otherwise, use the first part of the game to build up your collection of train cards. If you start placing trains too early, you may run into a situation where you're waiting on cards that aren't coming up or could be sitting in the hands of the other players. Outside of the Nordic and United Kingdom expansions, a fistful of train cars that are the wrong color for your routes means wasted turns.

Start in the Center

When you're ready to start claiming routes, start somewhere in the middle of your planned route and expand outward. This isn't as important while you're playing the AI, but you must keep human opponents guessing about your ultimate destination.

Mind the Gaps

Unless you have absolutely no other choice, never, never, never leave gaps in your line of trains. Other players will happily fill in the gaps and cut off your ability to link your routes. If another player slips up and leaves an obvious gap, fill it in with trains of your own unless you don't have any to spare.

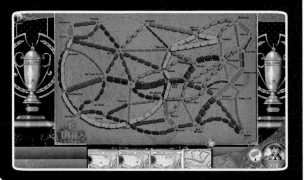

AI Challenge

The AIs specific to certain expansions (Asia's Kwaibot, Europe's PoirBot, India's Beretonbot, Nordic's SantaBot, Pennsylvania's ThomsonBot, Switzerland's EscherBot) offer the stiffest challenge on their respective maps.

Short Routes Mean Fast Starts

On maps that are primarily short routes (United Kingdom and India, for example), get an early jump on claiming routes. This is especially important when double routes aren't in effect due to the number of players in the game.

Tunnel Trouble

Depending on the expansion, you must be prepared to spend up to three additional cards to claim a tunnel route. While you don't lose your train cards for failing to claim a tunnel, you essentially waste a turn and also tip off opponents to the direction you want to go.

Station Situation

Each unused station in the Europe expansion is worth four points at the end of the game. If placing a station nets you fewer than four points, don't bother putting it on the board.

Single Locomotives OK!

Typically, you're better off drawing two cards blindly (and hoping at least one is a locomotive) than selecting a face up locomotive card. However, if you're playing the United Kingdom or Nordic Countries expansion, claim every locomotive you can. They're incredibly valuable in these expansions.

Mandala Bonuses

If your starting destination tickets allow for it, go for Grand Tour bonuses rather than longest train. It only takes two qualifying destination tickets to earn the same points as the longest train. With a large enough circle, you may earn the longest train bonus anyway!

An Early Start on Stocks

Because lower stock certificate numbers serve as a tiebreaker for determining scores in the Pennsylvania expansion, you should start claiming routes earlier than you would on other maps.

UNKILLED

Developer	**Madfinger Games**
Publisher	**Madfinger Games**
Year Released	**2015**
Platforms	**Android, iOS, Windows Phone**
Type	**First-person shooter**
ESRB Rating	**T**
Cost	**Free to download**

$ IN-GAME PURCHASES
In-game currency
(gold and money)

Game Overview

Unkilled is a first-person shooter that takes place in New York City. Take part in a zombie-killing action campaign with 150 missions, or annihilate other players in an online duel. Multiplayer is unlocked at rank 4.

In-App Purchases

When levels are completed, you're given the option to double your rewards by watching ads. If you choose not to pay for the in-game currency, watching ads would be a wise decision since many upgrades are quite pricey. If you do decide to buy currency, many upgrade options are far easier to get. Gold is especially pricey and something that you don't want to spend willy-nilly, so be careful.

Character Selection

After you complete the story mode tutorial, you're asked to choose your hero. You have five choices. You can unlock the other characters later in the game, so your choice is not permanent. After comparing the initial character stats and what they sacrifice for other stats, we've chosen Joe. Here's a stat comparison.

Joe:	**Survivor:**	**Sam:**	**U.S. Ranger:**	**Clark:**
Universal Specialization	Assault Rifle Specialization	Sniper Rifle Specialization	Heavy Machine Guns Specialization	Shotgun Specialization
HP 100	HP 95	HP 90	HP 105	HP 100
Walk 3.6	Walk 3.6	Walk 3.8	Walk 3.5	Walk 3.7
Run 4.7	Run 4.9	Run 5.1	Run 5.0	Run 4.6
Special Skills: Movement Speed and Instant Reload	Special Skills: Rapid Regeneration and Ammo Clip Capacity	Special Skills: Burst Regeneration and Headshot Damage	Special Skills: Better Accuracy and Kevlar Helmet	Special Skills: Additional Damage to Limbs and Faster Reload

Blue Puzzle Pieces

When you kill a zombie and a blue puzzle piece drops, make sure to pick it up. The blue puzzle pieces are blueprints for more weapons.

Key:
HP (health),
Walk (walking speed),
Run (running speed)

Intel (White and Blue Cubes)

Watch out for white and blue cubes called intel; these items are used to upgrade your hero's stats. If you miss the intel, don't worry—after a few seconds it's automatically picked up and given to you. Once you have enough intel (and money) you can upgrade your hero's skill tree, which increases Attack, Defense, Utility, and Gadgets.

Upgrading Weapons

Some missions require you to use a certain weapon type (the first is mission 4, a heavy-machine-gun mission). So don't focus just on one weapon type, but instead gradually build and upgrade all weapon types.

Sniping

In heavy-machine-gun and sniper missions, you are required to manually shoot instead of aiming and having the game shoot for you. Snipers have a very high bullet penetration and can shoot through multiple zombies—if you line up your shots correctly. In sniper missions, you also need to lead your shots if your target is moving. Snipers don't instantly hit the target like they normally do when using a sniper outside of these missions.

Red Barrels

In the fifth mission, you encounter red barrels. You can aim your crosshairs over one to automatically shoot it (like you do with zombies) and it'll explode. To get the most out of these, let the zombies that are coming from the red barrel's vicinity mass up, and then shoot the zombies that are not near it. When the side with more zombies is larger, shoot the barrel to explode the mass. The explosion radius is huge. You could also "train" the zombies in circles until you have a large horde of them, then lead them toward the barrel and shoot it. Red tanks and fire extinguishers can also be blown up, but the fire extinguishers have a smaller explosion radius.

First Boss: Sheriff

The first boss you encounter is in level 10. Sheriff is a large zombie with chest protection. Since he wears a shield on his chest, you need to aim for his limbs and head. He does large amounts of damage with his melee hits and fireball attacks. To dodge the melee attacks, run around them. To dodge the fireballs, simply move left or right out of their trajectory.

Nukleon Zombies

Nukleon is another special zombie type. Nukleon emits a radioactive aura, and if you stand in range, you'll get radiation poison that damages you over time. If Nukleon starts to charge up, either run or kill him fast. If you don't, you'll take heavy damage. Use medium- to long-range weapons to take him out while taking as little damage as possible.

Minesweeper Zombies

Minesweeper is a zombie with a large bomb inside his stomach, and if he gets too close it detonates, possibly killing you and all the zombies around you. Since the explosion can also kill other zombies, try to manipulate his path by leading him to a horde of zombies and then blowing him up there.

Dodger Zombies

The Dodger zombie is a football athlete who charges you whenever given the chance. He is protected almost everywhere except for the stomach and back. Shoot his stomach when he's in front of you, but if he charges you, dodge him and shoot him in the back before he turns around. The Dodger has two more variants, each with increased speed: the Linebacker and the Quarterback. If you're hit by one of these zombies, you'll be knocked to the ground.

Butcher Zombies

The Butcher is a deadly foe in close quarters. His hand is an enormous blade that's used to cut you to pieces or, when shot at, is used as a shield. He is virtually ineffective from medium to long range. Another great way to take this beast out is with explosives. Make sure to dodge his charge attacks and hit him in the back while you can. When his shield is up, he primarily tries to block his head, but his large legs are exposed. When his shield is up, use a sniper to be more accurate while aiming for his head. Butcher has a lot of health, so aiming for the head is in your best interest (as is the case with most zombies).

Multiplayer Tips

In multiplayer level duels, you're pitted against another player. The first to five kills wins. Multiplayer is a great way to get resources fast. Here are a few tips to beat your opponent in this mode.

Sniper Cover

Try to stick to areas where you can see and shoot your opponent, but where they can only see as little of you as possible. Your head is the smallest target, and if this is all they can see, then you'll likely dole out more damage before they can get a shot on you—especially if you are using a sniper.

Shotgunning

If you are using a shotgun, collect power-ups as often as you can since one of them is a power rush. Power rush lets you do increased damage, and with a shotgun, this would be very destructive.

Health

When you kill your opponent, you don't regain full health; instead, your enemy drops a small health pack. Be careful while going for this health power-up. The returning opponent knows that location will be a good place to find you next.

Headshots

As with zombies, headshots are everything. Avoid just aiming for the body or you'll be missing out on a lot of damage. If your opponent picks up the big head power-up, hide. With this power-up—as the name implies—your head becomes larger and they'll have an easier time getting headshots.

VAINGLORY 5V5

Developer	Super Evil Megacorp
Publisher	Super Evil Megacorp
Year Released	2014
Platforms	Android, iOS
Type	Multiplayer online battle arena
Age Range	9+
Cost	Free to download

$ IN-GAME PURCHASES
Cosmetics, chests, battle pack

Game Overview

Vainglory 5v5 is a multiplayer online battle arena (MOBA) game where two teams of five player-controlled heroes compete against each other to destroy the other team's **Vain crystal**, which lies inside the opposite team's base. Vainglory boasts fluid combat and stunning graphics that can compete with other popular MOBAs.

What You Need to Know

The In-Game Interface

The Vainglory **HUD** is fairly standard. The items presented (from left to right) are: the map, usable items, healing flask, skills, scout cams, indicators and quick chat, home base teleport, help, scoreboard, the shop, and the quick-buy button. Above your hero a green bar showcases your current **health** level and a blue bar shows your current **mana.**

Map

The map shows the location of the three lanes and the two bases. The heroes' locations are indicated by small portraits.

Usable Items

Items that have active effects are shown on the left side of the screen. Tap to activate an item you want to use.

Indicators and Quick Chat

Five options at the top right of the screen can be used for quick communication with your teammates: a **green** icon that can be used to indicate something of interest, a **yellow** danger icon to indicate that a teammate should get away from some kind of danger, a **blue** icon to indicate that you are headed somewhere, and a **white** icon to indicate that your teammates should converge on a location. The **purple speech bubble** contains a list of many quick chat options that may be helpful.

Healing Flask

On the left side of the bar that houses your skills there's the button for the healing flask. This item grants you a small amount of healing but has a 120-second cooldown.

Skills

Your skills are located in the bottom middle of your screen. Every hero has two skills and an ultimate ability.

Scout Cams

Everybody starts the game with two **scout cams**. Scout cams can be placed to provide vision in an area for a certain amount of time or until destroyed by the other team. Additional scout cams can be purchased at the fountain shop.

Home Base Teleport

Located in the bottom right corner of the screen alongside other icons is the **warp icon**, which allows you to teleport back to your Vain crystal after a set amount of time. This teleport can be interrupted if your hero takes damage.

Help

Next to the teleport icon is the help icon. Tapping it shows you a page with information detailing your selected hero's skills and passive perk. The button labeled More Info shows you the damage type, energy cost, damage value, and cooldown of the skills and ultimate ability of the selected hero. This page also shows the stats of your selected hero, such as health, energy, and armor.

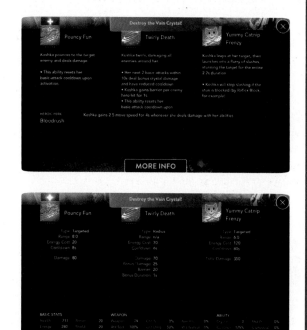

Scoreboard

The scoreboard shows a great deal of helpful information about the current state of the battle. It shows you and your teammates' purchased items as well as your team's and the opposing team's current kill/death/assist values.

Shop

Tapping the shop button takes you to the shop page, which features several categories of items that can be used to add beneficial effects and skills to your character. The **Recommended** tab helps choose an item build that best benefits your selected hero. The **Weapons** tab presents you with items that are usually built for increasing your hero's damage. The **Crystal** tab shows items that increase the strength of abilities.

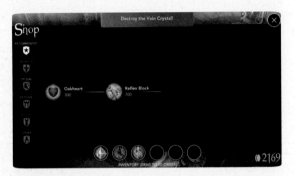

The **Defense** tab deals with items that generally make your hero more durable. The **Utility** tab shows items that might be helpful, but their usefulness may vary greatly depending on the situation. The **Other** tab shows items that are consumable (like the weapon or crystal infusion, which temporarily boosts attack power or cooldown speed, respectively), provide vision (like the scout cam), and provide less intensive temporary skills (like the contracts).

Quick Buy Button

The quick buy button is on the right side of the screen and features an image of the next item up on the Recommended tab of the shop page. This allows you to swiftly purchase the next item necessary for your selected hero's build without having to navigate the shop menu.

Modes

5v5

This is the standard 25-minute Vainglory battle mode. In 5v5 you and your team must attempt to win the three lanes from the other team as you push your way toward the opposing team's base turrets and then finally to their Vain crystal, where you attempt to deplete its health bar.

In this game mode, there are also jungles where your team can secure extra gold by defeating neutral enemies, but these neutral enemies and their gold can also be taken by the opposing team. A river separates the sides of the map. Along the river there are two shops with powerful items, as well as spawn points for dangerous but rewarding neutral foes. When moving with the flow of the river your hero has increased movement speed.

3v3

This 20-minute game mode is much the same as the 5v5 except there are only three members on each team, and at different times there'll be unique creatures that spawn. First there's a **sentry** that'll protect your team's jungle and attack any enemies that get too close. The next enemy to spawn is the **gold miner**, who accumulates gold over time and provides a great gold reward to the team that manages to defeat him. The final enemy to spawn, the **kraken**, is very useful. The kraken is very tough to defeat, and doing so may require the help of your teammates, but when she is defeated she'll fight for the team that defeated her and will help to push toward the Vain crystal and destroy turrets.

Blitz

This five-minute game mode is designed for a quick and fun brawl. The team's objective is to reach 15 points. Players earn one point for defeating an opposing player and three points for destroying the opposing crystal sentry, the middle sentry, or enemy turrets. In Blitz players start at a higher level and have more gold to help escalate the level of play early on.

Battle Royale

In this 10-minute game mode players constantly clash in a single lane as they attempt to destroy the opposing team's turrets and make their way to the enemy's Vain crystal. Heroes are selected at random from the entire Vainglory roster, for everyone in the game. In Battle Royale, players can purchase items at the start, but once they leave a barrier surrounding the sanctuary they cannot return to purchase items until they respawn.

Heroes Tab

Tap this option to be taken to the entire *Vainglory* hero roster. From this page, you can select new heroes to purchase as well as a wide array of cosmetics for each hero. You can also select a hero to see their abilities and even get general tips on how to play them. You can also purchase talents for each hero that are usable in certain game modes.

Party and Social Tabs

In the Social tab, you can see and add new friends as well as join a guild or a team. From this list of friends, you can create a group and start playing from the Party tab.

In-App Purchases

From the Market tab, you can purchase an array of cosmetics for each hero and purchase chests that drop a random blueprint for a cosmetic. You can also purchase a battle pass, which provides the chance to earn more rewards from every match. It also grants some bonus gifts.

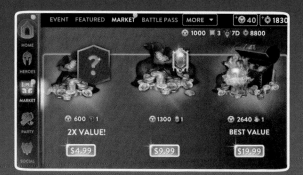

Securing Last Hits

Make sure that you practice attack animation timings for the heroes that you like to play, because making sure that you can secure the gold from being the last to hit a minion can be the difference between a win or a loss for your team, especially when you are playing the carry position

Knowing Your Role

Not every hero is the same. Some heroes are more focused on a supporting role. For example, Ringo cannot necessarily stand at the front of a fight and is much more suitable for a ranged attack, while other heroes, like Koshka, can hold their own and easily secure the farm from jungle minions.

Jungle Shops

Running back to the base every time you need to buy an item can be quite time consuming. The next time you need to quickly get a new item, try visiting one of the shops in the jungle.

Map Awareness

It is very important to know what the rest of your team is up to and where the enemy is showing up on the map. Making constant use of the map can help you and your team formulate the next plan of attack or prepare to defend a location.

Teleport Back to Base

If the outcome of a fight does not feel like it's going to be in your favor, then there is nothing wrong with running away to teleport back to the fountain to heal. Your team can benefit much more from a living hero than from a dead one that must take time to respawn.

THE WITNESS

Developer	Thekla, Inc.
Publisher	Thekla, Inc., Nvidia Lightspeed Studios
Year Released	2016
Platforms	PlayStation 4, Xbox One, Microsoft Windows, Xbox 360, iOS, Android
Type	Adventure puzzle
Cost	$9.99 iOS, $39.99 other platforms

$ IN-GAME PURCHASES
None

Game Overview

The Witness is a solo adventure puzzle game. You wake up on an island alone and are left to do puzzles and explore to find clues about who you are and how to get home. The game has over 500 puzzles, each with its own unique way of completing it.

What You Need to Know

Controls

When you spawn into the game you have to walk toward a door and open it. You are given the controls, but you may feel more comfortable if you go into your menu at the top left and invert the controls. Tap on the screen to move where you want to go. Double-tap to run. To stop in place, hold the screen with two fingers. To side-step, swipe the direction you want to go with two fingers. To zoom in, pinch the screen out, and to zoom out pinch in.

Getting Out of the Starting Area

To exit the starting area, you need to open a door. Near the door is a panel with three cords coming out of it. To open the panel up to complete the puzzle inside, you first need to activate the three cords, which are triggered by completing three other puzzles around the room. Follow the cords to locate the puzzles. Once you've completed a puzzle, its cord turns yellow. Complete all three to turn all cords yellow to make the exit door panel puzzle active.

Yellow Maze Puzzle

The circle marks the start of the puzzle. Simply tap and hold it to move your line around the maze. A pulsating white dot appears. You must lead your line to that location to find your way through the maze. If two or more start circles are on the maze, you only need one to complete one path.

Black and White Square Puzzle

In these puzzles, the task is to separate the white squares from the black squares while also getting your line to the end of the puzzle.

Multicolored Blocks Puzzle

Multicolored block puzzles require you to move through the maze separating each group of colors from other groups of colors so that different colored blocks will never be grouped together. Blocks of the same color do not have to be grouped with each other but have to be sectioned off from other colors.

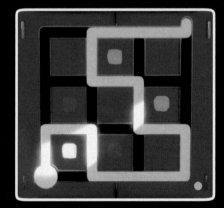

Symmetric Puzzle

These puzzles require you to lead two identical lines to an exit. One is a mirror copy of the other. If you move one line, another line is drawn symmetrical to it on the other side. To complete the puzzle, both lines need to make it to the exit point. Avoid dead-ends as much as possible.

Black Dots Puzzle

The black hexagon dot puzzle is simple: Cross the line over every dot and find the exit. The puzzle can't be completed without every dot being passed over.

Tetris Block Puzzle

The Tetris block puzzles can be quite tricky. The trick is to draw the tetromino shape while making sure you have the tetromino symbol inside the shape you've drawn.

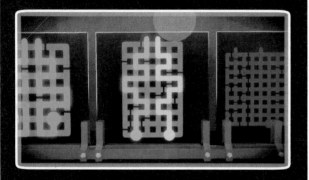

Elimination Mark Puzzle

Elimination marks are little upside down Y symbols that appear in blocks within the puzzle. The number of elimination mark symbol blocks determines how many rules you need to break in the puzzle to complete it—they could all be the same rule being broken. The block where the rule is being broken (for example, a white block could now be sectioned off with black blocks), must be sectioned off with the elimnation mark breaking its rule. You must always section off an elimination mark with the block that the mark is breaking the rule for.

Star Puzzle

With the star puzzles, you cannot have more than two stars of one color on the same side of your line. For example, if you have four stars of the same color in a panel, split them into two groups and complete the maze. If there are four stars of two different colors, they can be the same group. The only rule you have to keep in mind is if it is the same color, you can only have two of those same colors in a group.

Environmental Puzzles

You need to use the environment to solve this type of puzzle. This is not the only puzzle that requires environmental help, but it is one of the first you encounter. Use the apple on the tree to see which exit to lead your line to. If you mess up on the next puzzle, you'll have to start from the previous one.

Other environmental puzzles can be found throughout the world, and you have to locate them as well as solve them. They are actually a part of the world. Other environmental puzzles include:

◆ Desert puzzles, in which you use the light from the sun or reflection of water to solve it

◆ Jungle Puzzles require you to use sound, by moving the line up or down depending on the pitch of the sound (or across it if it's in the middle)

◆ Shady Tree Puzzles are completed by tracing the shadows of tree limbs to get to the exit

◆ To complete Monastery Puzzles, you need to position yourself to find the correct path and trace that path to the exit

WORLD OF GOO

Developer	2D Boy
Publisher	Nintendo, 2D Boy, Tomorrow Corporation, Brighter Minds Media, Microsoft Studios
Year Released	2008
Platforms	Android, Nintendo Switch, Wii, Windows, iOS, Linux, macOS, BlackBerry
Type	Puzzle
ESRB Rating	E
Cost	Paid download

 IN-GAME PURCHASES
None

Game Overview

In *World of Goo* your objective is to construct links of **goo balls** with available resources to deliver a set number of balls to a pipe while also avoiding hazards. It's a single-player strategy puzzle game. If you want to find a way to compete against other people, the game offers a level where the main task is to just build up. You get more goo balls to build up with in this level by collecting additional balls through pipes that are not needed to pass the level.

World of Goo features five chapters and 37 levels. The chapters are: The Goo Filled Hills, Little Miss World of Goo, Cog in the Machine, Information Superhighway, and the Epilogue.

Just Starting

In the first level, simply build up by dragging and dropping a goo ball. It may be tricky to see at first, but you'll know if the ball is in range and what it looks like before you drop it if you look at the white highlighted line connected to the starter box of goo balls.

Stacking & Tower Support

While stacking the goo balls, make sure to build tower support every so often, or it'll start to fall over. Depending on the level, you may not be able to build a foundation because you may have to build across a gap. If provided, use the balloons to keep your goo structure from falling over. Balloons can be moved to different areas of your goo network and put back into your structure if you no longer need them.